THE DIVINE DESIGN

The Untold Story of Earth's and Humanity's Evolution in Consciousness

LORIE LADD

I dedicate this book to all the courageous humans navigating their miraculous evolution. Thank you for your courage, commitment, and compassion to take one step in front of the other and lead humanity into a new world.

ACKNOWLEDGMENTS

First, I would like to thank my family for their unconditional love and support. I don't know if I could have finished the book without your gentle love cheering me on. Thank you for seeing in me what I sometimes could not see in myself. I am endlessly grateful for your support.

I would like to thank Joe Garrido who has been by my side since the moment I put paper to pen. Your encouragement, love, and undying support means more than you will ever know. You lifted me up when I didn't believe in myself. You reminded me of why I was writing the book. You kept me going when I wanted to quit. Thank you for you!

I would also like to thank my best friend Brandy Littles for all of your undying support, love and encouragement. I don't know where I would be without you. Thank you.

And finally, to my beautiful online community that stretches to all corners of the Earth—thank you for your support. Thank you for allowing me to be a part of your evolution. Thank you for standing side by side with me as we courageously navigate this planetary shift.

I love you, I honor you, and I see you.

CONTENTS

Introduction 1

CHAPTER 1: THE DESIGN OF THE 5D EARTH 5

    1.1 The Intention and Experiment 7

    1.2 What is the Evolution in Consciousness? 8

    1.3 The Four Steps of Evolution 9

    1.4 Choosing the 5D Field 11

    1.5 Creating the Galactic Federation of Light 12

    1.6 Creating the 5D Earth Plane 13

    1.7 Creating Physical Forms 15

    1.8 Creating Resources for Survival 16

    1.9.Designing the Sun 17

    1.10 Creating the Eight Micro-Quantum Universal Laws 19

CHAPTER 2: THE DESIGN OF THE 12D GRID 25

    2.1 Connecting Earth to the 12D Grid 27

    2.2 Opening the 12D Grid 28

    2.3 What is a Collective Consciousness? 29

    2.4 How Consciousness Exists in the 12D Grid 30

    2.5 Traversing the 12D Grid 35

    Summary 37

CHAPTER 3: THE 5D HUMAN FORM 39

    3.1 The Intention 39

    3.2 Light Codes 40

    3.3 The Role of DNA 41

    3.4 Two Types of DNA 42

    3.5 The Electrical Grid System 44

    3.6. The Channel 45

    3.7 Twelve Energy Centers 45

    3.8 The *I Am* Presence and the Higher Self 50

    3.9 The Etheric Body 51

    3.10 The Subtle Bodies 52

    3.11 The Energetic Field 54

    3.12 The Light Quotient 56

    3.13 Entering the Human Form 57

CHAPTER 4: EXPERIENCING THE 5D EARTH 61

    4.1 Masculine and Feminine Frequencies 61

    4.2 Creator Beings 62

    4.3 Creating a Human Life 62

    4.4 Telepathy 64

4.5 Nourishing the Form 65

4.6 Time 66

4.7 Aging 67

4.8 Death 68

CHAPTER 5: EARTH'S FALL FROM GRACE 69

5.1 How Earth Shifted Into the 3D Field 69

5.2 Earth's Timeline Shift 81

5.3 Clearing the Earth 83

5.4 The 5D Human Experience 84

5.5 The 4D Human Experience 86

5.6 The 4D Races Experience 87

Summary 88

CHAPTER 6: THE DESIGN OF THE 3D EARTH 89

6.1 The Physical Redesign 89

6.2 The 5D Grid 90

6.3 The Moon 92

6.4 Water 95

6.5 The Physical Redesign of 3D Forms 95

6.6 Universal Laws 98

6.7 Creating the Akashic Record 102

6.8 Sex, Date and Location of Birth 103

6.9 Core Foundational Consciousnesses 104

6.10 Contracts 106

6.11 Family Maps 107

6.12 The Blueprint for Incarnation 110

Summary 112

CHAPTER 7: CREATING THE 3D HUMAN BODY 113

7.1 Restructuring DNA 114

7.2 Light Quotients For the 3D Human 115

7.3 3D Human Body Versus 5D Human Body 117

7.4 The Energetic Field 117

7.5 Ego Structure 118

7.6 Higher Self 119

7.7 The *I Am* Presence 120

7.8 Subtle Bodies 121

7.9 Twelve Energy Centers 122

7.10 The Etheric Body 125

Summary 126

CHAPTER 8: THE BEGINNING OF THE LIGHT WORKER ... 127

8.1 Incarnating into the 3D Human Form 127

8.2 Volunteer & Lightworker 127

8.3 The First Call for Light Workers 129

8.4 Two Groups of Light Workers 130

8.5 The Impact of the Light Worker 131

Summary 133

CHAPTER 9: THE OPENING OF THE EARTH'S 5D GRID 135

9.1 The 12D Grid 136

9.2 Energetic Assistance 137

9.3 Connecting with the Human 137

9.4 Connecting with the Earth 139

9.5 Physical Assistance 140

9.6 Zones 141

9.7 Physical Connection with the Human 144

9.8 Working with the Human 146

9.9 Closing the 5D Grid 147

CHAPTER 10: 4D RACES 151

    10.1 Entering Onto the Earth 153

    10.2 The Galactic and Reptilian Beings 154

    Summary 155

CHAPTER 11:

ABDUCTION, HYBRIDIZATION, AND IMPLANTS 157

    11.1 The Abduction of the Human: A Three-Step Process 157

    11.2 The Abduction Program 164

    11.3 Hybridization Programs 165

    11.4 Creating the Hybrid Being 166

    11.5 The Human and Hybrid Connection 170

    11.6 Implants 171

CHAPTER 12: THE REPTILIANS AND THE HUMANOID 175

    12.1 Pulling Energy out of the Human 175

    12.2 Entering the Human Form 177

    12.3 The Creation of Humanoids 178

    Summary 180

CHAPTER 13: SECOND FALL FROM GRACE;
SECOND CALL FOR LIGHT WORKERS 181

13.1 The Unique Role of the Second Call Light Worker 182

CHAPTER 14: CLEARING THE EARTH 185

14.1 The Process 186

14.2 4D Beings Shifting into 3D Forms 187

14.3 Physical Contact with Humans 189

14.4 The Clearing of the Reptilians 193

14.5 The Clearing of the Humanoids 194

14.6 Engagement with 4D Races Off-Earth 196

CHAPTER 15: THE CLARION CALL:
THIRD CALL FOR LIGHT WORKERS 201

15.1 Three Groups of Light Workers 203

15.2 The Beacons of Light 203

15.3 The Soldiers 204

15.4 The Pioneers 206

Summary 208

CHAPTER 16: THE HARMONIC CONVERGENCE 209

16.1 Higher Dimensional Consciousnesses Entering the 5D Grid 209

16.2 Awakening the Light Worker 211

16.3 Earth Anchored into the 5D 212

Summary 216

CHAPTER 17: THE PHYSICAL EVOLUTION 217

17.1 The Multi-Dimensional Human 220

17.2 The Multidimensional Experience 222

Summary 225

CHAPTER 18: THE QUANTUM FIELD 227

18.1 Review: The 12D Grid 227

18.2 What is the Quantum Field? 228

18.3 Humans and the Micro-Quantum Field 231

18.4 Creating in the Micro-Quantum Field 233

18.5 Future and Past Lifetimes 235

18.6 Humans and the Macro-Quantum Field 236

Summary 237

CHAPTER 19: PARADIGMS 239

    19.1 Karma and Karmic Cycles 241

    19.2 Past Lives 248

    19.3 DNA 250

    19.4 The Akashic Records 250

    19.5 Clearing the Akashic Records 251

    Summary 254

CHAPTER 20: FINAL STATEMENTS 255

About the Author 259

INTRODUCTION

I was on a bus slowly winding its way up to the powerful site of Machu Pichu when *The Divine Design* entered my reality. As the bus was approaching the site, my body began to increase in vibration. All the noise on the bus quieted, and I started to shift into an altered state. I heard a soft, gentle voice say, "This is your book. You are writing Earth's story." I was confused, as I had no idea I would be writing a book, nor did I think it would begin on a bus.

I asked the voice, "What is my book?" The voice responded, "You are writing the historical account of Earth and humanity's evolution. As the bus stopped at the entrance to Machu Pichu, before I could even exit the bus, I received the download for the entire book. It was one of the most intense and magical moments of my life. I gathered my backpack and began to walk off the bus slowly. I could feel my body vibrating at a frequency much higher than it typically holds.

I receive downloads all the time from my Guides. I had never received a download as large and as quick as I did at that moment. It was as if my Guides wanted to make sure that I heard them but also understood the magnitude of the information delivered to me.

As I slowly walked the ancient land of Machu Pichu, I knew I was not alone. I could feel potent Higher Dimensional Beings around me, guiding me through the land. These Beings were the ones that spoke to me on the bus and provided the downloads that would later become *The Divine Design.*

When I asked who they were, they responded, "We are the Galactic Federation of Light, and we are here to assist you in writing your first book." There was a familiarity to these Beings. I felt at home in their energy. I knew I had been waiting my entire life to reconnect with them and fulfill the contract of writing this book.

As I walked through Machu Pichu, they shared the entire book with me as if we were sitting together at a table. They spoke to me through energy and showed me visual scenes like a movie. I knew at that moment I was the vessel that would write the story of Earth's and humanity's heroic journey, dictated by the Galactic Federation of Light (GFOL).

I had no idea this was the book I would write. I had no idea Machu Pichu was the location where it would all be downloaded. I had no idea the GFOL would be telling me the story, and I had no idea all that was going to be revealed to me—and eventually to you.

This book is Earth's story told by the GFOL. If it is difficult to wrap your head around these Beings, I encourage you to trust there is a reason you are holding this book in your hand.

I had never heard of most of the information that they provided to me. It was complex. I received many concepts that I had to sit with for days, sometimes weeks, in order to break them down into digestible concepts. I drew graphs, pictures, diagrams—anything that would allow me to dissect and understand the complex information I was receiving. My brain would twist like a pretzel trying to comprehend how and why certain events occurred.

It was my role to simplify the complex concepts into basic and digestible terms. It was imperative to create a book that any human could pick up and understand.

The Divine Design is a short analysis of what has transpired over millions of years. Our history is much more complex than what I was able to summarize in *The Divine Design*. Please see the book as a clift note version of a very complex and very detailed history of Earth and Humanity.

Although it plays out like a science fiction book, everything you are about to read occurred on the Earth, and you have a memory of it all.

This book spans approximately 10–15 million years, from the human linear perspective. One of the qualities required for reading this book is an expanded perception of time. Your time frame is linear, thus long and slow. The GFOL do not exist in a time-space continuum. They experience everything in the now. I did my best to quantify the time frames accurately, but please don't hold firm to exact dates and times described within *The Divine Design*. Three thousand years to you is a moment to the GFOL.

This book is designed to break you free from the chains of illusion the 3rd dimension creates through paradigms, beliefs, behaviors, and systems. *The Divine Design* will ask you to step into new paradigms and hold concepts that may or may not make sense. It will ask you to drop all desire for scientific proof because scientific proof only exists within a 3rd dimensional field. I am sharing a quantum perspective where our science doesn't exist.

I wrote *The Divine Design* through the lens of neutrality. There is no right or wrong, good or bad. There is no judgment around how Earth's journey has played out. I encourage you to set aside any preconceived notions or judgments and walk through the pages of this book with the neutrality this process requires.

You may find yourself experiencing moments of deep resonance followed by the inability to comprehend what you are reading. Both are okay. There is a reason you are holding this book. I wrote it to remind you of your story and your history with Earth.

The Divine Design was written to remind you of how it all began, why you are in your physical form, and the divine orchestration of it all so that you can begin to remember that nothing is chance. You are a divine design within a larger divine design. You are awakening to the massive experiment that Earth intended and that you agree to take part in now.

As you read through *The Divine Design*, I hope it resonates deep within your Being and activates a knowingness you have always held within your body.

I hope you find your story within these pages. I hope it reminds you of how courageous and committed you are for being in the physical form. I hope it brings clarity to your life. I hope it allows you to trust your human journey is a gift, and it is much more significant than what the human eye can see.

The Divine Design is your story, and I am humbled to have received the downloads allowing me to write this historical book. Thank you for being a part of this miraculous and courageous evolution. I hope this book brings you peace.

Chapter 1

THE DESIGN OF THE 5D EARTH

Let us start from the beginning. All Consciousness began from the same Source, which many in your field of Consciousness refer to as God. Source is a word used by the human to attempt to understand the beginning of Consciousness. It allows the human to hold or conceptualize the unnamable. Words are conceived within the dimension one finds themself in. Consciousness itself does not have a *word* associated with it. The human needs words to understand its experience. Throughout this book, we will use human words to describe that which has no name.

Source exists as a vibration, a sole tone, a single breath that never stops, a heartbeat that continues to expand. Source is a single vibration that has no beginning and no end. There is no definition, no description, no label; it just is. It exists in no time or space, and yet it holds everything. It is a concept, one that the human mind grapples with because Source is beyond experience. It is all and nothing at the same time.

Humans have touched the spark of Source, entering its one unified field of nothingness. When the human consciousness enters it, there is a feeling of complete bliss and oneness. These are simply words used to describe that which is difficult to describe.

Source exists in the space of oneness. It has nothing to experience other than the one unified field of its spark. As one unified field, it can only experience itself by existing outside itself. Source uses individual sparks of its own consciousness to experience itself. It pulsates or splits an aspect of its Consciousness and sends it into the quantum field. That unique Consciousness holds its own energetic frequency based on its energetic spin. The frequency creates an experience. The Consciousness that split from Source becomes its own energetic expression with its unique experience. Every individual Consciousness existing in the now, including you, is created in this way.

Let us break this down for you. Consciousness is energy, and energy spins. The spinning of energy creates a frequency that produces a vibrational tone. The frequency dictates the dimension the Consciousness is experiencing. The dimension establishes how Consciousness experiences itself.

A dimension holds a spectrum of consciousness to be experienced within it. A spectrum of consciousness is the available experiences a Consciousness (you) can access. The higher in the dimensional field, the smaller the range of consciousness and the fewer experiences a Consciousness will have to experience. The lower in the dimensional field, the larger the spectrum of consciousness and the more experiences a Consciousness will have to experience itself.

For instance, in the 3rd dimensional field, the human can access thousands of consciousnesses to create an experience. They can access fear, love, joy, peace, and so on. However, in a higher dimensional field, like the 5D field, the spectrum of consciousness is not as large, and thus there is less consciousnesses for the human to access in order to experience itself. The 5D field does not hold fear, greed, lack, control, and so on.

As Source began splitting itself into unique Consciousnesses, these energetic expressions of Source began to play within a quantum field. The quantum field is an energetic space allowing infinite possibilities of expression through frequency and dimension. All that ever is, was, and will be resides in the quantum field. All Consciousnesses that split from Source exist in the quantum field. Every experience that has, could, or will be experienced is held in the quantum field. All dimensional fields exist within the quantum field. There are an infinite amount of experiences that can be had within the quantum field.

The quantum field holds universal laws allowing Consciousness to understand how to experience itself. These universal laws are a natural way of being, once separation from Source begins.

We want to expand on two universal laws: free will and the energetic field. Free will allows all Consciousness to create its own unique expression through its choice in frequency and dimensional field.

The energetic field surrounds each Consciousness as soon as they split from Source. The energetic field allows each Consciousness to experience the quantum field in a sovereign energetic container. Sovereignty provides for safety. A sovereign Consciousness is held in a safe field of its own light without any interference. Other Consciousnesses cannot impact a sovereign Consciousness within the quantum field unless it chooses to be impacted.

In the quantum field, Consciousness is free to create any experience and be any expression. It does this by shifting its frequency through intention and energy. It chooses what it wants to experience (intention) and shifts its frequency (energy) to enter the dimensional field to allow for that experience and expression. It is all choice.

Once Consciousness understands how the quantum field works, it can experience and play in lower dimensional fields. The lower fields allow for more experiences. Like we said above, the lower a dimension, the larger the spectrum of Consciousness and the more to feel and experience.

1.1 The Intention and Experiment

The Consciousness that is known as *Earth* split from Source at one moment and used intent and energy to create her current experience and experiment. We would like to point out the distinction between the Higher Dimensional Consciousness that created this experience and the planetary body holding that Consciousness. We will be referring to the Higher

Dimensional Consciousness as Earth, she, or her, and we will be referring to Earth's form as the Earth Plane or Planet Earth.

Earth as the Higher Dimensional Consciousness split from Source and was experiencing itself in many different frequencies, forms, and dimensional fields. She decided she wanted to play in a low dimensional field. She wanted to experience shifting within lower dimensional fields while in a physical form.

She wanted to enter into a 5th dimensional form (the Earth Plane) within a 5D field and experience shifting into a 7th dimensional field within the same form. The Earth Plane would shift frequencies and dimensions while Earth as a Higher Dimensional Consciousness would experience that shift within the Earth Plane. This experience had never been done before.

If a Consciousness wants to move from one dimensional field to another, it will instantly shift its frequency to enter into and become another dimensional field. The Consciousness as an entire energetic body moves from one field to another.

What made this experience so unique was that Earth as a Consciousness would exist within a physical form (the planet), and the planet would move her into higher dimensional fields. It was the planet that would shift, not Earth. Earth was merely experiencing the shift through the physical form. This shift has been referred to as the evolution in Consciousness.

1.2 What Is the Evolution in Consciousness?

Evolution is the process of energy moving from a lower frequency and dimensional field to the next-highest frequency and dimensional field. The Earth and all Higher Dimensional Consciousnesses incarnated on the Earth Plane to experience an evolution through physical forms.

The experience of evolution is similar to driving a car. The Earth and the human or Higher Dimensional Consciousness are pushing on the gas, but it is the car—the human body and planetary body—that is speeding up and taking the human and Earth for a ride. The physical form takes Earth and the Higher Dimensional Consciousness on a ride into the next-highest dimensional field.

Earth and the Higher Dimensional Consciousness will be experiencing the 5th, 6th, and 7th dimensional fields without being anchored in that dimensional field. They remain as their Higher Dimensional Consciousness within the human form, yet they can experience lower dimensional fields through the physical form.

Evolution is experienced through steps. It occurs energetically and cannot be manipulated. It is the natural process of energy increasing in form. It begins and ends the same way for Earth and all Higher Dimensional Consciousness in physical form. There are four steps: acclimation, assimilation, tapping, and anchoring.

1.3 The Four Steps of Evolution
Acclimation

The first step in evolution is *acclimation*. The physical form continuously receives high frequency light from the Sun. As the light enters the form, it begins to acclimate it. Acclimation occurs when the physical form slows down the high frequency light to receive it into the body. If the frequency of the light is too high, the body won't be able to access the light and use it to shift into higher frequencies. The light will dissolve from the body. If the body acclimates, it will settle into the physical body.

Assimilation

Once the physical form acclimates to light, the body begins to *assimilate* it. Assimilation occurs when the physical form integrates the higher-frequency light into the lower-frequency light within the body. The higher-frequency light then either pushes the density or lower-frequency light out of the body or merges the denser light into the higher-frequency light. Either way, the physical form begins to increase its frequency as the lower density is moved out of the form or is integrated into the higher light.

Acclimation and assimilation occur naturally. The physical body is designed to evolve. It knows how to shift the light within its form into the next highest dimensional field. However, evolution requires the physical form and the Higher Dimensional Consciousness within the form to work together. The physical form will hold higher frequencies of light, but the Higher Dimensional Consciousness within the form, the Earth, and the human must consciously participate in the evolution. They must choose to experience and tap into the next highest frequencies and dimensional field. They also must feel and experience the denser lower-frequency light moving out of the body or merging into the higher light. The physical form acclimates to and assimilates the higher frequencies, but the Higher Dimensional Consciousnesses must choose, feel, and experience the energy shifts.

Tapping

Tapping into the next dimensional field is an essential step in evolution. As the physical form holds more light, the human aspect and the Earth can feel and experience the next highest frequency and dimensional field. They—the ego and personality—must begin to tap into and experience the Consciousness within that dimension.

For instance, when the human's 5D physical form is anchored into the 5D field, it will experience and create from this field. The body is holding 5D frequencies. As the form begins to assimilate and acclimate to light, it starts to hold higher frequencies of light, allowing the human to naturally tap into the next highest dimensional field, the 6D field. The human begins to be and feel the higher frequencies or higher states of Consciousness within that dimension. They feel it within their body because their body is holding the frequencies. All that is experienced during evolution is in the body. Tapping into higher frequencies of light and the next highest dimensional field allows the human and the Earth to practice being in higher states of Consciousness.

Anchoring

As the physical form continues to acclimate and assimilate more light, tapping into the next dimensional field, the physical form will *anchor* into that field. The physical form must hold over 80 percent of the frequency of that dimensional field to anchor into the next highest dimensional field. Once the body is anchored into a new dimensional field, it will physically stand in that field. The human or the Earth's reality is that dimensional field.

For instance, a 5D physical form is holding 100 percent 5D frequencies. As the body begins to acclimate and assimilate more light, the percentage shifts into 95 percent 5D and 5 percent 6D. The more light the body holds, the more the percentage shifts toward the 6D frequency until eventually the body holds 80 percent 6D. Once this occurs, the body is anchored into the 6th dimensional field. The form is holding a majority of 6D frequencies and is physically standing in the 6D field. The human's entire reality in every *now* is seen through the lens of the 6th dimension. The physical form is in the quantum field; therefore, at this point, it can still see and feel the 5th dimension, but the form is anchored and standing in the 6th dimension.

This process is how evolution occurs for both the Earth Plane and the human form. There is acclimation of light, assimilation of light, tapping into the next highest dimensional field, and then the anchoring into that field. We created the 12D grid to allow all physical forms to connect and anchor into the next dimensional field effortlessly.

1.4 Choosing the 5D Field

Earth chose the 5th dimension for a few reasons. It is the lowest dimensional field a consciousness can enter into that provides a physical form without duality. The 5D field allowed her to stay connected to the higher aspects of herself, including Source, her blueprint, and the quantum field. The 5D field also provided Earth a large variety of consciousnesses to experience and create from the now.

When Consciousness is in a 4D field or lower, there is a high probability of amnesia. Amnesia is experienced when a Consciousness is in a dimensional field that is dense enough to create a feeling of separation from Source and the quantum field. Imagine dimensions as a light that dims. As Consciousness moves into lower dimensions, the light begins to dim, and the Consciousness has a more challenging time staying connected, seeing who it is and what it is choosing. It forgets how Consciousness works, where it originated from, and why it is where it is.

In addition, the density within fields that are 4D and lower creates duality. Duality increases the variety of Consciousness experienced within the field. However, it also provides denser consciousnesses such as control, tyranny, and greed. Duality creates good and bad, right and wrong, positive and negative.

Earth wanted to be in a physical form, experiencing the lowest dimensional field without duality, while still staying connected to her Higher Dimensional Consciousness, the quantum field, her knowingness of who she was, and Source. The 5D field allowed for all of this, and so she began her experiment in the 5D.

Once she established her intent, she needed to create a team of Light Beings that would design the experiment and then support, guide, and watch over her as she moved through it.

1.5 Creating the Galactic Federation of Light

Earth sent out an energetic call for assistance in creating her experiment and for guidance through the experiment. We are the council of twelve Higher Dimensional Light Beings that answered her call.

Once we understood Earth's intention, we created the Galactic Federation of Light. We needed much more assistance designing the experiment and ensuring Earth would be safe to navigate the experiment.

We had thousands of Higher Dimensional Consciousnesses from many different dimensional fields answer the call. Most of these were Light Beings from larger collective consciousnesses existing between the 9th and 24th dimensional fields.

As the Beings were forming into one large Federation, we created councils. The councils allowed for groups of Beings within the Federation to have specific tasks and roles within Earth's large experiment. Each council contained about 120 Beings. Twelve Beings were in charge of each council, and each Being had ten Beings assisting them. Our council of twelve oversaw all councils within the Federation.

There are councils focused on technology to assist in clearing Earth's density. There are councils focused on the security of Earth, ensuring her physical form remains intact. There are councils focused on activating and upgrading Earth and humanity. There are councils focused on assisting all the physical forms on the Earth other than the human. Councils focus on assisting specific Light Workers incarnated in human form working in large communities such as government, religious, financial, and scientific. The councils and all Light Beings within each council play a significant role in Earth's evolution.

1.6 Creating the 5D Earth Plane

The Earth Plane was the first thing we created after the Galactic Federation. We created this physical body through intent and energy instantaneously.

It may be challenging to conceptualize how a planet is created instantaneously through intent and energy, yet everything in the quantum field is created in this way.

When we intend to create a physical form from energy, first we must see it, feel it, and understand its frequency. When creating the planet, we use the energy of our own vibration, the 12th dimension, and we intend that energy into a planetary form within the lower dimensional field, the

5th dimension. Creation can only occur within the dimensional field one is standing in. Therefore, we created all forms, including the Earth Plane, from 12th dimensional energy.

The energy we are alchemizing into the 5D exists in what are called *light codes*. These codes hold the intention of what we are creating—the physical 5D Earth Plane.

We intended the vision of the physical form into the 12D light codes through energy and telepathy. You can imagine circles of light, if you will, swirling in front of you. With your intention and visualization, you intend the light to hold the form you are creating.

We energetically infused the light codes with the intended physical form, the planet. The codes held the physical intention energetically. We then slowed the energy of the light codes down from a 12D frequency to a 5D frequency.

As the light codes slowed down, they began to form the intent held within the 12D light codes. The light within the codes alchemized into a denser crystallized matter, creating the intended form.

The codes automatically shifted into the physical form because they held the intention of that form within their light. The form is created when energy is slowed down.

The 5D planet became a crystalline physical structure. What began as an intention in the 12th dimension turned into a physical form in the 5th dimension.

The design of her form was always to allow her to shift into a 7D field. We knew that whatever we created needed to be able to sustain a 7D field. A form that holds less density allows an easier transition shifting into light.

We chose a shape that would allow for the ease of energy to flow through and around the planet and provide the ability to hold mass. We created a disk-like elongated form that would enable her to expand more easily. This shape wasn't too wide or too thin. It allowed the form to hold density and be physical yet not take up too much mass, which would make shifting dimensional fields more difficult.

Once we created the initial 5D form, we began to make some subtle energetic touches within the form. We needed to ensure Earth's Consciousness could reside within this form. We created through intent an etheric body similar to the human etheric body that would hold her Higher Consciousness while in the 5D form. This energetic body would allow her a safe experience shifting from 5D to 7D. We designed an energetic channel that would allow Earth to stay aligned and connected to the quantum field, ourselves, and all other aspects of her, including Source. We also designed an energetic field around her form to ensure she would remain sovereign within the experience.

1.7 Creating Physical Forms

One of the unique aspects of Earth's experiment was that she wanted to allow Higher Dimensional Consciousnesses to experience this shift with her. These consciousnesses would have the option to enter a physical form on her planetary body. They would be able to experience a very low dimensional field without having to be anchored in that dimensional field. Like Earth, they, too, would be moving their Consciousness into a 5D form to experience the 5D field.

We needed to design 5D physical forms on the planet that would allow Higher Dimensional Consciousnesses to incarnate onto the 5D Earth Plane to participate in her experiment.

We created every physical form in the same way we created the Earth Plane, through intent and energy. First, we needed to intend a specific form. For instance, when we chose to create what a human refers to as a tree, we had to visualize the form. We had to know all the details of how we wanted that tree to look and feel. Once we held the intention of the tree, we took 12D light codes holding the intention of the form and shifted the codes down into a 5D frequency. Instantaneously the form would appear on the Earth Plane. Every form we created held a Higher Dimensional Consciousness within it.

Similar to the Earth Plane, every physical form was created with an energetic field around it, a channel within its form, and an etheric body to hold the Higher Dimensional Consciousnesses light quotient while participating on the Earth Plane.

We created thousands of physical forms at this time: animals, flowers, trees, rocks, crystals, insects, birds, plants, dragons, fairies, mermaids, whales, and more. We created every physical form you see on the planet now, and every physical form has a Higher Dimensional Consciousness within it. This was one of the most creative and enjoyable aspects of designing the Earth Plane.

1.8 Creating Resources for Survival

Once we had the thousands of forms created, we needed to create resources that would allow the physical forms to survive on the Earth Plane. Two resources were imperative in keeping the forms functioning: air and water.

Air was created from energy particles and was the conduit that moved energy within the 5D field. It was also what provided breath within many of the 5D forms. We created forms that would need to move energy and blood to stay alive. The breath is what would keep the energy and blood moving. Air allowed for breath, and breath fed the body.

Water was another resource necessary for the 5D form to survive. All 5D forms had water within their form. Water is a conduit for the form. It is a physicality that moves energy through the body with ease. It assists the body in integrating higher frequencies of light in order to shift into the next dimensional field.

Air and water were two necessary resources needed to maintain the well-being of all 5D forms; however, the Sun was the most essential component necessary in Earth's design. Without the Sun, Earth's intention and all life on her would not be able to survive.

1.9 Designing the Sun

The Sun was the most crucial design in keeping the Earth Plane and all living forms on the Earth alive. We had two intentions when creating the Sun: to assist the planet and all physical forms on the planet in the evolution, and to maintain life on the planet.

We created the Sun the same way we created everything else, with intent and energy. The Sun was created as a 9D form, and it holds a Higher Dimensional Consciousness within its form. We placed the physical Sun in close proximity to the Earth to ensure a close connection throughout Earth's experiment. Many humans are under the impression that the Sun is far away in linear time and space, but that is just not the case. Humans only see things in physicality, yet all that is seen in the sky is within the quantum field. Linearity does not exist in the quantum field. What looks to be physical in nature, existing light years away is actually Consciousnesses within a form held in the quantum field where time does not exist. Distance in the sky is an illusion once you leave the 3D field.

The Sun is much closer to the Earth than is believed. It's the divine design of this experiment.

The color you see from the Sun is the light creating the color when it hits the Earth's atmosphere. The air, physical density, and oxygen make colors from frequencies. As the Sun emits higher-frequency light from its form, the color will shift into a lighter yellow.

We sent out a call for a Higher Dimensional Consciousness to assist Earth in providing the light, as the Sun, to Earth. The Higher Dimensional Consciousness that answered our call has a close relationship with Earth. Both Consciousnesses have experienced each other many times within the quantum field.

The Higher Dimensional Consciousness resides within the form called the Sun. The physical Sun you see has a living Consciousness within it right now. The contract between the Consciousness within the Sun and the Consciousness within Earth is powerful and crucial.

We designed the Sun to emit two distinct types of light to the Earth Plane and all physical forms on the planet. The first type of light is sunlight, which provides life or *prana* to the planet and all 5D forms. Direct sunlight provides fuel for the physical forms. All 5D forms are created from light codes, which are energy. The 5D form needs energy— light—to survive, and it needs to have a constant flow of energy in and out of it. This light was necessary for all living Beings and the planet to survive. Without the Sun, Earth and all Beings on her would perish.

The second type of light is made from higher-frequency light codes sent down onto the Earth Plane for all 5D forms to shift into higher dimensional fields. Light codes from the sun are designed to increase the light frequency within the 5D forms and activate the light codes within the forms.

The Sun holds many different frequencies of light codes. The frequency of the Earth Plane and all 5D forms on her will dictate what high frequency light will be emitted from the Sun. The light codes are always at a higher frequency than the Earth Plane and 5D forms, yet not so high that the forms cannot assimilate, acclimate, and anchor the light. It is a delicate balance. The Sun can accelerate or slow down the frequency on the Earth Plane based on the light codes it sends down. It's a unique and powerful relationship between the Consciousnesses within Earth and the Sun. They are deeply connected and constantly communicating with each other. The Sun holds a pivotal role in Earth's experiment; without it, evolution and life on the planet could not exist.

We didn't need to create much other than the Sun, water, and air for the forms to survive. As 5D consciousnesses, they can create and intend anything they may need while in a 5D form, including food.

Food was not necessary for us to create because 5D physical forms survive on energy. In the 5D field, there is no consumption of any other physical form, including animals, plants, and flowers.

All Higher Dimensional Consciousnesses within a 5D form see all other 5D forms as Consciousness choosing to participate in a 5D field, not as something to consume or use for their benefit. It is a different mentality than in the 3D or 4D field. All 5D forms do, however, have free will. If they want to design and create foods to digest, they can do that through intent and energy.

1.10 Creating The Eight Micro-Quantum Universal Laws

A basic proponent that exists within the quantum field are universal laws. There are four universal laws that exist for the entire unified quantum field. There are also universal laws that exist within a micro-quantum field. The Earth's experiment was within a micro-quantum field. Therefore, we had to create specific universal laws for all Consciousnesses to follow when they entered onto Earth. Before we share these laws, let us first describe the four universal laws in which all Consciousness exists in the quantum field.

The Four Quantum Universal Laws

These four universal laws were designed by the natural flow in which energy moves, creates, and exists. These ways of being were not designed by Source. They were created by the flow design of natural energy itself.

The four Quantum Universal Laws are:

1. Free will
All Consciousness can create, design, and be in any frequency at any now moment within the quantum field. When Consciousness splits from Source, it understands that it is free. It can choose and create its experience at will in any moment. It is not tied or stuck in or with any experience.

2. All Consciousness holds an aspect of Source
When Consciousness splits from Source, it holds within its frequency an aspect of Source. It contains the oneness that everything stems from

and remains connected to it while in the quantum field. Every Consciousness carries an aspect of Source within it regardless of what frequency it holds.

3. Intent creates experience

Consciousness creates all experience through intent and energy. Energy creates a frequency that dictates the experience. Depending upon the frequency consciousness is existing in, intent can manifest instantaneously or take time. The slower the frequency of Consciousness, the slower intent will manifest into an experience. A 3D consciousness intends an experience, and it can take months or years to appear. A 5D consciousness intends an experience, and it can happen within that moment.

4. Frequency dictates dimensional field

All Consciousness holds a frequency, and that frequency allows the Consciousness to reside in a specific dimensional field. If a Consciousness wants to experience a lower or higher dimensional field, it must shift its frequency either up or down to match the frequency within that dimensional field. For instance, a consciousness holding a 5D frequency can enter a 3D field by slowing down its frequency and moving into that dimensional field. A Consciousness holding a 3D frequency can enter a 5D field by increasing its frequency and moving into that field.

The Eight Micro-Quantum Universal Laws

There are also universal laws that are created within micro-quantum fields. Micro-quantum fields are dimensional fields within the quantum field holding their own unique experience, such as the Earth's experiment. Earth's experiment was in a micro-quantum field. We created a 12D grid around the Earth that created this micro-quantum field. We will go into more detail on the 12D grid in the next chapter. Any consciousness that chooses to move into this micro-quantum field will abide by the laws.

The reason micro-quantum fields have laws is to allow for homeostasis within the field. The universal laws will hold the intention of the experiment while maintaining free will. When a consciousness enters or chooses to experience a certain micro-quantum field, it agrees to play within that experiment's set of rules, thus allowing free will but holding the experiment's intention.

We designed eight laws within Earth's micro-quantum field that are still in place now and provide a framework for Higher Dimensional Consciousnesses that choose to participate in Earth's experiment.

These eight laws are:

1. The Galactic Federation of Light are Earth's Guardians.
2. There is a 12D energetic grid around the Earth's Experiment.
3. The light quotient exists within the physical form.
4. The light quotient remains consistent.
5. The Consciousness that incarnates is connected to its light.
6. The Consciousness that incarnates must vibrate at a 6D frequency or higher.
7. Source is held within the physical form.
8. The Earth Plane cannot be physically destroyed.

The Galactic Federation of Light: Earth's Guardians

As we have stated before, Earth chose a group of Higher Dimensional Consciousnesses to design, guide, and protect her as she moves through her intentional shifts in Consciousness. The GFOL are overseeing the entire experience and ensuring that she succeeds in her intention.

The 12D Grid Around the Earth's Experiment

There is a 12D energetic grid around the Earth's experiment. This grid provides a container for Earth's intention to play out without interference or disruption from other outside Consciousnesses. We will provide more details on the grid in the next chapter.

The Light Quotient Exists within the Physical Form

Every Higher Dimensional Consciousness that drops down into any physical form on the Earth Plane brings in a percentage of their light. The percentage is based on the frequency that the human form is holding. The higher a physical form's frequency, the more light it can hold. For example, if the physical form is in a 5D frequency, it can hold between 10 and 15 percent of the Higher Dimensional Consciousness's light. If the form is in a 3D frequency, it can hold between 3 and 10 percent of its light. This percentage of light is called the light quotient.

The Light Quotient Remains Consistent

The Higher Dimensional Consciousness that incarnated into the physical form holds the same percentage of its light quotient throughout its entire experience on Earth. The light quotient does not change. If a consciousness brings in 6 percent of its 12D Consciousness, that 6 percent remains the same throughout its human journey regardless of shifts in frequencies within the human body.

The light quotient does not shift into a higher percentage of light as the physical form shifts into higher frequencies. The human form is shifting in order to allow the Higher Dimensional Consciousness within the form to experience itself in different dimensional fields within the same physical form.

The Consciousness that Incarnates is Connected to its Light

When a Higher Dimensional Consciousness enters the human form, it moves into the etheric body. The etheric body is an energetic field within the physical body designed to hold the Consciousness incarnating into the body.

The Consciousness within the etheric body becomes a light body while in the physical form. The light body is designed to energetically connect the Higher Dimensional Consciousness in the form to the larger collective Consciousness it existed in prior to dropping down into form.

An energetic cord connects the Higher Dimensional Consciousness within the human form to its larger Consciousness outside of the form. This cord vibrates at the frequency that the Higher Dimensional Consciousness resides in outside of the form. For instance, if a Higher Dimensional Consciousness dropped into a human body from a 9D Pleiadian collective, the energetic cord would vibrate at a 9D frequency. The cord is within the 12D grid because the collective Consciousness, Pleiadian Consciousness, is also within the grid.

The Consciousness that Incarnates must Vibrate at a 6D Frequency or Higher

Any Consciousness that drops into a physical form on Earth must be holding a 6D frequency or higher. If the Consciousness in the form is holding a 5D frequency, the form won't shift into the 6D. The Consciousness in the form does not increase its frequency. The physical form is shifting frequencies. Therefore, if the Consciousness within the form is at a lower frequency than the form is moving into, it won't be able to shift. The Consciousness will keep the form in the 5D frequency. The Consciousness incarnating into the physical form must hold the frequency that the form will eventually shift into.

Source is held within the Physical Form

The Higher Dimensional Consciousness incarnating into the physical form will hold an aspect of Source within the form. Source is known by many different names, including Allah, God, Creator, to name a few.

The Earth cannot be Physically Destroyed

If any Consciousness on or off the Earth tries to destroy the planet, the GFOL, with the assistance of other Higher Dimensional Consciousnesses, can intervene. This intervention can play out in many different ways, depending upon what is for the highest good of Earth and all Consciousnesses on it. This is the only time we can intervene.

Now that you understand how the Earth was designed and the universal laws that exist within Earth's experiment, let us describe how we hold this experiment together in an energetic grid.

Chapter 2

THE DESIGN OF THE 12D GRID

Earth was creating an experience we had never seen before that was both challenging and exciting. She was going to be allowing Higher Dimensional Consciousnesses to participate in her experiment both on and off her physical form.

As we stated in Chapter One, all consciousness that separates from Source enters the quantum field and has free will. Free will states that any consciousness can choose every moment without interference from any other consciousness.

We knew that all Higher Dimensional Consciousnesses entering Earth's experiment could freely create their realities. We could not intervene nor could Earth. We set up universal laws that would ensure some sense of order in the experiment, but we could not intervene unless the Earth Plane was going to be physically destroyed.

We knew we needed to create an energetic grid around Earth and her entire experiment to maintain a sense of order and control without interfering. The energetic grid would hold everything that exists in any now moment while participating on or off the Earth Plane.

All Higher Dimensional Consciousnesses participating on or off the Earth Plane are within the grid. All physical and non-physical forms we created were within the grid. Any experience, creation, dimension, and reality that could occur by any Higher Dimensional Consciousness participating with the Earth are within the grid. Everything that is seen, felt, heard, and experienced on the Earth Plane is filtered through a lens held within the grid.

We knew that the grid we designed needed to hold at least a 7th dimensional field. Earth was held in a 5D form within a 5D field. Her form was going to be shifting into a 7D frequency and a 7D field. The grid had to hold at least the frequency the Earth Plane was going to be shifting into. We also knew that many Higher Dimensional Consciousnesses would be entering into the field to participate. We needed the grid to hold high enough dimensional fields that the Higher Dimensional Consciousnesseses entering the grid would be able to exist within the grid.

We settled on a 12th dimensional grid. We chose a 12D grid for two reasons. One, it was a frequency high enough for any Higher Dimensional Consciousness to enter it and remain without too much difficulty. Two, it would allow the 5D Earth Plane to eventually shift into the 12th dimension if she chose.

We designed the energetic grid through intention and energy. First, we intended it into being. We knew we were creating a grid that would hold ten dimensions, the 3rd to the 12th. We intended the grid without the 1st and 2nd dimensional fields because those frequencies are too low for Higher Dimensional Consciousnesses to experience themselves in physical forms.

Once we had the intention in place, we visualized the grid, the role it would play, and the frequencies it would hold. We created a collective energetic pulse out from our energetic forms that was vibrating at a 12D frequency. The grid was instantaneously created and vibrating in a 12D frequency.

We then wrapped the grid and its energetic pulse around the Earth's form. It was not on the Earth Plane. It was in the quantum field. The grid could not be viewed from the Earth Plane as it was in a 12D field. It is around the Earth but in a much higher frequency, wrapping the entire experiment around its grid. Only if you were vibrating in a 12D field or higher would you be able to see the energetic grid.

The 12D grid holds ten dimensional fields. Each dimensional field is a distinct and separate energetic grid, and each field holds a spectrum of consciousness that can be experienced within it. Imagine the 12D grid as one large cloud and each dimensional field within the cloud is its own separate cloud.

From a distance, the 12D cloud looks like one dense physical form, but as you get closer and move into the cloud, you realize its moisture, and as you move into the moisture, you can see other clouds or dimensional fields. What looks like one physical cloud is actually ten separate clouds or dimensional fields. As you energetically move into each cloud, you no longer see the cloud but simply the spectrum of consciousness within it. The 12D grid is merely consciousness holding ten unique dimensional fields similar to the sky holding moisture that looks like clouds.

All ten dimensional fields exist in the same now moment within the quantum field. They can be accessed by any Higher Dimensional Consciousness within the 12D grid as long as the consciousness is holding that frequency. Therefore, any Higher Dimensional Consciousness, including Earth and the forms on her, have the opportunity and ability to enter any dimensional field within the 12D grid.

2.1 Connecting Earth to the 12D Grid

Once the grid was designed and in place, we created a replica of the 12D grid and placed it within the Earth Plane. We did this because we needed to energetically connect Earth and her physical form to the 12D grid. This would ensure that her consciousness as well as her physical form would be energetically connected to all 10 dimensional fields regardless of which dimension her form was vibrating at in any now moment. She held all dimensions within her form. She could potentially access any of the dimensions at any now moment if her form vibrated at that dimensional frequency.

2.2 Opening the 12D Grid

Once we designed the 12th dimensional grid and connected it to the Earth's physical form, we then sent out a call or energetic pulse providing an opportunity for any Higher Dimensional Consciousnesses to enter the grid and participate in this unique experiment.

We opened the grid by lowering its vibrational field to a 6D vibration. We then sent out an energetic pulse into the quantum field. The energetic pulse holds the frequency of the intention we set. This intention provided an opportunity for any Higher Dimensional Consciousness to participate and experience Earth's grand experiment. The quantum field holds all consciousness that ever split from Source; therefore, when we sent the pulse out, all consciousnesses received the pulse.

Once the pulse was received, Higher Dimensional Consciousnesses had the opportunity to choose. All consciousness understood this was an experiment. They knew it was an opportunity to experience lower consciousnesses in lower dimensional fields without being that consciousness. We had many consciousnesses that chose to participate.

To enter the 12D grid the Higher Dimensional Consciousnesses had to be in a 6D frequency or higher. As we stated in Chapter One, any consciousness entering a physical form must at least exist in the dimensional field the Earth Plane and physical form are shifting into. The Higher Dimensional Consciousnesses entering the grid would have the opportunity to enter physical forms on Earth. Therefore, they had to hold a 6D frequency or higher regardless of whether they chose to enter into a physical form or not.

We opened the grid once. If a Higher Dimensional Consciousnesses chose to exit the grid once they were in it, they would not have the ability to enter back in.

We keep the grid shut to ensure the least amount of interference from any other Consciousnesses within the quantum field. If we kept the grid open and held the intention that consciousness could come and go, it would be more difficult to maintain a contained and safe environment for Earth to evolve in physicality. It would allow for more variables. We wanted to create a space with the least number of variables in a field where all consciousness had free will. The only way we could guarantee that was by intending for the grid to stay closed.

We closed the grid the same way we opened it. We intended the frequency to shift back into a 12th dimensional field, and then we held an energetic pulse around it that prevented any further consciousnesses entering the field.

Once the grid was closed, we had hundreds of thousands of Higher Dimensional Consciousnesses from a variety of dimensional fields now within the 12D grid. The highest frequency within the grid is the 12th dimensional frequency. Regardless of what dimension a Higher Dimensional Consciousness existed in prior to entering the grid, they needed to hold an aspect of their consciousness within this 12D frequency.

2.3 What is a Collective Consciousness?

Before we begin to share how Higher Dimensional Consciousnesses are held within the 12D grid, we want to explore the idea of *consciousness*. All consciousness is sovereign and holds its own field of experience and expression. It chooses what consciousness it wants to experience or feel.

When multiple Higher Dimensional Consciousnesses choose to experience a unique expression of consciousness in specific frequencies and dimensional fields, they will all hold the same frequencies within the same dimensions. They create and become a collective of consciousness or what the human refers to as a *collective consciousness*.

A collective can hold a variety of frequencies within one dimensional field or a variety of frequencies within a few dimensional fields. If a collective is holding one dimensional field, the entire collective will be experiencing the same spectrum of consciousness held within the same dimensional field. If a collective is holding two or three dimensional fields, the entire collective will be experiencing a much larger spectrum of consciousness.

The larger a collective, the more dimensional fields are within that collective. A collective becomes larger by more consciousnesses choosing to enter it and experience it. Typically, the largest collective we have seen has three dimensional fields within it. This means that a consciousness within that collective can be holding a variety of frequencies, and depending upon which frequency it chooses, that will place it within one of three dimensional fields. The dimensional field it chooses will provide it with the spectrum of consciousness to experience.

Imagine each collective consciousness as a cloud. A Higher Dimensional Consciousness chooses to experience that cloud and enters it. You can imagine it as a light jumping into a larger light. Upon jumping in, it agrees to experience itself as the spectrum of consciousness or consciousnesses and dimensional fields or field within that collective. The Higher Dimensional Consciousness becomes the collective it moves itself into. It experiences itself as that collective consciousness.

Higher Dimensional Consciousness can also choose to experience themselves outside a collective. This is referred to as *an individual consciousness*. Essentially, all Consciousness that separates from Source becomes an individual consciousness, always holding an aspect of Source within its field. All collective consciousnesses are made up of individual consciousness. Everything in the quantum field is an aspect of Source experiencing itself as an individual consciousness, choosing to be separate in experience or collective in experience. In the quantum field, we see many more collectives than we do individual consciousnesses.

2.4 How Consciousness Exists in the 12D Grid

Both collective consciousnesses and individual consciousnesses volunteered to drop into the 12D grid. In each collective consciousness, there are thousands of individual consciousnesses. For example, the Pleiadian collective is the entire collective consciousness. A Pleiadian would be an individual consciousness within that collective.

When a collective or individual consciousness enters into the 12D grid, only an aspect of its consciousness enters the grid. We have referred to this in Chapter One as the *light quotient*. Only a percentage of the collective's or individual's consciousness enters into the grid to experience Earth.

Imagine the collective or individual consciousness as a pie. A piece (percentage) of the pie enters into the grid. The remainder of the pie exists outside the grid. The collective or individual consciousness enters the 12D grid with a percentage of its light, which we call the light quotient.

The collectives and individual consciousnesses that enter into the 12D grid are holding a variety of different frequencies varying from the 40th dimensional field to the 6th dimensional field.

Consciousnesses that existed beyond the 40th dimensional field never chose to enter into the grid. There are two reasons for that. One, they were experiencing themselves in a frequency that did not desire to feel a 5D field. The 40th dimension is a very high frequency, and it experiences itself very differently than 5th dimensional consciousness. Two, it's very challenging for a Higher Dimensional Consciousness holding a 40th dimensional frequency to shift down into a 12D field.

All Higher Dimensional Consciousnesses that enter the 12D grid have to be able to hold themselves in a 12D frequency within a 12th dimensional field. The higher the frequency, the more difficult this becomes.

The Higher Dimensional Consciousnesses do not have to shift down into a 12th dimensional frequency; they just need to hold their frequency within that dimension. It is similar to you, holding a very high frequency within your human form, entering into a room with humans holding a much lower frequency. They may be yelling, fighting, and discussing low frequency topics, and yet, you are standing in the room holding your frequency. It may be challenging to stay in your frequency, but you do it.

This is the experience for Higher Dimensional Consciousnesses when entering into the 12D grid. The challenge of being in the 12D grid is dependent upon their frequency. If an 8th dimensional consciousness entered into the grid, it would not be challenging. Its frequency is lower than the 12D, so it can easily hold itself in the grid. If a 25th dimensional consciousness entered into the grid, it may have a more challenging time. We had to ensure that all consciousnesses, regardless of the frequency and dimensional field they held, could safely and comfortably be held within the 12D grid.

We decided to create zones or physical forms within the 12D grid that would allow any collective or individual Consciousness in any dimensional field to remain within the grid while participating with Earth.

These physical forms would hold Higher Dimensional Consciousnesses that were entering into the 12D grid. It is very similar to the Earth's physical form (the Planet) holding Earth (the consciousness) or the human's physical form holding a Higher Dimensional Consciousness within.

We knew that each zone or form we created would only be able to hold a certain amount of consciousness. We had to ensure all collective or individual consciousnesses entering the 12D grid would be held within the grid. Therefore, we created thousands of zones.

We would like to preface that currently there are many more zones in the 12D grid than what we originally designed. As the Earth experiment progressed, more zones were created by the collective or individual consciousnesses within the grid.

Each collective and individual consciousness had free will, and as they began to experiment with the lower frequencies, they began to multiply or create more of their own consciousnesses as well as new consciousnesses. We will go into more detail later in the book. What is important to understand is that the zones we created in the beginning have multiplied a thousand times over in linear terms.

We created these forms the same way we created anything else, through intent and energy. It took a now moment to instantaneously create the zones. We intended to create forms ranging from the 5th to the 12th dimension.

We took 12D light codes, shifted them into 5th–12th dimensional frequencies, and created a variety of different forms. Each form had the ability to hold specific frequencies and dimensional fields.

For instance, if we were creating a 10th dimensional form with the intention of holding Higher Dimensional Consciousness in a 15th–20th dimensional field, we would slow the 12D light codes down into the 10th dimensional field and intend a form to arise in order to hold the 15th–20th dimensional consciousnesseses. This form would look like what a human would call a star.

All the forms we designed at this time created what the human calls the sky. They are referred to as stars, planets, suns, and moons. When there are groups of forms together, it is referred to as solar systems, galaxies, and constellations.

Once we had the zones created, the Higher Dimensional Consciousnesses can then enter into the grid and move themselves into one of these zones. They remain within the zone throughout their entire experience with Earth.

The majority of forms we created are what the human calls stars and star systems. These forms were easy for us to make as they required very little form and were able to hold consciousnesses existing between the 7th and 40th dimensional field. Most individual and collective consciousness that dropped into the grid were held in some sort of form that resembles a star.

The size of the collective consciousness would dictate whether it would enter into a single star or multiple stars (creating a star system). A collective's size is determined by the number of individual consciousnesses held within the collective entering the 12D grid.

For example, let us refer to a collective consciousness as a *group*, a consciousness as a *person,* and a bus as a *zone*. If a group dropped down into the grid with 50 people, that would be considered a small group; it could fit into one bus. However, if a group dropped down into the grid with 150 people, that would be considered a large group and would fit into three buses. This is how stars and star systems worked with collectives.

If a small collective enters into the grid, it will move into one star. For instance, the collective the humans call Polaris is held in one star due to the small size of its collective when it dropped into the grid.

If a large collective drops into the grid, they would be held in multiple stars, creating a star system. Star systems hold much larger collectives. For instance, the collective the humans call Orion is held in many stars due to the large size of its collective.

When you combine stars and star systems together, you get what the human calls *galaxies* and *solar systems*. It's all just individual and collective consciousnesses within forms we have created in order to exist within a 12D grid.

Another zone we created is what the humans have called planets, moons, and suns. These zones were created to be more dense and physical than the stars and would hold individual and collective consciousnesses holding 6th and 7th dimensional frequencies. They could also enter stars, but many chose and were more comfortable in planets, moons, and suns.

We created hundreds of planets, moons, and suns. Currently, there are more planets, moons, and suns than what we created in the beginning. They are holding individual and collective consciousnesses that exist within a 4th and 5th dimensional frequency. Later in the book, we will discuss how 4th and 5th dimensional consciousness got into the 12D grid.

Every form we created is holding Higher Dimensional Consciousness experiencing itself within that form. The form is not the consciousness. It is holding the consciousness. For instance, what the human would call a Pleiadian is thought to be a star being—or another name the human created—because it resides within a star or stars. However, a Pleiadian is actually a Higher Dimensional Consciousness residing within a form called a star. It is neither a Pleiadian nor a star being. It is a Higher Dimensional Consciousness participating in Earth's experiment. The linear human mind creates a name in order to understand it and believes it is from the form it is residing in. The Higher Dimensional Consciousness within the "star" does not come from that star system. It is merely holding an aspect of its consciousness within that form.

All of the forms we created hold Higher Dimensional Consciousness yet can be seen by the human as physical forms in the sky. The quantum field holds both the physical form and the Higher Dimensional Consciousness. What is seen and experienced depends on the frequency of the one seeing. There is simultaneously a dense form and a Higher Dimensional Consciousness within the form.

The human can only see the frequency and dimensional field their body is holding. For instance, a star in the sky may be holding a 7th dimensional collective Pleiadian Consciousness. When the human looks up at the sky, it will only see a physical form reflecting the same dimensional field as their body. A 3D Human will see a 3D form. A 5D human will see a 5D form. However, within that physical form is 7D Consciousness. If the human were holding a 7D frequency, it would be able to look up at the star and see consciousness, not form.

We created a sky that is filled with individual and collective consciousness participating with and in Earth's experiment. All of you reading this now incarnated from one of these forms holding an individual or collective consciousness, and many of you visit these forms regularly.

2.5 Traversing the 12D Grid

Once all the individual and collective Consciousnesses entering the grid moved into forms and we closed the grid, they began to create ways to traverse the 12D grid. There were many ways a Higher Dimensional Consciousness could travel through the dimensional fields within the 12D grid. Many moved through intent and energy. They knew how the quantum field worked, and they would shift their frequency in a now moment to move into another dimensional field. However, as they began to work with and participate with the Earth Plane and the humans on the

Earth Plane in the lower dimensional fields, they began to create physical moving forms that would allow them to traverse the lower dimensional fields with more ease and grace.

These forms are what the human calls *craft* or *ships*. They were created like anything else in the quantum field, through intent and energy. Consciousness within the 12D grid would intend light codes to hold the physical form of a craft. They would shift the light codes into a 5th, 6th, or 7th dimensional field and, instantaneously, a craft would appear. They created the craft in these lower dimensional fields, as these were the three closest dimensional fields to Earth and humanity. It would be much easier to interact and connect from craft within these three fields.

Any Higher Dimensional Consciousnesses, regardless of the frequency and dimensional field it held, could energetically move themselves into a craft while remaining within their frequency. So, even if a craft was in a 5th, 6th, or 7th dimensional field, a 12D Consciousness could shift their frequency down into a 7D field and enter the craft.

Crafts were and still are one of the most miraculous creations within the 12D grid. There are hundreds of thousands of these craft currently around the Earth Plane and accessed within the 12D grid.

Craft allow Higher Dimensional Consciousnesses to have a more intimate and palpable experience with the Earth Plane and humans. Craft provide a place where the human and the Higher Dimensional Consciousnesses can connect. The human's etheric body had the ability to travel into the craft and receive teachings, healings, activations, or anything else that is desired by the human. This occurred for the human in the dream state and the waking state.

There are also many Councils, including us, that reside in craft. These councils are designed to focus solely on assisting humanity and Earth through their evolution. They must remain physically close to the Earth Plane to monitor every now.

We are currently holding ourselves in a craft and have been for around 15,000 linear years. It allows us to be in close dimensional proximity with Earth while remaining in our own frequencies.

Everything we created within the 12D grid, including the grid itself, has a purpose. The grid allows for a contained environment to ensure the Earth's safest outcome. The forms allow all individual and collective Consciousnesses to reside within the 12D grid and participate with and on the Earth. It is all part of the divine design.

Summary

The 12D grid holds everything. It holds all galaxies, star systems, solar systems, and anything that the human linear mind can imagine or believe to exist. Every experience that was had, is being had, or will be had on the Earth is held in the 12D grid.

This concept may be challenging to understand because the 3rd dimension uses the belief system of science to explain its surroundings. Science is a beautiful tool. It allows the human to understand the physical 3D reality. However, it is truth that can only hold validity within a 3D lens, and this entire experiment and all that exists within it is seen through a 12D lens.

Science can only take the human so far, and then one must turn to energy. Everything was designed with energy and exists as energy. It is not the human's fault they are unable to see the entire energetic design. We hope through the pages of this book, you begin to remember what you have always known and have just forgotten due to the density within your field.

As you begin to understand just how large the 12D grid is, you will see that nothing created is a mistake. It is all a divine design. Perhaps the most miraculous aspect of this design and experiment was the human form itself.

Chapter 3

THE 5D HUMAN FORM

Once we had the 12D grid in place, we then designed the human form. We selected a group of twelve Higher Dimensional Light Beings within our Federation to design and create the form. These Beings are known by the humans as the Lyrans, Orions, and Andromedans. They created the human 5D form the same way we created the Earth Plane and all physical forms on the Earth, through intention and energy.

There are similarities to the design of the human form and all other 5D forms. They all were created from 12D light codes, have an energetic field around their form, hold an energetic channel within their form, and can hold a quotient of the Higher Dimensional Consciousnesses light within their form. However, the human form was a much more complex creation because it holds different intentions and experiences than all other forms on the Earth. It was designed to allow Higher Dimensional Consciousness to create, engage, and navigate the 5D field differently from all other forms on the Earth Plane. This required more design characteristics to ensure its success in the 5D field.

3.1 The Intention

We began with the intention, the visual characteristics, and the purpose of the human form. First, we needed to visualize a physical 5D human form. We knew we would have both masculine and feminine forms that would stand upright in order to navigate the physical terrain. We had to ensure the forms could physically experience the 5D field. We visualized ears, noses, mouths, eyes, and the external feet and hands.

We created the internal body, including the organs, bones, skin, nerves, ligaments, and cells to ensure the form could stay alive while on the planet. We intended and visualized a model for the physicality of the human form.

Once we understood how the physical form would look, we created the purpose of the human form. We had three purposes for the human body;

1. The body had to hold a Higher Dimensional Consciousness within its form.
2. The body must allow the Higher Dimensional Consciousness to participate and engage in the 5D field actively and consciously.
3. The human form would have the ability to shift from the 5D field to the 7D field.

3.2 Light Codes

Once we created the intentions, we moved these intentions into 12D light codes energetically and telepathically. The light codes are what create the physical form. Remember, light codes are high frequency light that holds intentions and information allowing the creation of new realities, forms, and experiences. The codes shift or alchemize into different frequencies depending upon the intentions placed within them.

Once the intentions of the human form were placed within the light codes, we began to shift the codes down from a 12D frequency to a 5D frequency to create the physical human form. The codes began to alchemize and shift from light to a crystalline matter. The light codes created a human form that has a crystalline structure with a dense matter holding it together. In a now moment, we turned light into matter.

The 12D light codes were held in a 5D frequency, allowing the physical human form to appear. The light codes always hold the original

12D frequency. For example, the 12D light codes have now shifted down into a 5D frequency to create the human form; however, the 5D codes are also existing in the 6th, 7th, 8th, 9th, 10th, 11th, and 12th dimensional frequencies.

The activation of light codes occurs when the human form shifts into higher frequencies. This shifting will naturally activate the light codes, allowing the codes to shift frequencies as well. When light codes activate, the human has new information that is held in those higher codes. For example, when codes shift from a 5th dimensional field to a 6th dimensional field, the information held in the 6th dimensional codes are now accessible by the human.

Once we had the human form designed and in a 5D physicality, we needed to create a way to hold the light codes within the form. They needed to be held in a unique way to allow the codes to potentially activate within the human form. This is where we designed the twelve strands of DNA.

3.3 The Role of DNA

We designed a structure that would hold the 5D light codes within the human form. This structure was crystalline in nature yet had a dense matter covering the structure. The crystalline structures are made up of twelve strands. The twelve strands hold the light codes in place within the human form. These strands are what the human calls DNA.

DNA is simply the physical crystalline strands holding the light codes. DNA is not the human form. The light codes are the human form. DNA is not the Consciousness that dropped down into the form. DNA is the term humans use for the container that holds the light codes. It can be confusing for the human as DNA has been synonymous with creating life and form. However, it is light codes within the DNA strands that create all life and form seen in the physical reality.

DNA strands are necessary to hold the physical form in the dense 5D field. It is the strands that allow the form to exist. The light codes could not exist within the form without the dense structure of the DNA.

41

DNA strands only exist within Earth's experiment in the 6th, 5th, 4th, 3rd, and lower dimensional fields. Earth's entire intention was to evolve from a lower dimensional field into a higher dimensional field. The DNA strands were the perfect solution to create, in a dense physical reality, a physical form with the ability to shift into higher dimensional fields.

As the physical human form shifts into higher frequencies, the light codes shift as well, and eventually the DNA strands will shift into the light codes. When the human form reaches the 7th dimensional field, the physical form is almost all light. There is very little physical density in the form. When this occurs, the form doesn't need DNA strands to hold the light codes and human form in place. The light codes can exist as light within the 7D form.

Twelve strands were chosen because the light codes held 12th dimensional frequencies. It took thousands of light codes to create the human form. To ensure all the light codes could be held within the form, we designed twelve DNA strands. This number of DNA strands holding light codes allowed more of the codes to be expressed and expanded within the human form. If we only had four strands, we would not have been able to get all the necessary light codes needed to create the physical form into the human body.

The first five DNA strands hold all the 5D frequencies necessary for the Higher Dimensional Consciousnesses to begin their human journey. They won't need to activate the first five strands. They are activated and experienced as soon as the Higher Dimensional Consciousness incarnates into the form.

The human will access the remaining seven strands as the physical body increases its frequency and activates the light codes held in those strands.

3.4 Two Types of DNA

There are two types of light codes held within the DNA strands. The first set of light codes is designed to create the human form and is the same for every human form. These codes are a template for the human form and make up 10 percent of the DNA.

The second set of light codes is designed to create the human experience chosen by the Higher Dimensional Consciousness. It includes their intention for incarnating or the *divine blueprint*. It holds all their multidimensional abilities and skills they want to access as they shift into higher frequencies. It holds the characteristics they chose for their human body, including male or female; size and average weight of their body; color of their skin, hair, and eyes; and the location on the Earth Plane of their birth. These codes also hold the family system including ancestral lines, parents, siblings, and extended family. This second set of light codes makes up 90 percent of the DNA.

The Higher Dimensional Consciousness brings these codes in with them and stores them in the twelve strands of DNA. The codes hold the Higher Dimensional Consciousness's blueprint and specific abilities or ways of being while in the human form.

The Higher Dimensional Consciousness that incarnates into the human form is not made of DNA, nor does it hold DNA within its Consciousness. It is a Higher Dimensional Consciousness choosing to participate in a 5D form that was created by light codes held in DNA. The DNA strands were designed strictly by us in order to hold both sets of light codes that allow the experiment to take place. Outside the 12D grid, DNA does not exist. The only way a Higher Dimensional Consciousness within the 12D grid could hold light codes within DNA structures is if the Consciousness itself was designed within the 12D grid. This did eventually occur on the Earth but not for millions of years after we designed the 5D human form. We will discuss this in more detail later in the book.

DNA was created by us for Earth's experiment, and at that time, all Higher Dimensional Consciousnesses incarnating into the human form were not made of DNA.

Both sets of light codes are designed to activate and turn on within the human body. Once they activate, they hold different roles. Both sets of light codes are activated when the human form shifts into higher frequencies. The human form shifts into higher frequencies when the light from the sun enters the human body. As the frequency within the body increases, it increases the frequency of the light codes within the DNA. This increase in frequency activates the light in the higher frequency and the light codes turn on.

As the first set of light codes activate, they allow the human form to navigate and experience the next highest dimensional field. As the second set of light codes activate, they allow the human access to more of their multi-dimensionality, including new ways of being, new abilities, and new skills they did not have in the lower frequencies and dimensional field.

The light codes within the human form hold twelve dimensional fields and frequencies. They have the potential to activate within the 5D human form and allow the form and the Higher Dimensional Consciousness to access the seven remaining dimensional fields.

This is the divine design. This is the natural process of evolution in physical forms.

3.5 The Electrical Grid System

Once we had the physical form created, we then designed the electrical grid within the form. The grid was a map, as well as a container, for the Higher Dimensional Consciousness incarnating into the human form. It connected the Higher Dimensional Consciousness into the human form and provided a safe container for it to remain and experience the human life. It aligned the Consciousness to the quantum field, as well as assisting it in navigating the dense 5D form and the 5th dimensional field.

The electrical grid is made up of twelve energy centers, the Higher Self, the *I Am* Presence, the subtle bodies, the light quotient, and the ego structure. You can imagine it like a hard drive for a computer. The hard drive allows the computer to function. The electrical grid system within the 5D form allowed the Higher Dimensional Consciousness to function and navigate within the 5D field while aligned and connected to the quantum field.

3.6 The Channel

The design of the electrical grid began with the channel. The energetic channel was placed into the human form to act as a conduit for all energy, light, and consciousness to move in and out of the human form. Without the channel, the human form would not be able to navigate the 5D energetic world nor hold the Higher Dimensional Consciousness that would enter into the human form.

The channel runs above and within the human form. You can imagine the channel as a freeway system moving light in and out of the human form.

3.7 Twelve Energy Centers

Once we had the channel connected into the human form, we created the twelve energy centers. These are what humans might call *chakras*. These centers were the foundation for the grid and the most important component to the success of a Higher Dimensional Consciousness incarnating into the human form.

The twelve energy centers were designed to allow light to move in and out of the physical form as well as allow the Higher Dimensional Consciousness within the 5D form to experience, navigate, and understand the 5D field while simultaneously remaining connected to the quantum field. All twelve centers exist within the energetic channel.

The twelve energy centers move up the channel in numerical order starting with the first energy center found at the lowest part of the channel within the body and the 12th energy center located at the highest part of the channel outside the body. All twelve energy centers hold a unique purpose. They spin counterclockwise to move the light through the form and keep the form clear.

There are four reasons why there are seven energy centers within the form all spinning counterclockwise:

1. To move the light and consciousness into the form
2. To filter and connect the higher consciousness within the form to the quantum field
3. To allow the physical form to evolve
4. To keep the form clear

The first, and most basic yet important purpose, is to move the light into and through the human form. The energy centers must spin to move the light through the body.

The second purpose is connecting the Higher Dimensional Consciousness within the form into the quantum field. The quantum field is any frequency and dimensional field outside the 5D field. Connecting into the quantum field allows the Higher Dimensional Consciousness to experience and connect into the *I Am* Presence, Higher Self, and Source, as well as all the individual and collective consciousnesses outside the 5D field and the intention for incarnating into the human form.

The third purpose is to allow high frequency light from the Sun to enter the human form, increasing its frequency and ability to access higher dimensional fields. When high frequency light from the Sun enters the channel, the seven energy centers pull the light into the form, allowing the acclimation, assimilation, and anchoring of the light into the form.

The fourth purpose of the seven energy centers is to filter and clear all 5th dimensional consciousness out of the physical form. All external experiences the 5D human has in the 5th dimensional field is made up of consciousness. Because the experience is in a 5D field, the consciousnesses that make up that experience are in the 5th dimensional frequency.

The consciousness of that experience must enter the channel and be filtered into the human form to allow the 5D human to understand the experience. The consciousness moves into the channel, and the 5D human form dissects it into an emotion, thought, and behavior. For example, a 5D human has an interaction with another 5D human. That interaction is an external experience that creates consciousnesses that move into the human form through the channel allowing the human to filter and understand the experience.

All 5D consciousness created by an external experience must move through and clear the channel. It is the spinning of the energy centers that moves the 5D consciousness through the channel. If consciousness cannot move through the channel, it will remain in the energy centers and clog the channel. If the channel becomes clogged, it will be difficult for the Higher Dimensional Consciousness to connect to the quantum field as well as its Higher Self, *I Am* Presence, Source, and intention for being in the human form. It will also create density in the human form, slowing down the human body's ability to evolve into higher dimensional fields.

The spinning of the seven energy centers is like the oil that keeps the engine running. It allows the evolutionary process to occur by filtering 5D density out of the form and providing a clear channel for the high frequency light to filter in. The less density the form holds, the easier it is for the form to increase in frequency. When the centers spin fast, it is difficult for any external consciousness to remain within the channel. The consciousness will be moved quickly through the channel.

We knew that as long as the energy centers remained spinning, the human form and the Higher Dimensional Consciousness within the form would be able to navigate the 5D field and shift into higher frequencies and dimensional fields.

Energy Centers 8–12

The five energy systems outside the physical form, 8–12, allow the Higher Dimensional Consciousness within the form to connect to the Higher Self, *I Am* Presence, and Source. These energy centers also provide access to the micro-quantum field within the 12D grid, including all Higher Dimensional Consciousnesses outside the 5D grid and the entire quantum field beyond the 12D grid.

The eighth energy center is the first center outside the physical body and is about ten linear inches above the human head. It is designed to hold the Higher Self. The Higher Self is an aspect of the Higher Dimensional Consciousness within the form. Energy center nine is designed to provide the human form access to all Consciousnesses within the 12D grid. Centers ten, eleven, and twelve are designed to hold the *I Am* Presence. The *I Am* Presence is also an aspect of the higher consciousness within the form. These three energy centers provide access to the quantum field outside the 12D grid, as well as Source consciousness.

Energy Centers 1–7

The seven energy centers within the form are designed to allow the higher consciousness incarnating into the form to navigate and filter the 5D field while maintaining a connection to the quantum field. The centers move up the channel in numerical order beginning with the first center at the base of the channel and arriving at the seventh center at the top of the channel in the form.

The first energy center, also referred to by the 3D human as the Root Chakra, is designed to anchor and hold the light down onto the Earth Plane. It allows the consciousness within the human form to feel secure and safe while experiencing the 5D physical reality.

The second energy center, referred to by the 3D human as the Sacral Chakra, is designed to allow the consciousness to experience physical pleasure. It opens the physical body to energetic sensations creating physical pleasures. This can be energetic touch from another human form, activations increasing the human frequency, digestion of energetic frequencies creating physical sensations, and so much more.

The third energy center, referred to by the human as the Solar Plexus Chakra, is the power vortex. It is where the human consciousness in the form can connect into the quantum field and access their multi-dimensional abilities beyond the 5D field. It is also the center where the human form can clear, purge, and release any density out of the form.

The fourth energy center, referred to by the human as the Heart Chakra, holds the *I Am* Presence. It holds the frequency of love and oneness. This center allows the consciousness to connect into all other consciousnesses outside of its 5D physical form, as well as Source.

The fifth energy center, referred to by the human as the Throat Chakra, is designed to act as the higher dimensional communicator. It allows the human to access multiple ways to communicate beyond the 5D field in order to access the higher dimensional realms.

The sixth energy center, also referred to by the human as the Third Eye, is designed to allow the human access to the quantum field. The human can experience and participate in higher dimensional fields and frequencies while in physical form.

The seventh energy center, referred to by the human as the Crown Chakra, is the access point into and out of the human form. It opens the human form into the quantum field and the other five energy centers. It is the entryway for all external light and consciousness to enter the human form.

All seven energy centers work together. They all must be open and spinning to work successfully. We chose seven centers because they provided a perfect balance of density and light within the form. We had to make sure that the density of the 5D form and the frequency of the light entering the form could co-exist. The energy centers are designed to spin light. If we had too many energetic centers spinning light, it would increase the frequency of the human body too quickly and short circuit the physical form. If we didn't have enough energy centers, the physical form would not be able to circulate the light coming into its form. The energy would become clogged within the channel and essentially halt the natural process of evolution. Seven centers provide the perfect balance for the form and the light.

We knew that as long as the energy centers remained spinning, the human form and the higher consciousness within the form would be able to navigate the 5D field and shift into higher frequencies and dimensional fields.

3.8 The *I Am* Presence and the Higher Self

Once we had the twelve energy centers designed, we needed to ensure that the Higher Dimensional Consciousness incarnating into the human form would stay connected to itself and receive guidance as it navigated the 5D field.

The consciousness would be held in a very dense 5D form, experiencing a dense 5D field. As soon as it entered the 5D human form, it would experience its reality through the lens of the 5th dimensional field. We designed the *I Am* Presence (IAP) and Higher Self (HS) to assist the Higher Dimensional Consciousness in staying connected to its own frequency and in navigating the 5D field within the 5D form.

When the Higher Dimensional Consciousness incarnates into the human form, we split an aspect of its consciousness into two distinct lower frequencies, creating two unique constructs: the IAP and HS. Both constructs are an aspect of the Higher Dimensional Consciousness in a lower frequency and are placed within an energy center inside the channel.

The IAP is placed in the 10th, 11th, and 12th energy centers. It remains within those three centers throughout the human experience. The IAP is holding a frequency between the 10th and 12th dimensional field. The role of the IAP is to connect and align the human to Source Consciousness. Creating the IAP and placing it inside the human channel provides a direct road map connecting the consciousness in human form to Source and to the remembrance that all is one.

The HS plays a more direct role in the 5D human life. It was designed to navigate the Higher Dimensional Consciousness in physical form through the 5D field. The HS was placed in the 8th energy center and is holding a 6th–8th dimensional frequency. Placement and frequency were necessary to ensure the human could access the HS while in the 5D field in each moment.

The HS is connected to the blueprint, which is the intention the higher dimensional consciousness had in incarnating into the human form. The

HS knows, and holds the awareness of, how and why the consciousness is in the human form. It understands the quantum field, the entire Earth experiment, and where the 5D human form is going in its human life. It serves as the eyes for the higher consciousness within the physical form. The HS can see through the denser fields from a higher vantage point. It guides the consciousness through its 5D human life.

The HS is energetic, not physical. It guides the human internally and filters all messages as energy through the human body. It sounds like the human's inner voice. The human aspect and the HS are communicating and navigating life together in each moment and it feels like an intuitive knowingness.

The design and placement of the IAP and HS allow the Higher Dimensional Consciousness to connect into these aspects of itself as soon as it enters the human form.

3.9 The Etheric Body

Once we had the IAP and HS designed, we needed to ensure that the Higher Dimensional Consciousness could safely exist within a dense 5D human form. The consciousness incarnating into the human form is in a much higher frequency than the form.

It did not make sense to have the Higher Dimensional Consciousness existing throughout the entire human body. Its high frequency could and most likely would short circuit the physical form, causing energetic damage. The Higher Dimensional Consciousness would need to be contained. We needed an energetic field that could hold the consciousness while in the human form.

We created what the human calls the etheric body to perform this task. The etheric body is an energetic field within the human form holding the Higher Dimensional Consciousness. It allows the consciousness to safely navigate the 5D field.

Another reason we created the etheric body was to allow the Higher Dimensional Consciousness to experience and travel into the quantum field while in the human form. The etheric body provides the consciousness and the human aspect an ability to connect into these other dimensional fields. The etheric body is the vehicle that allows for inter-dimensional travel while remaining in the physical form.

When the etheric body travels outside of the human form and the 5D dimensional field, it remains connected to the physical form through an energetic cord. It never splits or separates from the form. This allows the Higher Dimensional Consciousness and the human to always stay connected to the physical body. It also allows the ego and personality the ability to consciously remember the inter-dimensional travel.

The etheric body is not a bridge, a communicator, or a filter for consciousness. It is an energetic field that holds the Higher Dimensional Consciousness in physical form and allows for inter-dimensional travel both by the higher consciousness and the 5D human aspect.

The etheric body is an intricate part of the human design. Without it, the Higher Dimensional Consciousness would not be able to incarnate into the human form.

3.10 The Subtle Bodies

Once we designed the etheric body, we needed to create a way for a Higher Dimensional Consciousness to navigate and understand the 5D field within the human form.

The Consciousness was going to be navigating an external world with an infinite number of experiences. These experiences were made up of consciousness and would be digested and filtered into the human form in order to understand the external reality. We needed to create a way for the human body to filter these experiences (consciousnesses) through the physical form. We came up with the design of the mental and emotional energetic bodies or what the human calls the mental and emotional subtle bodies. They were designed as an energetic field and were placed within the human form to filter all external consciousness entering into the form.

Consciousness is energy. Energy creates all external experiences in the 5D field. Any external experience the 5D human has is consciousness. For the human to understand that external experience, it must digest the consciousness that created that experience. Digestion occurs when the consciousness of an external experience enters the human channel and is filtered through the two subtle bodies. The subtle bodies process the consciousness into emotions, thoughts, and beliefs that allow the human to understand the experience. This happens instantaneously.

Every consciousness within the 5D field holds a unique frequency; therefore, each external experience holds unique frequencies. The frequencies of an experience will dictate the emotions, thoughts, beliefs, and behaviors experienced by the human.

The emotional body filters the consciousness into an emotion or feeling. The mental field filters consciousness into an idea, thought, or belief. These ideas, thoughts, or beliefs can create constructs, programs, patterns, and paradigms that dictate a way of being in a 5D field. They allow the human to understand their reality. The emotional and mental bodies create all human behaviors.

All consciousness—the emotions, thoughts, beliefs, and behaviors— in a 5D frequency within the 5D field is experienced as neutral. It is purely consciousness being experienced by the human. There are no polarities or dualities creating judgments or attachments. Consciousnesses are not experienced as feeling *bad* or *uncomfortable* but are simply honored, felt, and moved out of the physical form. The consciousness does not remain within the form and clog the channel. The experience of neutrality allows for all emotions, thoughts, beliefs, and behaviors to move through the human channel and out of the body without remaining within the form creating density.

Here is an example of how these two subtle bodies work:

A 5D human encounters a large living crystal and engages with the crystal. The interaction is the external experience, and that experience is made up of consciousnesses. When the human has the interaction with the crystal, they digest the consciousness creating the interaction. The consciousness enters the channel and is filtered by the emotional and mental bodies. The emotional body may filter the consciousness into emotions such as joy, peace, love, expansion, or oneness. The mental body may filter the consciousness into ideas or beliefs such as: *This crystal can heal. This crystal can increase my frequency. This crystal activates my heart chakra.*

The external experience is understood through the digestion of the consciousness held within the experience and is filtered through the subtle bodies. The subtle bodies are imperative in providing an understanding of the human's external world.

3.11 The Energetic Field

We now needed to create an energetic field around the human form that would allow the Higher Dimensional Consciousness to navigate and experience all external experiences in the 5D field.

We knew the human form would be interacting with many different external 5D experiences and energies. Every experience is made up of consciousnesses holding a frequency. The energetic field would allow the human to navigate and feel all the external energies and experiences while remaining sovereign.

Sovereignty provides a sense of safety for the human. It allows the human to feel safe, free, and empowered while in a human body. It also allows the human to feel safe to experience itself as its energetic signature without being impacted by the external world. A human's energetic signature consists of the frequencies their body is holding at any given moment. Their signature is what expresses itself as the human based on the frequency of the body. Creating sovereignty was essential in providing the human the safety to navigate the large spectrum of consciousness within the 5D field.

We also needed the physical form to be able to feel and navigate all external energies in the 5D field. Everything experienced on the 5D Earth Plane is energy; therefore, the only way a human can understand its world is through energies. The human body had to be able to feel all the external energies to allow the human to navigate and understand their world. The energetic field provided the human the ability to navigate, experience, and understand all external energies.

The energetic field extends 18 inches or 46 cm out from the physical body and circles the form. You can imagine it like a bumper around the physical form. When the human engages with the external world, the energetic field around the physical form connects to the energies. The human form literally bumps into the energies or consciousnesses of all experiences. It is through this bump that the consciousness enters the physical form and is filtered through the subtle bodies, and so allows the human to understand the experience.

All physical forms, including the Earth Plane, have an energetic field around their forms. These energetic fields are how all physical forms, human and non-human, connect and communicate. Although there are languages the human uses to communicate, the first form of communication is energetically filtered through the interaction of the energetic fields.

For example, a human encounters a dolphin. The human's energetic field connects with the dolphin's energetic field and an energetic communication occurs. The human feels certain emotions, and the dolphin feels certain emotions. This is also how humans engage with each other. Each human's energetic field connects into the other's energetic field, and there is an energetic exchange first before there is a verbal exchange.

Because the energetic field provides sovereignty, the human is not impacted or effected by another human or non-human's energetic field. The fields merely touch each other to communicate.

The energetic field will vibrate at the frequency of the human form, and that is what is felt between human and non-human. Each human form will hold a unique frequency vibrating out of the energetic field, and this will allow the human to navigate the expansive external world while remaining sovereign.

3.12 The Light Quotient

Once we had the entire physical form complete, we were ready for the Higher Dimensional Consciousness to enter the human form. All Consciousnesses incarnating are energetic, existing as light. We knew the physical form would not be able to hold 100 percent of the Higher Dimensional Consciousness's light. The density of the form would short circuit and shut down.

We had to find the percentage of light all Higher Dimensional Consciousnesses could incarnate with and still allow the human form to function. This is what we have termed the *light quotient,* and it refers to the percentage of light the consciousness brings into the human form.

The light quotient was an extremely important and fragile aspect of the human design. We had a variety of Higher Dimensional Consciousnesses incarnating that were holding frequencies ranging from the 6th to the 40th dimensional frequencies. We had to find a quotient or percentage of light that would ensure all Higher Dimensional Consciousnesses could enter the form safely regardless of their frequency.

The way we found the light quotient was by experimentation. We asked for the Higher Dimensional Consciousness to take a percentage of their light and move into the human form. We wanted the consciousness to bring in as much of its light as possible without short-circuiting the form. The more light it held in the 5D form, the easier it would be for the human to stay aligned and connected into the quantum field, their Higher Self, the *I Am* Presence, and their blueprint.

We knew that the human body could potentially only hold around 30 percent of a Higher Dimensional Consciousness's light. However, we were unsure if the body could function with that much light. We watched and measured as Higher Dimensional Consciousnesses began to incarnate into human forms and brought in their light. Very quickly, we realized that 30 percent was way too much light. The human body would shut down almost immediately.

After many incarnations and thousands of physical forms shutting down, we discovered that the 5D human form could only hold between 14 and 20 percent of the Higher Dimensional Consciousness's light, regardless of its frequency.

The percentage of light a Higher Dimensional Consciousness incarnates with is dependent upon their frequency. The higher the frequency, the lower the light quotient. For example, a consciousness holding a 28th dimensional frequency would only be able to bring in around 14 percent of its light. A consciousness holding a 9th dimensional frequency would be able to bring in around 20 percent.

Understanding the light quotient is extremely important as it allows the Higher Dimensional Consciousness to safely enter the human form. The light quotient never increases or decreases during the human experience. It is an aspect of the Higher Dimensional Consciousness held in the etheric body and remains stable through the human journey. The percentage remains the same as the physical human form shifts into higher dimensional fields.

3.13 Entering the Human Form

Once we had the light quotient set, it was time to allow Higher Dimensional Consciousness to enter the human form. We had never created such a delicate physical form holding a complex energetic system within it. We were unsure how the Consciousness and the human form would function together. We decided to experiment with a handful of Higher Dimensional Consciousnesses before we allowed the incarnation process to begin.

We started with consciousnesses from our own federation since we had the most knowledge of how the human form worked. Pleiadians, Lyrans, Sirians, and Orions volunteered and entered 5D human form. They experienced and played within the Earth's 5D field for what would be perceived in 3D linear reality as hundreds of years. They tested out all aspects of the 5D human design. Through these trials, we were able to trust the human body, and we were ready to allow Higher Dimensional Consciousnesses to enter the human form.

We sent out the call to all Higher Dimensional Consciousnesses that had entered the 12D grid and began to allow them to incarnate into all physical forms, including the human form. All Higher Dimensional Consciousnesses entering human forms at this time were volunteers, not Light Workers. The Light Worker was first introduced when the Earth Plane entered a 3rd dimensional field. We will discuss this in much more detail later in the book.

Any Higher Dimensional Consciousnesses incarnating into the human form at this time were volunteering for the sole purpose of experiencing both the 5D Earth Plane and the 5D physical form. There were tens of thousands of consciousnesses that incarnated. They entered adult physical forms rather than infant forms. We had to populate the Earth Plane with adult forms first, and then, as the human began to experience the 5D field, they could intend and create new human lives beginning as infant forms.

As soon as a Higher Dimensional Consciousness chose to incarnate, we provided them with all the details of how the 5D experience would work. We detailed all the universal laws that would take place when they entered the 5D field and form. We shared with them how the human form would hold their consciousness and how they would experience and navigate the 5D field within the form.

They understood they would be observers and not active participants. Once in the form, they could not actively lead the human life. The Higher Self would be guiding them through the human experience, and the ego would be keeping their form safe. The density of the form made it impossible for the Higher Dimensional Consciousness to lead itself through the experience. The consciousness was a frequency that could only exist and experience the 5D field by remaining within the etheric body. It would be a participant, a passenger.

We invited them to create their second set of light codes through intention and choice. The last thing we shared with the Higher Dimensional Consciousness was how they would enter the human form. We informed them of the percentage of light—their light quotient—they could bring into the human form. They took that percentage of light from their entire consciousness and created an aspect of themselves.

Once they had the aspect of themselves created, the first and second set of light codes, they intended the incarnation of themselves into the adult physical form on the Earth Plane. We will discuss how the Higher Dimensional Consciousness enters an infant in a later chapter.

In a single moment, they found themselves in the physical body on the Earth. They simultaneously created the physical form, moved into the physical form through the channel, and settled their light into the etheric body.

Once the consciousness entered the etheric body, it connected into the energetic grid within the form and began to experience 5D consciousness and the 5D field. It was experiencing the 5D physical world through the body's energetic grid, the internal subtle bodies, the guidance of both the ego and Higher Self, and the alignment into the quantum field. The consciousness began the human experience on the 5D Earth Plane.

Chapter 4

EXPERIENCING THE 5D EARTH

The 5th dimensional Earth was a unique and exciting opportunity for all Higher Dimensional Consciousness entering the 5D form. It was what the human calls Heaven on Earth. In this chapter, we would like to describe some of the unique characteristics and experiences of the 5D Earth and the human form. Many of you have lived in the 5D human form on the 5D Earth. We hope this chapter reminds you of what you have forgotten.

4.1 Masculine and Feminine Frequencies

We created a masculine and a feminine frequency that was experienced while in the 5D field and 5D human form. Each frequency held different characteristics. The masculine frequency was experienced as strength, power, courage, independence, intellect, and mind-centered. The feminine frequency was experienced as soft, nourishing, creative, expressive, heart-centered, unified, empowered, and open. There are many more characteristics that can describe these two frequencies; these are the most common traits. Each 5D human held a balance of the masculine and feminine frequencies within their form. They experienced themselves as an expression of both masculine and feminine frequencies.

The 5D human form was designed as either a male or female body. We created this distinction to provide a unique experience within the 5D form. The ability to choose between a male and female form provided the Higher Dimensional Consciousness unique experiences on the Earth Plane. The female human would navigate the 5D field slightly differently from the male human. Which form they incarnated into was a choice, and that choice was based on how and what they wanted to experience when they were on the Earth Plane.

4.2 Creator Beings

The 5D human was a Creator Being. They chose and created every moment instantaneously through intention and energy. Their choice came from their Higher Self and was always for their highest good. Any desire or need would be fulfilled in a now moment. They never created out of lack but out of love instead. All creations were for the betterment of humanity and the Earth Plane.

This is also how they created a new human life. We stated in the previous chapter that we originally populated the Earth Plane with adult humans. Infants and young children could not survive without the adult human. We seeded hundreds of human forms as adults first, and once we had enough human forms on the Earth Plane, the 5D human could begin to create human life. All human life would then begin as infants.

4.3 Creating a Human Life

Fifth dimensional humans create a new human life through intention and energy. It begins with two humans coming together with the intention of creating a new life. There is a masculine human and a feminine human. Both human forms merge their energetic fields into one unified field. As we stated in the previous chapter, each human has their own energetic field. When creating a new life, both humans come together and merge their fields to create one unified field of energy.

This is experienced by both humans as what can only be described as ecstasy within the human form. Both humans energetically become one in that moment. The energetic exchange creates a feeling of bliss, unity, love, creation, joy and peace. Once merged, they create an energetic intention. The intention begins as a thought: *Create a new human form.* The two humans bring an energetic frequency to that thought. The frequency creates an energetic blueprint. The blueprint holds the frequency of the new life that will eventually create the physical human form.

Once the energetic blueprint is set, the two humans create an energetic field to hold the blueprint. They create this field by pulling energy from the quantum space and moving it into a sub-field within their unified energetic field. The sub-field is where the form is created and eventually birthed. Imagine the sub-field as a cloud of energy. This cloud is formed within the one unified energetic field of both human forms and holds the energetic blueprint for the human form.

Once the energetic field is created, the two humans send out an energetic call to any Higher Dimensional Consciousness outside the Earth Plane within the 12D grid desiring to enter a 5D human form and experience the Earth Plane. A Consciousness answers the call and energetically connects with the two 5D humans. An energetic agreement is made among all three Beings.

Once the agreement is made, the humans begin to separate back into their own unique fields. The energetic sub-field and blueprint they created remains within the female form until the completion of the human design. The female form always holds the blueprint, energetic subfield, and 5D human form. There is no other reason for this other than the intention of the female body within the 5D field. The female body births the child.

The 5D human form does not have the same type of physical organs as the 3D human form. It doesn't hold eggs or any other physical way in which a human life is created in the 3D field. The 5D human creates everything, including a human life, through energy and intent. The female human form is designed to hold the energetic subfield, blueprint, and eventually, the crystalline infant form.

The human form is created through light codes that are held within the energetic blueprint set by the two humans. The light codes are what the 5D human brings into their intention when creating a new form. All light codes are held within that blueprint and are designed to create the new physical form.

While the form is created within the female body, she is honored and provided blessings and prayers. She is typically held in a sacred space of her choosing and remains there while the form is creating. She will sense energetically when the form is completely designed. This process does not take much time in the 5D field. If we were to provide a linear time frame for your understanding, we would say a few days to a few weeks. As soon as the form is complete, both humans who created the human form come back together to create a ceremonial space, and the woman births the baby into the 5D field.

The birthing process is similar to the 3D human birth in that it physically exits the human form out the birth canal. However, the experience of the 5D human birth is very different. Remember the 5D human form is crystallized. It is a merging of physicality and light creating a crystal form. This allows for the 5D birthing process to be more energetic and less physical.

When it is time to birth the infant, the female increases her frequency by intending the energy within her form to increase. Once she is holding a higher frequency, she calls in the Higher Dimensional Consciousness that will be incarnating into the new human form. In a single moment—simultaneously—the female pushes the form out of her body, and the consciousness drops into the infant form. The birth occurs in a now moment without any physical pain.

The creation and birth of a human form is sacred and intentional. The entire process is honored and experienced as a precious gift to both the Higher Dimensional Consciousness entering the form and the humans bringing the form into life.

4.4 Telepathy

All communication is telepathic in the 5th dimension. Language is not necessary. Telepathy in the 5D field is when two humans communicate

64

energetically through their physical bodies' energetic field. The human intends a thought that exits the channel and moves out from their energetic field as energy. The other human's energy field connects and feels the energy and receives the thought.

For example, two human forms are standing next to each other. One human chooses to say hello to another. They think the word *hello* intending it to be received by the other person. The thought creates an energetic frequency that moves out of the human's energetic field. The other human's energetic field feels the energy of the thought and receives the message *hello*. This happens instantaneously. There is no need for words.

Along with language, the 5D human can telepathically communicate in other ways. They can transcribe energy as information, messages, or thoughts, through sound, art, movement, and more. The human receiving the information will feel the energy held within the sounds, art, movement, or tones throughout their energy field. Once they feel the energy, they can translate the information held within the energy.

Telepathy is simply the human body sending out an energetic signal holding messages, information, or thoughts through their energetic field. Another human receives the energy through their energetic field and translates it into the message, information, or thought.

4.5 Nourishing the Form

The 5D human forms hold a vibration that doesn't require food. Food is density, and the human form doesn't require density to sustain itself. It requires *prana*, which we discussed in an earlier chapter. Prana can be viewed as liquid light that is received from the Sun and digested by the human form. This light charges the form and keeps the form alive.

If the 5D human chose to digest something, including plants, herbs, and flowers, they would intend and create these forms in their reality for the purpose of digesting them. They would not take from what is already alive and experiencing the 5D Earth Plane. Remember, all 5D forms were designed by us and holding Higher Dimensional Consciousnesses. The 5D human knew this truth. They were not going to take or destroy any living form. Therefore, anything a 5D human wanted to eat they would create and design for the sole purpose of experiencing digestible food. It was not necessary for their survival.

The 5D human also never digested an animal or any living organism. They not only knew it, too, was a Higher Dimensional Consciousness choosing to experience a 5D life, but their bodies did not crave animal or flesh of any kind. They never manifested or created any animals or living organisms to eat. The body holds frequencies that do not crave the density found in flesh.

The 5D human understood that, without the physical form, they could not participate on the Earth Plane. They adorned, cherished, honored, and loved the human form. They had a very strong energetic connection and communication with their human form. They knew what the physical form needed. They trusted the form as an aspect of their experience and knew the form was moving them through the evolution in their Consciousness.

4.6 Time

Time is an illusion created by a consciousness or energy slowing its frequency down into a time-space continuum, creating the slowing down of a now moment. The slow spin of the frequency creates the illusion of time. The slower a frequency spins, the slower the now moment will become and the longer it will be experienced through time.

Time is experienced very differently in the 5D field from the 3D field. The 5D field spins faster than the 3D yet is still slow enough to create the illusion of time. There is still an experience of a time-space continuum. Now moments are slowed down into time; however, the 5D human experiences time through the awareness of the quantum field. The 5D human can see and energetically tap into a past or a future, yet they know that everything is experienced in a now moment. The 5D human lives in a present moment state yet still experiences the passing of time. So, even though the 5D field holds a time-space continuum, the human is experiencing every now in the now. They don't feel the passing of time. They don't need to keep track of time. They understand it is the spin of the 5D field's frequency to experience itself and that spin creates the illusion of time.

4.7 Aging

The 5D human does not experience age in the same way the 3D human ages. There are two reasons for this. One, the consciousness chooses where along the developmental growth it wants to experience its human life. Two, the human form is holding a high enough frequency that the human form cannot experience physical aging.

The human form will developmentally grow from infant to toddler to child to adolescent to adult. The Higher Dimensional Consciousness chooses where its human form will stop along its development. They will experience the rest of their human life from this developmental place. For example, if the consciousness chooses to stop its growth at an adolescent, they will experience the entire human life as an adolescent. It is a choice. The human will not age beyond this developmental marker. Now this can seem challenging to comprehend, but once presented with this choice, most 5D humans choose to stop their growth around the 25- to 45-year mark. They have fully developed into the human form, and it's a very comfortable age to navigate the 5D field. But again, it's a choice that the Higher Dimensional Consciousnesses make.

The 5D human form is also holding high frequency light that won't allow the deterioration of the physical form. It's impossible for the human body to age, get sick, or hold illness. Illness and disease are consciousnesses that cannot exist in a 5D form. The body is holding too much light to allow it to enter. The light also provides the body with enough oxygen and life force that the blood, cells, and DNA are never deteriorating. The 5D body is able to stay young.

4.8 Death

Every Higher Dimensional Consciousness incarnating into a human form chooses when it will depart the human life. They may make this decision while in the human form or prior to incarnating into the human form.

The 5D human life typically lasts a few hundred linear years. This tends to be the time frame when most consciousnesses are ready to depart the physical form. Years are not experienced in the same way as in the 3D human field. Two hundred years in the 5D would feel like fifty years in 3D. Remember, time is still experienced but is sped up in the 5D.

There isn't an experience of death in the 5D. When the consciousness chooses to depart the form, it does so with ease and grace. It exits the form in the same way it entered the form. The Higher Dimensional Consciousness shifts itself out of the etheric body, moves through the human channel and out the 12th energy center, and merges back into its complete consciousness and the collective field it existed in prior to incarnating into the human form.

Once back with its complete consciousness, it will regroup and choose whether to come back into a physical form or stay in their collective consciousness within the 12D grid and participate from off the Earth Plane. It's always a choice with each incarnation.

Chapter 5

EARTH'S FALL FROM GRACE

Earth was a free-will planet with millions of Higher Dimensional Consciousnesses incarnating onto her. What occurred a few million years into her experiment was something we could never have imagined.

We have called this moment in Earth's history *Earth's first fall from grace*. Earth descended from the 5th dimensional field down to the 3rd dimensional field. It was a slow, meticulous process that occurred over millions of linear years.

5.1 How Earth Shifted Into the 3D field

There are seven key reasons for Earth's descent from the 5D field to the 3D field:

1. The variety of Beings entering human forms
2. Free will
3. Access to the quantum field
4. The role of the ego
5. The physical form's ability to anchor lower dimensions
6. The design of 4D races
7. The human form's frequency impacting the Earth's frequency

1. The Variety of Beings Entering Human Forms

One of the unique aspects of Earth's experiment was the ability for Higher Dimensional Consciousnesses to incarnate into forms on the Earth Plane. This ability was perhaps the most significant reason for her shift down into the 3rd dimensional field.

Thousands of different Higher Dimensional Consciousnesses entered the 12D grid. Their frequencies ranged from a 6th dimensional field to a 40th dimensional field. They each could create and intend their realities. Once inside the grid, they had free will to choose whether to incarnate onto the Earth Plane.

2. Free Will

The second pivotal reason for the fall into the 3rd dimension was free will. All Higher Dimensional Consciousnesses that incarnated into human forms have free will. They could create any reality within the 5D field without interference. We could not manipulate, stop, or control any Higher Dimensional Consciousness's creation once they entered into human forms. We had to let everything play out on the Earth Plane. This was one of the most challenging aspects for us. We had to allow and watch as Earth and humanity began shifting down into lower dimensional fields. We had to honor free will.

3. Accessing the Quantum Field

The third pivotal reason for the Earth's fall into the 3rd dimension was the human's access to the quantum field. The 12D grid and all Higher Dimensional Consciousnesses within the grid were in the quantum field. The Earth Plane and all humans on the Earth were in the quantum field. The 5th dimensional field was in a high enough frequency that all humans had access to the quantum field.

The quantum field holds all dimensional fields. If a human has free will and can access the quantum field, it can create realities in different dimensional fields. To understand this, we want to remind you of how a human experiences Consciousness and dimensions.

A Higher Dimensional Consciousness is energy. Energy is designed to spin. The spin of a Higher Dimensional Consciousness creates its frequency, and the frequency dictates the dimensional field they will reside in. The dimensional field will dictate their experience and density.

The slower a Higher Dimensional Consciousnesse's energy spins, the lower its frequency, the lower the dimensional field, and the more density it will hold. The higher their energy spins, the higher its frequency, the higher the dimensional field, and the less density it will hold.

Every dimension is made up of a spectrum of frequencies. This spectrum holds all the consciousnesses that exist within that dimensional field. The consciousnesses create every experience within that dimension, ranging from emotions to thoughts to behaviors, depending upon the dimension.

The spectrum of Consciousness experienced in any dimensional field is based on the frequencies within the dimension. The lower the dimensional field, the larger the spectrum of Consciousness and the more there is to experience. The higher a dimensional field, the smaller the spectrum of Consciousness, the less to be experienced. Lower frequencies allow for more experiences. Higher frequencies allow for fewer experiences.

Every dimensional field holds a spectrum of frequencies. Each frequency within that spectrum contains a variety of consciousnesses that create experiences. Think of a spectrum of Consciousness as linear. Now, of course, it's not linear, but this will provide a better understanding of how this connects and works in the quantum field.

A Higher Dimensional Consciousness that has split from Source will choose to move into a dimensional field by shifting their frequency into that field. Based on their frequency, they will settle into an aspect of that field's spectrum of Consciousness.

For example, a 5th dimensional field holds a spectrum of frequencies between 5.0 and 5.9. If a Higher Dimensional Consciousness holds a frequency of 5.5, they will find themselves in the 5D field experiencing consciousnesses ranging between 5.0 and 5.5. Their reality and all experiences will be based upon this spectrum of consciousness.

Any consciousness (experience) that does not hold the frequencies within that dimensional field will not be experienced. For example, lack is a consciousness that has a frequency around 3.0–3.5. It cannot be experienced in the 5D field. Greed is a consciousness holding a frequency around 3.0–3.4 and cannot be experienced in the 5D field. All Consciousnesses within a 5D field must hold a frequency ranging from 5.0 to 5.9. All Higher Dimensional Consciousnesses that want to experience the Earth would incarnate into a human body that is holding a frequency between 5.0 and 5.9. The human aspect is anchored into a 5D field. All of their experiences are within that 5D spectrum of consciousness. However, if their body increases in frequency, they will access higher dimensional consciousnesses. If their body decreases in frequency, they will access lower dimensional consciousnesses.

The human can also access higher or lower consciousnesses by choosing to tap into them so long as their body is holding a frequency close to the consciousness's frequency. For example, if a human is vibrating at a 5.1 frequency, they can easily tap into and access consciousnesses in a 4.9–4.6 frequency, such as control or persuasion. They have access to these new consciousnesses that are not in the 5D field. It's all a choice.

The human chooses their reality from the quantum field by tapping into and holding the frequencies they wish to experience. 5D humans began choosing to tap into the 4D frequencies. They began accessing consciousnesses in the 4th dimensional field. They started to have experiences that were not available in the 5D field, such as control.

We never intended or imagined that the Higher Dimensional Consciousnesses incarnating into the 5D human form would choose to experience lower dimensional fields. Free will and the quantum field allowed for that opportunity.

4. The Ego Structure

The ego played a pivotal role in Earth's fall from grace. When we originally designed the ego, its role was to keep the human form physically safe and alive. It was not designed to lead or guide the human form like it does in the 3D field. When the 5D human started accessing 4D Consciousness within a 4D field, the ego structure began to take on a slightly different role.

The 4D field holds a larger spectrum of consciousnesses than the 5D field, creating more experiences for the human. The egoic structure was unfamiliar with and never designed to navigate the 4D field. It became more active as it attempted to understand and keep the human form safe within the 4th dimensional field.

Keeping the human safe is experienced differently in the 4D field because there is duality in this field. Duality creates an illusion of polarities, allowing the human to feel good and bad or right and wrong. Experiences are judged, and there is an attachment to outcomes and experiences when the human is in a dimensional field that holds duality.

Duality does not exist in the 5D field. The 5D human does not judge or attach to any experience or outcome. There is no feeling of *bad* or *wrong* in the 5D field.

As the human experiences 4D Consciousness and duality, the role of the ego structure slowly shifts from keeping the human form physically safe to keeping the human form safe from uncomfortable, bad, or wrong experiences. The ego does this by creating beliefs around each Consciousness experienced.

When the human form starts to experience a 4D consciousness not found in the 5D field, such as control, the ego structure becomes more active to understand the Consciousness of control.

It has never felt the experience of control. The ego will pull the Consciousness (control) into its awareness to understand it. Once it understands the experiences of control, it will create beliefs around control. The beliefs will provide the human an understanding of how control works, allowing them to either choose to experience control or navigate away from it. The ego begins to label, manage, and create experiences based on beliefs.

For example, if control feels good to the human, the ego structure will create a belief around control that will allow the human to desire more of it. If the human does not like the experience of control, the ego creates beliefs around control that allows the human to desire less of this experience.

Another example would be authority. This is a consciousness holding a frequency around 4.6. It is not experienced in the 5D field. However, once the ego structure begins to feel authoritative, it creates beliefs around it. If the human enjoys feeling authoritative, the ego will have to create beliefs that will allow the human to desire more authority. If the human does not like the feeling of being authoritative, the ego will create beliefs that will pull the human away from experiencing authority. The ego's role in the 4D field begins to shift from physical safety to emotional safety.

As the human begins to choose to experience more 4D consciousnesses, their body will start to hold more 4D frequencies in their form. The ego will become more active while the Higher Self will become less prominent. The human begins to experience separation from the Higher Self. They hear and follow the ego more than the Higher Self. Instead of the Higher Self dictating and guiding the human, the ego structure begins to lead the human through the 4D field.

We watched as the humans began to separate from Higher Self. They allowed the ego to guide them through these denser consciousnesses. As the human continued to choose to experience these 4D Consciousnesses, they eventually began to anchor into the 4D field. We had no idea the human form could or would anchor into lower dimensional fields.

5. Anchoring into Lower Dimensional Fields

The fifth pivotal reason for the fall was the anchoring of the physical form into lower dimensional fields. Anchoring into a dimensional field requires the human body to hold 80 percent of its frequency in that dimension.

For example, a 4D human form is anchored into the 4D field when 80 percent of its frequency is in the 4D frequency. It may be holding some 5D and 6D frequencies, but most of the frequency in its form is 4D. The form is experiencing itself as a 4D frequency. The Higher Consciousness within the 4D human is experiencing a reality through the lens of the 4D field. It may feel 5D Consciousness or 6D Consciousness, but if it's anchored into the 4D field, its reality will be seen through the lens of the 4D field.

As we have stated in a previous chapter, the way the human understands and navigates its reality is by digesting external Consciousness, which creates an experience. The frequency of those consciousnesses move into and through the human form, shifting the body into higher or lower frequencies.

When the 5D human began to experience 4D consciousnesses, those consciousnesses moved into the 5D human form. The 4D Consciousness is a lower frequency than the frequency within the 5D human form. When it enters the human form, it will move slower. It holds more density. Imagine thicker, denser energy trying to move through a faster, clearer energy field. The denser energies slow down and can settle into the human body.

As the 5D human experienced 4D consciousnesses, the body began to hold 4D frequencies, slowly shifting the body down in frequency. The more 4D Consciousness the human experienced, the more the physical body held and shifted into 4D frequencies. Over time, as the human continued to choose to experience 4D consciousnesses, the body eventually anchored into the 4D field.

This did not happen overnight. We watched for millions of linear years as 5D humans began to access and experience the 4D field. The more humans accessed the 4D field, the larger the field became and the easier it was to access. The 4D field was expanded on the Earth Plane, and 5D humans were beginning to anchor into the 4D field.

Eventually, 5D humans in a 5D field stood on the same Earth Plane with 4D humans in a 4D field. Hundreds of thousands of human bodies held 4D frequencies and were standing in a 4th dimension and experiencing 4th dimensional Consciousness.

A human could now choose to incarnate into a 4D human form anchored into a 4D field or a 5D human form anchored in a 5D field. Both human forms and dimensional fields were available to experience on the same Earth Plane. The human's reality would be based on which human form and dimensional field they chose to incarnate into.

Let's provide a visual of what this looked like on the Earth Plane. For millions of years, the only dimensional field experienced by the human was the 5D. The only reality experienced by the human was in the 5th dimension. All humans were experiencing themselves in the 5D field. As humans began to tap in to, experience, and anchor into the 4D field, that field opened on the Earth Plane. There were now two dimensional fields energetically visible, based on how a human was choosing to experience their reality. There were 5D humans and 4D humans on the same Earth Plane. This is how the quantum field works and how the Earth started to shift down into lower dimensional fields.

6. Creating 4D Races

The sixth reason for the fall—and one of the most impactful events that ever took place on Earth—was the design and creation of *4D races*. Once the 4th dimensional field and the 4D human form became available for Higher Dimensional Consciousnesses to incarnate into, the design of 4D Beings and 4D races began to take place.

A *race* is a collective consciousness experiencing itself as a specific frequency. They are that frequency. The human, on the other hand, is not a race. They are Higher Dimensional Consciousness within a physical body experiencing a lower dimensional field. The Higher Dimensional Consciousness is not the 3D, 4D, or 5D form or dimensional field.

Higher Dimensional Consciousnesses that had been incarnating into both 5D and 4D human forms began to get curious about creating a 4D race that would exist in the 4D field alongside the 4D human form.

Instead of incarnating as a Higher Dimensional Consciousness into a 4D human, they wanted to create a Consciousness that would be 4th Dimensional. Its form and its Consciousness would be one.

Remember, one of the universal laws states that all Consciousnesses entering the 12D grid had to be holding a 6th dimensional frequency or higher. Fourth and fifth dimensional Consciousnesses could not enter the 12D grid and experience the Earth Plane. Creating a 4D race with a 4D form would bypass this universal law and allow any race designed by Higher Dimensional Consciousness to enter and experience the Earth Plane.

Creating a 4D race of Beings would allow for a completely new experience on the Earth Plane and in the 12D grid. The 4D races would not be connected to a Higher Self, to Guides, or to the *I Am* Presence of any other Higher Consciousness. They would be the 4D frequency. The 4D field would dictate their entire reality.

They would not have human DNA. They would not look like a human form. They would be created separately from anything we created and would experience the Earth Plane differently from the human.

Many Higher Dimensional collective consciousnesses wanted to design 4D races. These included the Grays, Anunaki, Zetas, Orions, and the Lyrans. These are benevolent Higher Dimensional collective consciousnesses. They hold frequencies between the 7th and 18th dimension. They were volunteering as benevolent Consciousnesses on the Earth Plane for millions of years prior to designing a 4D race.

Some of these names are currently perceived by many in your reality as darker Beings. That is because the Higher Dimensional collective consciousnesses created these 4D races, and humans gave them the same name as the Consciousness that designed them. The Grays are 11th dimensional Beings that created the 4D races that today humans call Grays. The Anunaki are 7th–9th dimensional Beings that created 4D races that today humans call Anunaki. They hold the same names, but they are very different Beings and frequencies.

There were many 4D races created at this time, and not all hold the names of the Consciousnesses that created them. Names and labels are only necessary on the Earth Plane. They allow the human to understand energy. The 4D races don't have names. They are known by their energetic signature and frequency, just like all Higher Dimensional Consciousnesses.

A Gray in the 4th dimensional frequency is known and understood by experiencing its energy. A Pleiadian in the 8D frequency is known and understood by experiencing its energy. It is the 3rd dimensional human that creates the need for names.

A 4D race was designed like everything else in the quantum field: through intent and energy. The Higher Dimensional collective consciousnesses were aware of how we created physical forms, including the human form, and used similar techniques. Their creation, however, was different from ours. They weren't creating a physical form; they were creating a new consciousness that was the physical form.

There are three steps in creating 4D races. First, they had to understand the energy they were designing: the energy of the 4D Consciousness. This first step was attained through their own experience of the 4D field in the 4D human form. The more they experienced 4D Consciousness in the human form, the easier it was to create a race in that field.

Steps two and three occurred simultaneously: they intended aspects of their frequency—light codes—to split from their Consciousness to become both the physical 4D form and the 4D Consciousness that would reside within the form.

First, they energetically split an aspect of their Consciousness into light codes holding the intention of a 4D consciousness and a 4D form. The light codes would create both the Consciousness and the form at the same time. They shifted the light codes down into a 4D frequency, creating the new 4D Consciousness or being.

Next, as soon as the Consciousness was created, it shifted into the 4D physical form. Instantaneously, there was a 4D consciousness—a Being—in a 4D physical form existing outside of themselves. This new aspect of the Higher Dimensional collective consciousness would be separate from them.

For example, the Grays intended to create a 4D Race using their collective consciousness. They created the light codes, infused them into a 4D frequency, and instantaneously, there was a 4D form holding the 4D consciousness. The new 4D Gray was an aspect of the 11th dimensional Gray. A 4D Being was designed and created in one now moment. They split their Consciousness, slowed it down to 4D frequency, and created a unique physical form from their light codes. Once the same 4D beings were created many times over, they had a race of 4D Beings, all with the same light codes and the same physical features.

Earth was now inhabited by 4D Beings that had very different intentions from humans. They were not volunteers experiencing the evolution. They were Beings created to experience the 4D field.

We never intended for Higher Dimensional Consciousnesses to create 4D races, and yet, with free will, we had to allow it all to unravel. Hundreds of 4D races were designed at this time and played a significant role in not only shifting the Earth down into the lower frequencies but also in bringing about the physical destruction of the Earth.

The 4D races on the Earth Plane were holding 4D frequencies, experiencing themselves in the 4D field. This extenuated and expanded the 4th dimension on the Earth Plane. As the 4D field continued to expand, Earth's frequency began shifting down into the 4D field.

Over time, the 4D races started accessing the 3D field to experience 3D Consciousness. They navigated the 3D field through choice and intent while remaining anchored in the 4D field. Their physical forms never shifted down into a 3D field. They would choose to tap into 3D Consciousness all while remaining in a 4D body.

However, the more these Beings accessed the 3D field, the more expanded the field became on the Earth. These Beings began opening the 3D field. This allowed the 4D humans easier access to the 3D field. Similar to how the 5D humans opened the 4D field, when 4D humans began to access 3D Consciousness, their bodies' frequencies slowly began to shift down.

Remember, the human form was designed to shift frequencies and dimensions. We created the form to evolve with the Earth Plane. It shifts frequencies. Therefore, when the 4D human form began experiencing the 3D consciousnesses, it was inevitable that the form would begin to lower its frequencies down into the 3D field.

7. The Impact of the Human Form's Frequency

The seventh pivotal reason for the fall was the impact the human form's frequency had on the Earth's frequency. We noticed that as the human form shifted into the lower frequencies, the Earth Plane was being pulled down into these lower frequencies as well. This changed our understanding of the relationship between the human form and its impact on Earth. There was a symbiotic relationship between the Earth Plane and the human body that eventually led to Earth's shift into the 3D field.

When a human form accesses lower consciousnesses in lower dimensional fields, the form slowly shifts into those lower frequencies. When a human form anchors into a lower dimensional field, the form is holding that dimensional field's frequency.

As humans began to access 4D frequencies and eventually anchor into the 4th dimensional field, we noticed the Earth Plane beginning to be pulled down into the 4D frequencies and the 4D field.

The human body was energetically impacting the frequency of the Earth Plane by shifting their own body's frequency. As hundreds of thousands of humans began to anchor into the 4th dimensional field, due to 80 percent of their body holding 4D frequencies, the Earth Plane began shifting into 4D frequencies and anchoring into the 4D field. The more humans anchored into the 4D field, the faster the Earth Plane shifted into the 4D field.

Earth did not intend to shift into lower frequencies. Humans had free will, and she allowed for free will; thus, she allowed herself to shift down as the human chose to experience the 4D field, but it was never her intention.

Remember, the experiment Earth laid out was volatile. There was and is room for many different experiences to unravel due to free will. She knew this, and we knew this. We put in place universal laws that would assist in keeping her experiment and intention on track. Had we known that human forms could pull the Earth Plane down in frequency, we might have created another universal law. Earth and we had to let the experiment play out.

It took millions of linear years, but eventually, we had an Earth Plane in the 5D field and the 4D field simultaneously. We had 5D human forms, 4D human forms, and 4D races on the Earth Plane.

There were 5D human forms existing in their reality and field while there were 4D human forms and 4D races existing in their reality and field. Both the 5D human and the 4D human were existing on the same physical Earth Plane, just in two separate dimensions. There was one physical Earth Plane being experienced, yet it held two dimensional fields, two realities to experience on the Earth Plane. There wasn't a separate 4D Earth Plane.

Over time, the 4D human slowly began accessing the 3rd dimensional field. They choose to experience 3D consciousnesses, allowing their bodies to hold 3D frequencies. As more 4D humans started accessing the 3D field and 3D consciousnesses, their bodies began to pull the Earth Plane down into the 3D frequencies.

Both the human form and the Earth Plane began to experience and hold 3D frequencies within the 3D field. It took millions of linear years, but we watched as Earth and humanity's frequency shifted from a 5D field to 3D frequencies. It was becoming extremely difficult for Earth to shift into the 6D field.

5.2 Earth's Timeline Shift

Earth was continuing to be pulled further and further into the 3D field. The 3D field was now being accessed by both humans and 4D races, and in so doing, they were experiencing and creating from the consciousnesses found within the 3D field. They were creating realities from fear, greed, power, control, manipulation, lack, and so much more. These realities created chemical, technological, and physical warfare on the Earth Plane.

Humanity was on a timeline that would see the physical destruction of the Earth Plane and all humans and non-humans on the planet. This timeline was inevitable because of the millions of humans who were now participating in the 3D frequencies and the overall frequency of the human collective and the Earth Plane.

A timeline holds the experiences and future outcomes that will be experienced by the human or the human collective. Each human holds their own unique timeline, and the human collective holds a timeline. Timelines are based on the frequency of the human or the human collective and are designed to shift if and when the frequency of the human or the human collective shifts. All timelines impact the Earth Plane and the Earth herself.

At this point in humanity's history, most of the human collective was holding 3D frequencies. Their timelines were reflecting these frequencies. If the human collective could shift their frequency up or down, the timeline would inevitably shift.

However, there were millions of humans experiencing 3D frequencies and creating a collective timeline that was about to destroy the Earth. It was at this moment we knew we would be intervening. One of the universal laws was that we had the ability to intervene if the Earth Plane was going to be physically destroyed. We were now going to be pivoting the entire Earth experience. We were going to pull her out of the human collective's timelines and allow her to choose a new timeline for herself and humanity.

There were two timelines we created for Earth to choose to step into at this moment of intervention:

1. We would shift her back into the 5th dimension, and she would start all over again in the 5D field.

2. She would shift herself back into the 5th dimension. She would begin again in the 3rd dimension with the intention of moving back into the 5D. Her physical form would be in a 3D field, and all physical forms on her would be in a 3D field. She would begin her evolution from the 3rd Dimension.

Earth has always been very conscious of her experience as well as the gift and power of free will and the quantum field. She recognized what was occurring on her, and she lovingly allowed for it to unravel. It was part of the experiment, even if it was not intended through her choices.

She knew by allowing Higher Dimensional Consciousnesses to participate in her experiment, there would be a multitude of variables and outcomes. She viewed us shifting her back into 5D as a disruption of free will and the quantum field. She trusted all that played out thus far and chose to begin number two, again in the 3rd dimension. She wanted to honor the experiment and do the work of evolving back into the 5D.

5.3 Clearing the Earth

Once this choice was made, we had to clear her entire physical form in both the 4th and 5th dimensions. Once the lower frequencies and dimensions were experienced and opened, we could not close or take them away.

We had to remove all human, non-humans, 4D races, and all physical forms in both the 4th and 5th dimension fields. We had to recreate her physical form in the 3D field. We had to recreate the human form and all other physical forms in the 3rd Dimension, and we had to send out the first call for Light Workers.

If we kept the 5D field on her while she began again in the 3D, this would only perpetuate the same shift down into the 3D by 5D humans. We had to clear the entire Earth Plane from all consciousnesses, physical and nonphysical, in any other dimensional field, to ensure she would only be experiencing herself in the 3D field. This allowed for the most direct shift into the 5D.

We cleared the Earth Plane in a single moment. However, it was experienced in the 4th and 5th dimensional fields as a 24-hour period. We used earthquakes, volcanic eruptions, and tsunamis to clear off most of the Earth. All the humans who experienced the events were surrounded by Higher Dimensional Consciousness. They were held in a field of light as they passed out of the physical form. It was beautiful even though it was physically destructive.

We ensured that these events were quick and that all humans, non-humans, and 4D races on the Earth Plane would navigate these clearings with ease and grace. The 5D human, 4D human, and 4D races experienced this clearing very differently.

5.4 The 5D Human Experience

The 5D human was aware of what was occurring on the Earth Plane. They were aware of Earth's shift into the 4th dimension and the timeline humanity was experiencing. They knew we would be clearing the Earth Plane with natural events for Earth to begin again in the 3D field. They were also aware that we would need humans to assist Earth back into the 5D field.

Every 5D human had four options to choose from once we cleared the Earth Plane.

The first option was to incarnate into a 3D human form and assist the Earth in shifting back into the 5D form, in a role now known as a Light Worker.

The second option was to incarnate back into a 3D human form as a volunteer experiencing the 3D field but not assisting the Earth in shifting into the 5D field. Both of these options would become available as soon as Earth was cleared, and we had redesigned the human body into the 3D frequency.

The third option was to transition out of the 5D human form and go back to the Consciousness it originated in prior to incarnating.

The fourth option was to assist the Earth while she was in the 3D by remaining in a 5th dimensional frequency within specific portals on the 3D Earth.

This last choice was a unique opportunity. If the Higher Dimensional Consciousness chose this option, they would remain in their 5D human form but energetically move into a portal we created within a physical structure on the 3D Earth Plane. They would anchor 5D frequencies onto the 3D Earth Plane as the Earth shifted from the 3D to the 5D. This had never been done before, but we knew it could have a significant impact in assisting the Earth Plane and the human in accessing and holding 5D frequencies.

It required us to open portals on the redesigned 3rd dimensional Earth Plane. These portals would be held within physical structures on the Earth and would hold the 5D physical forms and frequencies. We used mountains, pyramids, rock formations, and the ocean to hold portals.

This 4th option allowed the Higher Dimensional Consciousnesses in the 5D human form the opportunity to stay in the 5D field and frequency yet participate on the 3D Earth using these portals. Thousands of 5D humans chose this option. They have been holding the 5D frequency within the Earth Plane since she began her journey in 3D around 15,000 years ago. They played and are currently playing a significant role in Earth and humanity's shift into the 5D field. They were the first Light Workers on the 3D Earth.

Once all 5D humans chose one of the four options, they then either agreed to stay on the Earth and experience the physical clearing, or they exited the human form prior to the natural events occurring.

If the human chose option four, they would be shifted into a 5D portal as we were clearing off the Earth Plane. They could shift before the clearing, or they could experience the natural events and shift during the clearing. Either way, they would not transition or pass from the human form. They stayed with the human form and simply moved into a 5D portal off the Earth Plane. They would remain there until we had the portal created in the new 3D Earth.

If the human chose the first or second option and decided to exit the human form, they would move back into the Consciousness they existed in prior to incarnating and wait for the Earth Plane to be cleared.

If the human chose to experience the physical clearing, they would go through the natural physical events that would unravel. Once the human transitioned out of the human body (passed) the Higher Dimensional Consciousness would exit the human form and Earth Plane.

Regardless of which choice the human made, the Higher Dimensional Consciousness would have to wait for the Earth Plane and human body to be redesigned in the 3D frequency to incarnate back into the human form. Remember, we are describing this event as if it occurred in linear time and space. However, this event occurred in one linear 24-hour period, so the waiting that any Higher Dimensional Consciousness experienced was brief.

The humans who chose the third option, whether they stayed and ex-perienced the clearing or departed before the clearing, would move back into their original Consciousness they existed in prior to incarnating as soon as they departed the human form.

5.5 The 4D Human Experience

The 4D human's experience of the clearing was very different from the 5D human. The 4D field does not allow for the same awareness, understanding, and choice as the 5D human. The 4D human would not be aware of any choice they had in experiencing the clearing. They would all go through the natural events on the Earth Plane and transition out of the human form during these natural disasters.

The 4D human experienced these events feeling fear, sadness, panic, loss, and victimhood. The experience each 4D human had was based on the frequency in their human form. If they were holding higher 4D frequencies, they may have had less fear, confusion, and loss. They may have felt a sense of knowingness that all was well, knowing they were safe to transition from the human form. If they were holding lower 4D frequencies, they may have experienced much more fear, panic, fear, and lack of control.

The 4D human was unaware they could choose to exit the human form prior to the clearing. The 4D human was not holding a high enough frequency to make the same choices as the 5D human, and most experienced the physical clearing of the Earth Plane in their human form.

5.6 The 4D Races Experience

The 4D races held different physical forms from the human body. They held different light codes with different intentions; therefore, their experience on the Earth Plane was different from the other humans. They were connected to the quantum field, and they understood how energy worked. They were aware we were going to be clearing the Earth Plane, and they would have the choice to either exit the Earth Plane or stay and experience the clearing.

All 4D races chose to exit the Earth Plane. They departed differently from the 4D human form. They exited with their 4D forms and moved into a 4th dimensional field within the 12D grid. The 4D Being was its form; it wasn't separate from its form. If it chose to exit the Earth Plane, all of it, including its form, would depart the planet.

The human form is not the Higher Dimensional Consciousness within the form. When the Higher Dimensional Consciousness exits the Earth Plane, it transitions out of the human form, and the form stays on the planet. They do not take their human form with them.

The 4D races shifted out of the Earth's 4D field and moved into the 4D field inside the 12th dimensional grid. For the 4D races to remain in Earth's experiment, they had to hold themselves in the 12D grid within the 4th dimensional field. This 4D field is not the same 4D field that the Earth was experiencing. This is a separate 4D field off the Earth Plane in the 12D grid. If the 4D races wanted to experience the Earth Plane again, they would have to shift their physical 4D forms into Earth's dimensional field.

Earth was going to be shifting down into a 3rd dimensional field holding a 3rd dimensional frequency within a 5D grid around her. The 4D races remained within the 4D field and would not be able to physically enter back onto her form for thousands of years.

Summary

There are many reading this right now who will remember on an energetic level the pain and deep sadness that was felt during the fall from grace. You may have been there and courageously experienced the clearing. Many of you are the Light Workers that chose to come back onto the 3D Earth Plane to assist in shifting Earth and humanity back into the 5D. You have been on and with the 3D Earth for thousands of years. Many of you went back to your collective consciousness within the 12D grid and chose to reincarnate in the last 100 years. And many of you may have watched this entire clearing from off the Earth Plane and incarnated at this time to assist in the most miraculous shift in a collective consciousness. There are so many ways in which each of you experienced this moment in Earth and humanity's history.

Currently, you are shifting into higher state of consciousness and remembering what you went through on Earth, your role in this evolutionary process, and how deeply you love the Earth and humanity. It's a gift that all of you have been journeying with the Earth for millions of years, and you are with her now.

Chapter 6

THE DESIGN OF THE 3D EARTH

It was around 15,000 linear years ago when we redesigned Earth into a 3D form. Although we had no idea Earth would ever be experiencing herself in a 3D field, we knew we could create a form that would allow her to shift back into the 5D field and beyond.

This new physical reality for Earth required us to ensure three important qualities within her redesign:

1. Earth would be able to evolve back into the 5D field from this dense dimension.
2. Earth as the consciousness could exist within a 3D physical form.
3. The physical form could exist in a 3D field.

For these three things to take place, we had to redesign her physical form and her energetic field. We also had to change the way all Consciousnesses on and off the Earth Plane would interact and experience the 3rd Dimensional field. We began her redesign with a 5D grid around her form.

6.1 The Physical Redesign

We began Earth's redesign with her physical form.

Her redesign occurred in a single moment, just as her original 5D form was designed within a single moment. We took her 5D form and energetically shifted it down into a 3D field. When we did this, the shape of the Earth changed slightly.

In the 5D field, it was a disk-like elongated form, circular, but stretched out, not round. As we shifted the form into lower frequencies, it squeezed into a more circular shape. The 3D Earth Plane was more round than oval. It also held much more matter because it was holding lower frequencies within a denser dimensional field.

The 5D Earth had a thin crust of matter around a crystalline center. It existed mostly of crystalline light. The 3D Earth was a much larger body of matter with Earth's consciousness within the body. It did not hold a crystalline center.

When we cleared the 5D Earth, almost everything was wiped off the planet, including all physical forms. We did keep most Continents, all mountain ranges, and all oceans. In her redesigned form, we made five unique changes that had not been necessary when she was in a 5D field. We created a 5D grid. We designed a Moon. We added more water on her form. We created 3D physical forms to hold 5D consciousness, and we created more universal laws.

6.2 The 5D Grid

When Earth was originally designed in the 5th dimension, she was held within one grid, the 12th dimensional grid. All Higher Dimensional Consciousnesses volunteering on her physical plane were within the 12D grid.

During Earth's shift down into lower frequencies, 4D races had been created. Although these races were not on the Earth Plane as we were redesigning her form, they were now within the 12D grid. They could access Earth at any time.

We had 4D races within the 12D grid that had played a role in shifting Earth and humanity into lower frequencies. They now could enter back onto the Earth Plane and perhaps play the same role again in shifting Earth and humanity into lower frequencies.

We had to ensure that they would not be able to participate on the 3D Earth Plane. If we allowed 4th dimensional races access to the planet, Earth's ability to shift back into the 5th dimensional field could, and most likely would, be compromised.

We needed to create an energetic grid that would keep 4D races from entering onto the Earth Plane. The grid had to be vibrating at a frequency higher than the 4D races. This is because any consciousness, including 4D races, can only access the dimensional field they are existing in or a lower dimensional field. It is impossible for a Consciousness to experience and move into a higher dimensional field unless they are anchored into that dimensional field.

We chose to create a 5D grid around the Earth, knowing that 4D races could not penetrate or access the grid. The 4D races were anchored into the 4th dimension as 4D consciousness. They were not 5D consciousness. They were not holding 5D consciousness. They could only anchor into a 5D field if they chose to shift into the 5D field and no longer be 4D Beings. And if they chose to no longer be 4D Beings and shift into 5D consciousness, we wouldn't need to worry about the possible compromise they could have on Earth's frequency. Fifth dimensional consciousness is experienced very differently from 4D consciousness.

We knew as long as we had 4D races in the 12D grid, the creation of a 5D grid would allow Earth and humanity to evolve without the interference from 4D races. We created the grid like we did everything else in this divine design, through intent and energy. We intended the grid to hold Earth in a sovereign field and vibrate in 5D frequencies. We pulled energy from the 12D field we were anchored into and shifted the energy into a 5D field. The grid instantaneously formed around the Earth body. It's an energetic grid surrounding the Earth, not on the Earth Plane.

All Consciousnesses within the 12D grid energetically understood the intention and role the 5D grid played, including the 4D races. They knew they would not have access onto the Earth unless we opened the grid.

The 5D grid was a significant design of the 3D Earth Plane. It ensured that Earth and humanity would have the ability to anchor back into the 5D field without the interference of any other Consciousnesses.

6.3 The Moon

When Earth was designed in 5D, she held a balance of both a masculine and feminine consciousness. These consciousnesses are vibrational signatures or tones experienced as what the human calls either masculine or feminine energies. We are not speaking of male or female, as the human designation of male or female is based on their anatomy. We are referring to two consciousnesses that exist as energy and are experienced as unique characteristics.

Only dimensional fields that hold form experience masculine and feminine energies. These fields are the 3rd, 4th, 5th, 6th and 7th dimensional fields. Beyond the 7th dimensional field, the two unique vibrational consciousnesses merge into one unified consciousness. There is no separation, and thus, there isn't a masculine or feminine.

What may be important to point out as you read this section is that any Consciousness that is in the 3rd to 7th dimensional field may experience Higher Dimensional Consciousness existing in an 8th dimensional field or higher through the lens of being masculine or feminine. Meaning, if a 3D human interacts with a 9D Consciousness (i.e., a Pleiaidan) they may experience that Pleiadian as being male or female. They are feeling specific aspects of the Pleiaidan's energy field that feel similar to a feminine or masculine energy.

The 3D human perceives this Pleiadian to be female because they are filtering the energies though their 3D lens. Feminine energy holds specific emotions, feelings, and ways about it. When the human feels these same energies in the Pleiadian, they associate it with feminine energy. The Pleaidian is neither male nor female but a unified field of many consciousnesses. They do not hold a dominant masculine or feminine. Both energies are merged into one energy.

As Consciousness shifts into a 7th dimensional field or lower, there is a unique and separate vibrational experience of masculine and feminine. These two consciousnesses split and are experienced as two separate frequencies. Any Higher Dimensional Consciousness including the human that is in a 5th to 7th dimensional field is balanced in these two consciousnesses. They hold both masculine and feminine energies equally within them.

Any Higher Dimensional Consciousness, including the human that is in a 4th or 3rd dimensional field, experiences an imbalance of the two consciousnesses. They will experience a pull or a need to be in one more than the other. They will identify and take on or express the qualities of one consciousness over the other.

Since Earth and humanity began again in the 3rd dimensional field, they will be experiencing the imbalance of the masculine and feminine energies. Humanity will have a choice as to which of the two consciousnesses they will more often experience. This choice will be unconscious. They will merely choose ways of being that will either be in the masculine frequency or the feminine frequency. Their reality will be dictated by this consciousness. If humanity chooses to experience more of the masculine consciousness, their reality will be expressed through more masculine energies, such as repressed emotions over expressed emotions, power over flow, mind over energy, force over surrender, and so on.

Earth and her balance of masculine and feminine will be impacted by the choice humanity makes as to which consciousness they will more often experience. She will not have the ability to balance out both energies until the frequency within her form increases to a 5D field. This is also the case for all humans. They will experience an imbalance of these two energies until their own physical form begins holding 5D frequencies.

The human will experience masculine consciousness more easily than feminine consciousness because feminine energy spins a bit faster. It is more challenging for the human to tap into the consciousnesses and hold it in their bodies. The human body is in a low frequency, and it's much easier to hold and access the slower masculine energy than the faster feminine energies.

It also takes longer for masculine energy in the human form to shift into higher frequencies. Therefore, when a human holds more masculine than feminine energy, it will have a more difficult time shifting into higher frequencies.

We understood all of this, and we knew it was very probable that the masculine energy would be more pronounced while in the 3rd dimensional field. The human collective would most likely be unconsciously choosing masculine energies over feminine energies. This had the potential to create difficulty in Earth and humanity shifting into the higher frequencies.

We needed to create a physical form that could assist Earth with the imbalance of masculine and feminine energies while she was evolving. This form would interact with the physical Earth Plane and humanity, allowing them to hold more feminine energies as they evolve.

We created what the humans call the Moon for the purpose of energetically connecting the Earth Plane to feminine consciousness. The Moon was created from a 9th dimensional council of Light Beings within our Galactic Federation. It was created the same way all other physical forms were created, through intent and energy.

The Light Beings within the 9D council intended the form and its purpose. They wanted the Moon to be similar to the shape of the 3D Earth Plane. They held the intention of assisting and balancing Earth and humanity with feminine consciousness. They took these intentions and encoded them into 9D light codes. They then shifted the 9D light codes down from a 9th dimensional frequency into a 3rd dimensional frequency in order to create the physical Moon.

Once the Moon was created in a 3D field, we then asked for a Higher Dimensional Consciousness within the 12D grid to volunteer and enter the Moon's physical form. We needed a Consciousness to hold feminine energy within the Moon's form to energetically connect with the Earth and transmit this feminine energy onto the Earth and humanity.

Once we had the Higher Dimensional Consciousness enter the physical Moon, we connected the Moon to the Earth Plane through an energetic cord of light. This cord of light allows for a constant flow of feminine energy between the Moon, the Earth Plane, and humanity.

The Moon infuses feminine frequencies down onto the Earth Plane and all humans on her in order to balance out the masculine frequencies. Again, the balancing of these two consciousnesses is imperative in shifting into the 5D field. The Moon played and plays an important role in Earth's evolution.

6.4 Water

Once we designed the Moon, we then began to redesign aspects of Earth's physical form. We knew her form was going to be in a 3rd dimensional field that was denser than the 5D. She would be holding more matter than light. We needed to ensure that the density of her form would be able to shift into higher frequencies.

We knew water was a conduit for energy. It assists high frequency light to move through dense physical forms more easily. Water is also a solvent that assists in breaking down density and alchemizing it into light.

We knew if we added more water to Earth's 3D form, she would be able to shift into the 5D field with more ease. Water would assist the Earth Plane in not only anchoring into higher dimensional fields, but in alchemizing the density of her form into light.

We chose to add more oceans on her body. The 5D Earth had two large bodies of water. The 3D earth had five. We also added more lakes, which created more rivers. We created a 3D Earth that was two-thirds water. This still has a significant impact on her ability to shift into the 5D field.

6.5 The Physical Redesign of 3D Forms

The next part of our redesign concerned 3D physical forms that would hold 5D consciousness on the Earth Plane. We knew if we had physical forms holding 5D consciousness, both the human and the Earth Plane could access this 5D consciousness without yet being in 5D consciousness.

This was a way for us to allow higher frequencies to be anchored onto the Earth Plane before Earth and humanity had anchored them into their forms. This redesign had a powerful impact on the evolution. It allowed humanity and the Earth Plane to access 5D frequencies.

The moment Earth began again in the 3D field, we created physical forms that would hold 5D Consciousness. These were trees and non-human living forms, such as mammals, reptiles, birds, amphibians, and sea life that would be in a 3D form holding 5D consciousness.

Trees

We chose trees because we knew they could exist on the Earth Plane for thousands of linear years and needed very little to survive. They were powerful Beings on the 5D Earth, and we knew they could play a pivotal role in the evolution.

We redesigned 5D trees into 3D physical forms. Their physical form had to be in the 3D field, or it could not exist on the Earth Plane. We then asked for 5D Consciousnesses to volunteer and drop into these 3D forms. These consciousnesses would hold their 5D frequency while existing within in a 3D form. Their role was to anchor and hold the 5D frequency on the Earth.

Every tree on the Earth Plane has a 5D Consciousness within it that chose to incarnate to anchor 5D frequencies for the sole purpose of assisting Earth and humanity in their evolution. This was and still is extremely beneficial for the evolution.

Trees are alive, they energetically breathe, and they are communicating in every moment with humanity and the Earth. Although not many humans are aware of the consciousness a tree holds, if they connect energetically or physically to a tree, they will experience 5D frequencies.

Non-Human Living Forms

We also created 3D physical forms that hold 5D frequencies yet allow Higher Dimensional Consciousnesses to incarnate into these forms. This was very different from what we created with trees. Trees were 5D Consciousnesses. They incarnated as a 5D consciousness and held that Consciousness within the form of a tree.

We wanted to allow Higher Dimensional Consciousnesses to participate on the Earth Plane not just as humans, but as other living physical forms while having a significant impact on the evolution. The Higher Dimensional Consciousnesses that chose to incarnate into the 3D physical form—mammals, reptiles, birds, amphibians, sea life—would be experiencing life in 5D frequencies while living in a 3D physical form. Their forms were holding and anchoring the 5D frequencies that would slowly assist Earth and humanity in their evolution.

To allow the 3D physical form to hold 5D frequencies, we had to ensure that the physical body could filter the 3rd dimensional consciousnesses experienced from the external world through the form. It was imperative that the 3D frequencies not get stuck within the physical body, potentially pulling the form into a 3rd dimensional field.

We chose to place twelve energy centers and millions of meridians within these physical forms. Meridians are energetic cords that move energy throughout the body. The 3rd dimensional consciousnesses from the external world are able to move through the physical form with ease, allowing the form to remain holding 5D frequencies.

Every mammal, reptile, bird, amphibian, and form of sea life is holding a Higher Dimensional Consciousness within it that chose to incarnate in order to anchor 5D frequencies onto the Earth.

When the 3D human encounters any of these physical forms, they can energetically and physically experience 5D frequencies. The human can experience 5D consciousness without yet holding it in their body. They are experiencing the frequencies that their own physical body will eventually shift into.

The designing of all the mammals, reptiles, birds, amphibians, and sea life was one of the most powerful moments we had while redesigning the Earth Plane in the 3D. We knew the powerful impact these physical forms would have on humanity and the Earth's evolution. They anchored and continue to anchor 5D frequencies.

6.6 Universal Laws

Universal laws were very important in Earth's redesign. Universal laws allow for a sovereign and safe experience for both Earth and all Higher Dimensional Consciousnesses incarnating onto Earth.

We maintained all the universal laws that existed in the 5D field; however, due to the density of the third dimensional field, we added a few additional laws. These universal laws are agreed upon and followed by Earth and all Higher Dimensional Consciousnesses both incarnating onto Earth and existing within the 12D grid.

The 5D Grid

The first law we put into place was the 5D grid around the 3D Earth. We discussed this grid earlier in the chapter, but it is important to note that it was also a universal law allowing us to maintain a safe and sovereign field for Earth and all Consciousnesses entering down onto the Earth.

Amnesia

The second law was amnesia. Amnesia is experienced by any Higher Dimensional Consciousness that incarnates into a physical form on the 3D Earth Plane. It is the inability to remember who the Higher Dimensional Consciousness is, why they are in the physical form, and how Earth and the quantum field work.

The reason amnesia occurs is because of the density of the 3rd dimensional body. When a Higher Dimensional Consciousness incarnates into a 3D form, their light is dimmed by the density of the 3rd dimension. It is as if a veil has been gently placed over the Consciousness's light. Their ability to stay aligned and connected to their frequency and knowingness is weighted down by the density of the physical form.

If the physical form can shift into higher frequencies, the heaviness or density of that form lightens, and the veil that has dimmed the Consciousness within the body begins to lift. The Higher Dimensional Consciousness within the physical form begins to feel its frequency. It remembers who it is as light in form incarnated into a body on the Earth Plane.

All Higher Dimensional Consciousnesses understood this law and knew they would experience amnesia once they incarnated into the human form. They also knew what would be required to remember who they were while in the physical form. It wasn't a choice to forget. It was an aspect of being in a 3D form within a 3D field.

The Fifty Percent Light Quotient

The third law created was the 50 percent light quotient. This law states that once the Earth Plane is holding 50 percent of the light needed to anchor the 5D field, it could not be shifted or pulled back down into a lower light quotient by any external circumstance. She is locked into the trajectory of the 5D field regardless of what occurs on her physical form due to human behaviors, external energies, and or any other external experience. It also states that, at the 50 percent quotient, Higher Dimensional Consciousnesses may assist the Earth and humanity on, as well as off, the Earth Plane.

The Earth Plane's light quotient is the way we measure the progress of Earth's evolution, shifting from a 3D field to a 5D field. The light quotient is the amount of light the Earth Plane is holding within its form. This light quotient creates a frequency that emanates out from the Earth's form. This emanation creates the energetic field around the Earth Plane. We measure the Earth Plane's light quotient by connecting to its energetic field and feeling its frequency. The frequency tells us the amount of light the Earth Plane is holding and where it is along its evolutionary path.

We use numbers and percentages as a way of expressing an energetic experience through the lens of the 3rd dimension. However, frequency is constantly moving along a spectrum and that spectrum does not exist within a numerical field. Using numbers allows the human to have a better understanding of what we are referring to, but it is important to remember that percentages and numbers do not exist in the quantum field. We are only using it to communicate what is occurring on an energetic level.

Remember, Earth is a Higher Dimensional Consciousness held within the form called the Earth Plane. It is her form, and not the Consciousness, that is shifting frequency.

When Earth began in the 3rd dimensional field, her light quotient started at zero, which means the light she needs to hold in order to reach the 5th dimensional field was at zero. As Earth begins to evolve and hold higher-frequency light in her body, that percentage will increase. Her light quotient will go up. When Earth has anchored into the 5D field, her light quotient will be at 100 percent.

We knew, based on Earth's experiences in the 5th dimensional field, that there are many external probabilities that can play out once Higher Dimensional Consciousnesses incarnate into human forms. These probabilities, based on free will, can pull humanity and the Earth Plane into lower frequencies.

We wanted to ensure that once Earth hit a percentage of her light quotient—regardless of what may be occurring on the planet—she would not be able to be pulled back down into a lower quotient and lower frequency. We chose 50 percent as the tipping point that would enable Earth and humanity to move into the 5D field regardless of any external influences—including human influence.

Another aspect of this law allows off-planet Higher Dimensional Consciousnesses that are supporting humanity and the Earth to begin to actively engage and assist on the Earth Plane. Prior to hitting the 50 percent mark, all Higher Dimensional Consciousnesses had to assist off the Earth energetically. This law allows the Consciousnesses to energetically move themselves down into lower frequencies to assist humans in a more palpable and tangible way.

The purpose for this part of the law is to allow the human to receive guidance in a more physical manner. The human will begin to feel, see, hear, and receive from the Higher Dimensional Consciousness. Through this connection, humans will begin to awaken much faster and evolve into the higher states of consciousness.

Incarnation Requirements

The fourth law is an original law from the 5D that has been adjusted to match the new 3D frequency of Earth. The law states that any Higher Dimensional Consciousness incarnating into a physical form must be holding a frequency at or higher than the dimensional field the Earth Plane is shifting into. In this instance, the Earth Plane is shifting into the 5th dimensional field; therefore, any Higher Dimensional Consciousness incarnating into a 3D physical form must hold a 5D frequency or higher.

The Akashic Record

The fifth law was the design of the Akashic Records. The Akashic Record is a map or a navigational tool for the Higher Dimensional Consciousness incarnating into the 3rd dimensional human body. Only the human form has an Akashic Record. All other physical forms do not require an Akashic Record because of the simplified nature of their designed life. They are solely focused on survival, and all choices are based on that need. The human has a much more complex life, and the records were a tool to assist the human.

There are two reasons we saw a need for an Akashic Record and both were based on the density of the 3D field.

The first reason is the amnesia. Once the Higher Dimensional Consciousness incarnates, the human will not remember who they are, why they are in the human form, and how to navigate the 3D field. They will need records that will guide them through the human journey. There wasn't a need for an Akashic Record in the 5D field because the human form was in a much higher frequency allowing the human to remember who they are, why they incarnated, and how to navigate the 5D field.

The second reason for the Akashic Record was the duality, polarity, and large spectrum of experiences within the 3rd dimensional field.

The 3D human will be navigating a dimensional field with an infinite amount of experiences held in polarity and duality. The humans' free will to create and choose their reality will be dictated by right or wrong, good or bad, positive or negative. Duality and polarity unconsciously drive the experiences chosen by the 3D human.

We needed to ensure that the Higher Dimensional Consciousness had a somewhat organized and outlined human journey without the distractions from the 3D field.

The Akashic Record would guide the human through their life using the records created as the signposts. It is the role of the Higher Self to connect into these records and guide the human through their journey. The human may or may not be conscious of the guidance; nevertheless, the Higher Self follows the records and guides the human through their life.

6.7 Creating the Akashic Record

All Higher Dimensional Consciousnesses that incarnate into a human form create an Akashic Record for their human experience prior to incarnation. The records are designed within the quantum field offering an infinite amount of possibilities or consciousnesses to choose from. You can imagine the records like an energetic vault of information held in an energetic field. Each record is created through light codes. The light codes create the Akashic Record. Once the entire Akashic Record is designed, it is shifted into the human body's DNA upon incarnation. The Akashic Record is merely a large collection of light codes holding very specific information within the human form.

We connect with each Higher Dimensional Consciousness in the field of the Akashic Record. We show them how the 3D field will work and how the human body will hold their consciousness. We provide them with all the universal laws that will exist while they are in 3D field, and we show them what is energetically available to be experienced within that 3D field. Once they have the necessary information, they design the framework for their human journey.

Each time a Higher Dimensional Consciousness incarnates into a human form, they create a new Akashic Record. Each record is designed as a separate and unique human life. The Akashic Record holds the day, time, and physical location of birth, physical attributes, core fundamental consciousnesses, contracts, the family map, ancestral consciousness cords, and the blueprint or purpose for incarnating.

6.8 Sex, Date and Location of Birth

When the Higher Dimensional Consciousness enters the field of the Akashic Records to create its human life, they begin by choosing the sex, such as male, female. They then choose the day, time, and physical location of their birth, including continent, county, state, city, town, or any other location where they choose to be born. This is one of the most important decisions made within the Akashic Record as each continent and country allows for unique opportunities and experiences.

The physical location creates the foundation for the human and can dictate the entire human journey. If a Higher Dimensional Consciousness chooses to enter the human form in Africa during the 1800s, their experience will be drastically different from entering a human form in England at that same time. The physical location of their birth also dictates many physical attributes of the human form, including eye color, hair textures, body type, and facial features. The Higher Dimensional Consciousness simultaneously chooses the physical characteristic of its human body and the birth location as both decisions impact the other.

Although the choice of parents is what genetically provides the physical attributes, it is the location of birth that initiates the physical appearance of the human body. All physical attributes are designed by DNA, including eye, hair, and skin color, but the Higher Dimensional Consciousness chooses all of this prior to incarnating into human form based on the physical location of their birth and their birth parents.

Once the Higher Dimensional Consciousnesses chooses its sex, details for birth, and physical attributes, these choices are intended into light codes that create an aspect of the Akashic Record.

6.9 Core Foundational Consciousnesses

Once the Higher Dimensional Consciousness has choosen the sex, location of incarnation, and physical attributes, it then chooses core foundational consciousnesses. These consciousnesses will dictate and create the framework for many of the experiences the human will have during their life. Almost all experiences within the human journey will stem from these core foundational consciousnesses.

Typically, a Higher Dimensional Consciousness will choose six to ten core foundational consciousnesses to hold within their records. Each consciousness chosen vibrates in a 3D frequency and can be seen as a template that drives specific experiences in the human journey. Core foundational consciousnesses are chosen from the infinite amount of consciousnesses that can be experienced within the 3D field. A consciousness in the 3D field can be anything from abandonment, abuse, neglect, addiction, poverty, lack, murder, and greed to abundance, fame, unconditional love, safety, success, peace, and so much more.

Many of these consciousnesses are experienced by the human. However, when the Higher Dimensional Consciousness chooses one of these as a core foundational consciousness, it becomes the base that leads all other actions and decisions in creating a pattern of experiences within the human journey. Almost all of what is experienced within the human journey originates from one of the core foundational consciousnesses within the records.

For example, a core foundational consciousness such as abandonment will create experiences in the human life that will reflect abandonment. The human will unconsciously create experiences that allow for abandonment. These experiences will create belief systems, thought patterns, behaviors, wounds, traumas, and relationship patterns all stemming from abandonment. The human is unaware of the patterns that are being created through the Akashic Record.

When the Higher Dimensional Consciousness chooses these core foundational consciousnesses, they are doing so through the lens of neutrality. They are merely choosing consciousnesses to experience in a 3D field. They do not see them through the lens of duality. There isn't a right and wrong or a good and bad. It is an experience to have while in the human form.

However, once the Higher Dimensional Consciousness drops into the human form, they forget and get lost in the illusion that they are these experiences. The human does not remember the Akashic Record and filters all experiences through the lens of duality and polarity. There is a right and a wrong a good and a bad.

We know it can be challenging for the human to experience core foundational consciousnesses, but it was imperative in order to keep the human in a contained framework. The 3D field has a large spectrum of consciousnesses that can be experienced. If the human did not have the core consciousnesses framing their human journey, they would be moving all over the 3D spectrum. It would quite quickly create chaos and energetic breakdowns. We designed the core foundational consciousnesses, to create a more contained and stable experience within the 3D field.

Once the Higher Dimensional Consciousness chooses a core foundational experience like abandonment, for example, the energy of that consciousness is then intended into light codes. These light codes become an aspect of the Akashic Record.

6.10 Contracts

Once the core foundational consciousnesses are chosen, contracts are made with other Higher Dimensional Consciousnesses to allow these core consciousnesses to play out. Without Higher Dimensional Consciousnesses agreeing to contract with each other, the core foundational experiences would be held in the field of chance. They may not be experienced in the human journey. It was necessary the human had contracts to ensure these consciousnesses were experienced.

A contract is when two or more Higher Dimensional Consciousnesses agree to connect while in the human form in order to allow one or more of the humans to experience a core consciousness. These contracts are created prior to incarnating and held in the Akashic Record. Many are made with Higher Dimensional Consciousnesses that play the role of your family members, children, romantic partners, co-workers, friends, and acquaintances.

There are three important components to the contract:

1. The agreement to connect during the human life
2. The specific relationship between the humans
3. The core consciousnesses that will be experienced

Contracts do not hold specific details such as dates, times, or locations. Free will creates an inability to determine such details.

A contract is an energetic intention to experience a core consciousness. The contract is held within light codes and stored in the Akashic Record within the humans' DNA. The contract is activated when the two or more humans holding the contract connect in physical form. As soon as the humans meet, the light codes are activated, the energetic cord immediately connects the two human forms, and the contract begins.

The core foundational consciousness that is held within the contract and the Akashic Record will begin to be experienced. The human will feel the core consciousness based on the behaviors of the other contracted human.

For example, a Higher Dimensional Consciousness has chosen the core consciousness of physical abuse. They contract with another Higher Dimensional Consciousness, who agrees to play the abuser. Both agree they will experience their contract through a romantic relationship. The abused will incarnate as a woman. The abuser will incarnate as a man. When and how they meet is not determined.

When they meet in human form, the light codes holding the contract within their DNA is activated, and the energetic cord is formed between the two human bodies. The contract begins and the roles are played out.

Contracts are some of the most selfless acts the Higher Dimensional Consciousness can play out in human form. To be able to allow a Higher Dimensional Consciousness to experience what it is choosing in the human form is an honor and a gift.

We will discuss contracts in more detail in Chapter Eighteen. What we wish to remind you is that many of the relationships that you had in the past and currently have now were contracted prior to incarnating to fulfill the core consciousnesses you chose. Nothing is left to chance. Your Higher Self is always guiding you through your human journey with the map and guidance of the Akashic record you designed.

6.11 Family Maps

When the Higher Dimensional Consciousness is choosing its contracts, it also chooses its immediate and extended family. The family system, or what we call the *family map*, consists of the parents, siblings, children, and extended family.

This map is chosen for two reasons:

1. Agreements to play out contracts
2. Specific opportunities or experiences

Contractual Agreements

One reason for choosing family members is to play out the core consciousnesses. When creating the family map, many times it is the contracts that are agreed upon to allow for core consciousnesses to play out that create the map. The family is chosen based on the contracts within the core consciousnesses.

For instance, a Higher Dimensional Consciousness may choose abandonment as a core consciousness. It chooses to be a male. It will play the son in a contract with another Higher Dimensional Consciousness, who will play the mother. Mother has chosen a core consciousness of addiction. The son chooses a mom who has agreed to be an alcoholic in order to experience abandonment. The mother contracts with the son to experience addiction. The contracts not only create the opportunity for the core consciousness to play out but also create the family map.

The contracts are agreed upon prior to incarnation and will play out in divine timing. The mom and the son agree to this prior to the mom incarnating and years before the son will incarnate. Time does not exist outside of a dense linear continuum like the 3D field. These agreements and contracts are made together, yet it may take fifty human years in the 3rd dimension for a family member to enter the family map on the Earth Plane.

Experiences and Opportunities

Another reason for choosing family members in your human journey is to have specific experiences and opportunities. If you are choosing to experience poverty growing up, and yes, that is always a choice prior to incarnating, then you will intend parents into your family map that will match that intention. If you want to have the opportunity for success in a specific career, you may choose parents who will allow for that success to take place.

The choice of the family map is very detailed and planned out. The experiences, opportunities, and contracts held within the family map are never by choice. All has been agreed upon prior to incarnation.

The Ancestral Consciousness Cord

Not only does a Higher Dimensional Consciousness choose the family map, but in doing so, they choose the ancestral line that they want to be energetically connected to while in the human body. We call it an *ancestral consciousness cord.*

Ancestors are family members within the human's family map who are not currently alive. The consciousness cord is an energetic cord that connects the current family to specific core consciousnesses experienced by their ancestors.

When the Higher Dimensional Consciousness incarnates into a human form, they are immediately connected energetically to the ancestral consciousness cord. They will unconsciously feel throughout their life some of the ancestral core consciousnesses—such as lack, abuse, greed, and abandonment—through their own thoughts, beliefs, or even behaviors. It is unconscious in the human. For example, a human may have beliefs around lack but find no reason or purpose for having these thoughts. There isn't an individual, including a family member or an experience, that created the lack beliefs.

It's also possible for the immediate family to mirror and perpetuate the ancestral core consciousnesses. The family will play out lack beliefs and create a reality from these ancestral beliefs. This behavior can be unconscious for many humans, or the human will play in victimhood and blame their reality on their ancestors. Either way, the human learns specific ways of being based on the ancestral consciousness cord. This coupled with their own core consciousness creates and dictates much of the human's journey.

For instance, a Higher Dimensional Consciousness chooses to experience sexual abuse as a core foundational experience. They contract with another Higher Dimensional Consciousness and agree to connect in the human form through a family relationship. They then decide the role within the relationship. The abused will be a daughter, and the abuser will be the father.

They also both agree to incarnate into an ancestral consciousness cord that holds sexual abuse. Not only has the father agreed to be the abuser, but both father and daughter have agreed to tap into sexual abuse within their ancestral line. The father's behavior is connected to the ancestral cord. He has most likely been sexually abused and unconsciously perpetuates the ancestral cord of abuse. The daughter has chosen to receive the abuse and has the opportunity to clear or cut the ancestral line of that core consciousness if she is awake to the cord.

Both Higher Dimensional Consciousnesses then intend for the energetic contract and energetic ancestral cord to shift into light codes that will be held within their Akashic Record and brought into their human DNA when they incarnate.

The daughter is birthed into form. She is immediately connected to the ancestral consciousness cord. The father has been connected to the ancestral consciousness cord since he was birthed into form. He is unconsciously ready to play out the contract with his daughter as the abuser. When the two human forms meet, the energetic cord connects the two of them, and the contract and the core consciousness of sexual abuse can begin. We would like to state that a human can choose sexual abuse as a core consciousness and not choose that same consciousness in the ancestral lines. It's all a choice.

Ancestral consciousness cords are part of the Akashic Record chosen by the Higher Dimensional Consciousness and designed as part of the family map, and they influence many humans unconsciously.

6.12 The Blueprint for Incarnation

The last choice the Higher Dimensional Consciousness makes while creating the Akashic Record is the reason for incarnating. Every consciousness that incarnates into a human form has an intention for the human journey. We call this the blueprint for incarnation.

This blueprint can be as simple as intending to experience the 3rd dimensional physical reality or as complex as playing a role in shifting the Earth and human collective. There are millions of Higher Dimensional Consciousnesses that have chosen to simply incarnate to feel physicality and experience polarities. Humans find this hard to believe at times, but polarities are a unique experience. Simply experiencing Earth is a blueprint for millions of humans.

There are also millions of Higher Dimensional Consciousnesses that have chosen to incarnate to assist humanity and the Earth through the evolutionary shift in consciousness. These humans are commonly known as Light Workers.

The blueprint is intended into light codes. The light codes hold a specific frequency based on the blueprint. The light codes are then placed within the Akashic Record, and upon incarnation, they move into the human DNA. The Higher Self is connected to these light codes and will guide the human through their life based on this blueprint.

The human that has chosen to simply experience the 3D physical world will not need to awaken into their blueprint or have the blueprint activate within them. Their Higher Self is always guiding them.

However, if the human's blueprint holds a specific purpose that needs to be accomplished—for example, serving humanity's evolutionary shift in consciousness—then the light codes will activate and remind the human what they are here to do.

The light codes activate when the frequency of the human body mirrors the frequency of the blueprint. Many blueprints are activated at a very young age, and many are activated later in the human journey. The activation of the blueprint is intended upon by the Higher Dimensional Consciousnesses prior to incarnating. If they wanted to ensure they would awaken into their blueprint while in the human form, that intention would be held within the blueprint's light codes.

Every human form is holding their blueprint within their DNA. Not every human's blueprint will or needs to be activated. It isn't imperative that all humans are activated into remembrance, but most humans will become activated. This is part of the evolution in human consciousness; the light codes activate within the human DNA, and the human remembers who they are and why they incarnated regardless of the blueprint.

Summary

The Akashic Record is made up of light codes, all of which create the human experience. The light codes are infused into the human DNA at the moment of incarnation. The Akashic Record creates an intended map for the Higher Dimensional Consciousness to navigate the human journey.

Aside from the blueprint, all of the light codes that create the Akashic Record are held in a 3rd dimensional frequency.

When the human body is holding frequencies higher than the 3D field, the light codes within the Akashic Record held in the DNA that are in the 3D frequencies will begin to alchemize or dissolve. The Akashic Record will begin to dissolve. We will explain this is more detail in Chapter Eighteen.

When you see the perfection in the Akashic Record and you see that the Higher Dimensional Consciousnesses chose all of it, there is an ease and grace that can be experienced within the human journey.

Chapter 7

CREATING THE 3D HUMAN BODY

Once the Earth was redesigned in the 3D field, we had to redesign the 5D human form to adapt to the 3D field. There had never been a 3D human form.

We had to ensure three things during the redesign:

1. The physical form could exist within the 3D field.
2. The form could hold the Higher Dimensional Consciousness incarnating into it.
3. The human form could shift into higher dimensional fields.

As with the Earth, most of the design of the 5D human form was kept in place for the 3D form. It would have the same electrical grid, including the twelve energy centers, the energetic field, the channel connecting the human aspect with the Higher Self and the *I Am* Presence, the subtle bodies, and an ego.

What we did have to restructure was the DNA and the light quotient. These two components were imperative in allowing the physical form to exist in the 3D field and the Higher Dimensional Consciousness to incarnate into the form. The redesign of these two features would also ensure that the human form could shift into the 5D field.

7.1 Restructuring DNA

We began with the restructuring of the DNA in a 3rd dimensional frequency. As explained previously, DNA are light codes. Light codes are held in a structure within the human form called DNA strands. There are two types of light codes. The first set holds 10 percent of the DNA and creates the physical form. The second set holds 90 percent of the DNA. These light codes hold the Akashic Record and the higher dimensional abilities the human has the potential to awaken into during their lifetime.

The light codes that created the 5D physical form were held in a twelve-strand DNA crystalline structure.

The physical form was now going to be anchored in a 3rd dimensional field. Crystalline light codes cannot exist within a dense 3D form. We had to shift the frequency of the light codes down in order to be held within the 3D human body.

We discovered that carbon was a structure dense enough to hold the light codes. It's one of the simplest forms of matter in the 3D field. We also knew that carbon is malleable and could alchemize into a lighter structure as the human form increases its frequency.

We slowed down the frequency of the crystalline 5D light codes into 3D light codes. We then condensed the light codes into two strands of carbon DNA instead of twelve strands of crystalline DNA. The reason there are only two strands of DNA in the 3D human form is because the 3D human body is much denser than the 5D human body and can only hold a certain amount of light frequency within its DNA. Once we had the light codes condensed into a 3D frequency, a 3D human body can now be created.

The original 12D light codes are now contained within 3D light codes held within a 2-strand carbon-based DNA structure. This means all information that the human would ever need as it shifts into higher dimensional fields is held within its DNA. This includes the physical body's ability to shift into higher frequencies and the human's ability to access new ways of being as it shifts into higher frequencies. It is the frequency of the human body that will dictate the light codes that are available for the human to access.

A 3D human form holding 3D frequencies will only be able to access the 3D light codes. As the form holds higher frequencies, it will begin to access or activate light codes that are in higher frequencies. These codes naturally begin to alchemize from carbon to crystalline to light. This alchemization process allows the human to live as a multi-dimensional human within a physical form. This is evolution and is only possible through the shifting of light codes.

Redesigning the light codes into a 3D carbon-based structure allowed for the human form to exist in the 3D field as well as allowed for the human to experience and move through the evolution. It was the restructuring of the light quotient that allowed the Higher Dimensional Consciousness to incarnate into the human form.

7.2 Light Quotients for the 3D Human

Once we had the DNA designed, we focused on the amount of light quotient the Higher Dimensional Consciousness could bring into the physical form. As explained in Chapter Four, the light quotient is a percentage of the Higher Dimensional Consciousness's light that is held within the physical form when they incarnate. This is not what is shifting as the human evolves. The physical body evolves by shifting frequencies and dimensions. The light quotient remains in the same frequency and percentage throughout the human experience.

The 5D human form was able to hold 16 to 20 percent of the Higher Dimensional Consciousness's light. We found a balanced light quotient that enabled the highest amount of light the Consciousness could bring in without short-circuiting the physical form. We had to find that same balance in the 3D form.

We knew the light quotient would be much less due to the density of the 3D body. We also knew we had to be very careful how much light was allowed into the 3D human body. Each Consciousness dropping into the form was vibrating at a 6D frequency or higher. If we allowed 100 percent of a 6D Consciousness to enter the form, it would short circuit. The high frequency light would be so intense that the physical form would burn, and the organs would shut down. It's like putting your finger into an electrical socket. It would damage the physical body. Our goal was to allow as much light quotient as possible into the human body yet not so much that it would overload the body.

However, we knew, based on the density of the 3rd dimensional field, that the light quotient was going to be very low. Similar to what we did in the 5D human, we tested the amount of light that could be held in the 3D body.

Many Higher Dimensional Consciousnesses volunteered to incarnate into the 3D form, allowing us to gauge the amount of light the human form could hold. We started with 16 percent of their light quotient. We watched as the human body reacted and responded to the light. Through trial and error, we were able to discover that the 3D human form could function best with a maximum of 3 percent of light from the Higher Dimensional Consciousness.

The percentage fluctuated between 1 percent and 3 percent depending on the frequency of the Higher Dimensional Consciousness incarnating into the form. The higher a Consciousness's frequency, the less light it could bring into the form. For instance, if a 12th dimensional Consciousness incarnated into the human form, it could bring in 1–2 percent of its light. If a 6th dimensional Consciousness incarnated, it could bring in 3 percent of its light. The light quotient eventually increased over linear time as the human body began to increase its frequency.

When Earth began in the 3D around 20,000–15,000 linear years ago, the human form held 1–3 percent of a Higher Dimensional Consciousness's light. Ten thousand linear years later, the human form was holding around 4 to 5 percent, and just 500 linear years ago, it was holding around 6–7 percent. Currently, the human body can hold anywhere from 6 to 15 percent. As the Earth Plane and the human form increase in frequency, the light quotient for Higher Dimensional Consciousnesses incarnating into form will continue to increase.

7.3 3D Human Body Versus 5D Human Body

Once we had the DNA and the light quotient redesigned, we knew that the experience the Higher Dimensional Consciousness would have within the 3D human form would be very different from within the 5D human form.

The most significant difference is the connection with the electrical grid system within the body. We designed the electrical grid to be a navigational tool for the human. They could align and connect into the electrical grid and have a much easier time navigating the dense energetic fields. However, we realized that, due to the density of the 3D human form and 3D field, it was going to be much more challenging for the human to connect to the electrical grid. This meant it would be more difficult to remember who they are as Consciousness and why they incarnated into the body. They will live in the illusion of physicality. The 3D human would have a much more challenging time than the 5D human in remembering how the human experience works in physicality. They will create a very different experience with the electrical grid within their human form.

7.4 The Energetic Field

Let's begin with the energetic field. As stated in Chapter Three, there is an energetic field eighteen inches out and around the human form. This field holds the frequency vibrating within the body. The energetic field allows the human to navigate, experience, and understand the external world energetically.

The 5D human was aware of this field. They knew everything was energy. They understood their energetic field allowed them to interpret the physical world around them through energy. They were not caught in the illusion of physicality.

However, in the 3D field, the human does not remember that the external world around them is energy. The human body is so dense, and the light quotient is so low, that experiencing their energetic field is almost impossible. All the human sees is physicality, and thus, they believe everything internally and externally is physical. They are unaware they have an energetic field allowing them to process the energetic world. They forgot that they are contained within an energetic field allowing them to experience their life feeling safe, free, and empowered. It will take thousands of years and an increase in the human form's frequency until the human will be able to remember and feel their energetic field.

7.5 Ego Structure

The ego structure in the 3D human form is another component of the electrical grid system that is experienced very differently in the 5D human. The ego is an energetic structure we designed for the 5D human body to keep the human physically safe. The 3D human body is in a much denser physical field, with a large variety of consciousnesses for the human to experience. There is polarity and duality within the 3D field, creating a more complex human journey to navigate.

The ego will play a much larger role for the 3D human. It will not only navigate and maintain the safety of the physical body, but it will maintain the safety of the emotional and mental bodies as well. Its largest role is to ensure that the human does not feel pain, discomfort, trauma, anything that does not feel good.

The ego is held in its own energetic field. For the ego to function in the 3D human body we had to shift its energetic field down from a 5D frequency to a 3D frequency. This will allow the human to connect to the ego and easily follow its guidance. The ego will be the human's guide and it will sound like the human's internal voice.

7.6 Higher Self

In the 5D field, the Higher Self was responsible for guiding the human through its life.

The 3D human will have a very different relationship and experience with the Higher Self. The density of the 3D human body creates a more challenging connection into the Higher Self. As we stated in Chapter Four, the Higher Self is an aspect of the Higher Dimensional Consciousness. It resides in a slightly higher frequency in the 5D human body but a much higher frequency than the 3D body. It is held within the eighth energy center, connecting to the human body through the energetic channel. Unlike the 5D human form, the density within the 3D human form makes it almost impossible for most humans to connect with the Higher Self.

For instance, imagine you are trying to speak to someone through a long tunnel. You are on one end, and they are on the other. If the tunnel was clear, your voice would echo all the way to the end and be heard. However, if there were physical objects, such as people, water, or wind, clogging the tunnel, it would be much more difficult for your voice to reach the other person—if it reached them at all.

This is how the channel works in connecting the human to the Higher Self. There is always an energetic connection between human and Higher Self (the tunnel). However, the density within the human body (people, physical objects, water, wind) clogs the channel and creates a lack of clarity between human and Higher Self. The 3D human form is so dense in nature that connecting to the channel, and thus the Higher Self, can be challenging.

Along with the density of the human form, external experiences, including trauma, can create more density in the channel. The external experiences are energy. When the experiences enter the human body, if they are consciousnesses that the human does not want to feel through the body, they will remain in the body. These consciousnesses have the potential to clog or create more density within the human body, making it more difficult to hear the Higher Self. The more density, the more difficult it is to connect to Higher Self.

The role of the Higher Self for the 3D human is the same as for the 5D human, to guide them through their life. The nature of the 3D field makes it almost impossible for the human to be led by the Higher Self. Therefore, the 3D human follows the guidance of the ego while remaining energetically connected to their Higher Self.

It isn't until the 3D human body starts to hold higher frequencies that the human begins to connect into and embody the Higher Self. They will eventually follow the guidance of the Higher Self. Until then, the Higher Self's role for the 3D human is to be its internal compass if and when it can hear its voice. The voice will be the human's intuition, its knowingness. Although many humans are familiar with these terms and perhaps even listen to their intuition, it requires the body to hold higher frequencies for the human to connect and walk through life under the guidance of and as the Higher Self.

7.7 The *I Am* Presence

The *I Am* Presence (IAP), like the Higher Self, is another aspect of the Higher Dimensional Consciousness that will be experienced very differently for the 3D human than the 5D human.

As we stated in Chapter Four, the IAP is vibrating lower than the Higher Dimensional Consciousness but higher than the Higher Self. It is held in the 9th to 12th energy centers. Its role is to connect the human to Source Consciousness.

The 3D human is always energetically connected to the IAP through the channel within the electric grid system in the body, similar to the Higher Self.

Connecting into the IAP is much more difficult for the 3D human than the 5D human. Similar to the Higher Self, the density of the 3D human body creates a barrier to the channel and thus the IAP. The frequency of the IAP is much higher than the 3D body. It requires the human to connect and feel the IAP within their body.

Just like the Higher Self, the IAP is designed to be embodied within the human form, and it becomes easier for the human to connect into the IAP as the body increases its frequency.

7.8 Subtle Bodies

The role of the subtle bodies is to filter all experiences into the human body for the human to understand the experience. Remember, every experience the human has in the external world is made up of consciousnesses or energy. These consciousnesses move into the human body and are filtered through the emotional and mental subtle bodies creating emotions, thoughts, and beliefs.

The role of the subtle bodies in the 3D field is much more significant and prominent than in the 5D human form. This is because of the density within the 3D field. The density creates a much larger spectrum of consciousness than the 5D field. This allows for polarity and duality of emotions, behaviors, thoughts, and beliefs in lower frequencies.

Polarity creates opposites. One emotion can be felt in its opposite state; one thought can be had in an opposite state. For instance, if a human feels *love*, they can feel its opposite, *fear*. If a human has the thought: *I hate myself,* they have the ability to hold an opposite thought: *I love myself.* Polarity creates a multitude of consciousnesses to be experienced within the 3D human life.

The 3D field also holds much lower frequency consciousnesses than the 5D field. For instance, there is an opportunity for the human to experience sadness, anger, rage, fear, anxiety, stress, greed, and so much more. The 5D field does not offer these consciousnesses to be experienced.

Both polarity and the multitude of lower frequency consciousnesses create very active emotional and mental subtle bodies. These subtle bodies will be filtering a larger variety of denser consciousnesses into and through the human body than in the 5D human form.

For example, in the 5D field, two humans interact, and the exchange will result in the subtle bodies experiencing peace, love, union, and compassion. The event may elicit thoughts, such as *I am love; You are love; We are one; I am sovereign.*

In the 3D field, two humans interact, and because of polarity, there are a variety of ways in which a human could experience this one interaction.

For example, two humans encounter each other and have an exchange. That exchange creates an initial fight that ends in an agreement. The emotional body may begin the interaction filtering anger, frustration, fear, and rage. By the end of the interaction, the emotional body is filtering compassion, joy, and gratitude.

The mental body may begin by filtering beliefs and thoughts, such as *I am not liked; I am unlovable; I am not safe; No one understands me; I do not like this person.* By the end of the exchange, the mental body is filtering thoughts, such as *I am liked; I am safe; I am understood.* One experience can create many more thoughts, beliefs, and emotions for the 3D human.

Once the subtle bodies filter the experiences into the body as thoughts, beliefs, and emotions, these consciousnesses move through seven of the twelve energy centers within the human channel. As with the ego and the subtle bodies, these energy centers function much differently in the 3D human form.

7.9 Twelve Energy Centers

When we designed the 5D human form, we created twelve energy centers, seven within the form and five outside the form. These energy centers create a channel that filters consciousness (energy) in and out of the physical body. The energy centers are designed to spin in order to circulate and move the energy in and out of the physical form.

The 3D physical form will experience these twelve energy centers much differently from the 5D form. The consciousnesses of the 3D field are much denser than in the 5D and this density will impact and compromise the functionality of these energy centers.

There are three reasons the twelve energy centers are compromised:
1. The density of the human form
2. The density of consciousnesses experienced in the 3D field
3. The way in which the human experiences 3D consciousnesses.

The Density of the Human Form

A 3D human form is dense matter. It is difficult for energy to move smoothly through matter. It is like quicksand. It moves slowly. The human form is designed to hold seven energy centers within the channel inside the human body. These centers naturally spin to move all energy and consciousnesses through the human body. It becomes difficult for energy to spin fluidly and quickly in dense matter. The simple nature of the 3D human form slows the energy centers down. They cannot spin at their natural potential. If the energy centers are unable to spin quickly, energies and consciousnesses will have a much more difficult time moving in and out of the human body through the channel. The basic nature of the form's density slows the seven energy centers down.

The Density of Consciousnesses Experienced in the 3D Field

The second reason the energy centers are compromised is the density of the consciousnesses experienced within the 3rd dimensional external world. All experiences are filtered as consciousnesses through the human body. The 3D consciousnesses are dense and move much slower than 5D consciousnesses. Remember, the denser a consciousness, the slower it spins. The slower a consciousness spins, the longer it takes to move through the human channel. If a consciousness (energy) moves through the channel slowly, it has the potential of getting stuck and essentially clogging the channel.

The Way the Human Experiences 3D Consciousnesses

The third reason the energy centers are compromised in the 3D human body is due to the way in which the human experiences 3D consciousnesses. Every external experience creates a consciousness that will be felt as emotion for the human to filter through the seven energy centers. The denser an experience, the denser the consciousness thus emotion. For example, if a human has a fight—a very dense experience creating dense consciousnesses—the human will experience a dense emotion, such as fear or rage.

The denser consciousnesses typically do not feel good, and many times the human will avoid, suppress, or try to not feel the emotion. If the human is not able to feel the emotion that enters the form, the consciousness—the emotion—will remain within the body. It will first stop in the channel, then move into an energy center, and then perhaps move into other areas of the physical form. Remember, all consciousness is energy, and energy is designed to move. If the consciousnesses is not felt entirely, it will settle in the form. The seven energy centers assist all consciousness in moving through the body. If the human does not feel it all the way through, it will get stuck in the channel, energy centers, or other areas of the human body.

For example, experiences, such as abuse, or any trauma, will create dense consciousnesses, such as terror, fear, stress, anxiety, or neglect to enter the body. These consciousnesses will move much slower through the channel. If the human is unable to feel the experience completely, it will remain within the channel, energy centers, and body, clogging and blocking the centers and the channel.

If the human were to have external experiences, such as falling in love, listening to a joke, or watching a good movie, the consciousnesses created would be love, joy, peace, fun, or excitement. These consciousnesses are less dense. They are lighter and will move more easily through the human form. They also feel good, so the human is more likely to feel them completely, which allows the consciousness to move completely through the body. The more enjoyable an experience, the less density resides within the experience and the easier it is to move through the body. The less enjoyable an experience, the more density resides within the experience and the more challenging it will become for the human to feel the consciousnesses through the human form.

What eventually occurs is the human encounters many experiences that create dense uncomfortable consciousnesseses. The consciousnesses move slower through the human channel and energy centers. They don't feel good, and the human consciously or unconsciously chooses to not feel them. After multiple uncomfortable experiences, the channel begins to clog, and the energy centers slow down or eventually stop spinning completely. It is because of the denser consciousnesses experienced within the 3D field that the seven energy centers are compromised.

7.10 The Etheric Body

The etheric body is another component within the electrical grid system that is experienced differently for the 3D human. The etheric body, as stated in Chapter Four, holds the Higher Dimensional Consciousness within the human form. It is also the aspect of the human that energetically travels outside of the human body into other dimensional fields.

The human is designed to be connected and aware of the etheric body to consciously travel into other dimensional realms while simultaneously remaining in the human form.

The 5D human was consciously connected to the etheric body and could travel inter-dimensionally at any time. The 3D human body is holding more density than the 5D body. The density creates a barrier between the 3D human and the etheric body. This barrier makes it almost impossible for the human to remember there is an etheric body within its form that can travel inter-dimensionally.

The 3D human's etheric body will do most of its traveling in the dream state. During this state, the etheric body energetically departs the physical form and travels into other dimensions.

The dream state is a very active state for the etheric body. The 3D human rarely remembers anything that occurs; however, there is a lot that the human form and human receive during the sleep state. They experience upgrades, healings, activations, remembrances, teachings, and more.

As soon as the body is holding higher frequencies, the human begins to connect into the electrical grid. They naturally begin to remember they have an etheric body, and that body allows them to consciously travel inter-dimensionally if they choose. They will begin to remember what is occurring in their dream states, and they will begin to travel inter-dimensionally in the waking state.

Summary

The density of the human form, the density of the 3rd dimensional field, and the way in which the human experiences and processes 3D consciousnesses all result in a very different experience for the 3D human.

The human has a very difficult time connecting to their channel to receive guidance from Higher Self. They remain disconnected from Source and their own Consciousness. The human experiences trauma, and that trauma becomes stored in the human body. The energy centers begin to slow down and eventually may stop spinning. The body has the potential to create illness and disease.

It is inevitable that the 3D human will have a much more difficult time connecting into the energetic grid and receiving the benefits we designed the grid to offer the human. We knew we couldn't change the density of the human form or the dense 3D field the human would be experiencing. What we could do was ensure that the 3D human could exist, function, and evolve into higher dimensional realms, and that is what we did through the design of the 3D human body.

Chapter 8

THE BEGINNING OF THE LIGHT WORKER

8.1 Incarnating into the 3D Human Form

Once the Earth and the human form had been redesigned and anchored into the 3D field, we could begin to allow Higher Dimensional Consciousnesses to incarnate into physical forms.

Prior to incarnating, all Higher Dimensional Consciousnesses had to agree to the laws we had designed for the 3D field. They entered the human form with choice, free will, and an intention as either a Light Worker or a volunteer. They created their Akashic Record. They understood the dimensional shift down and the density they would be held in.

All Higher Dimensional Consciousnesses incarnating understood how the human form and Earth Plane worked. They courageously chose to move their light into a physical form and experience a state of amnesia indefinitely. This was one of the most exciting and courageous opportunities for Consciousnesses, and we were honored to be able to assist in this experience.

8.2 Volunteer & Light Worker

There were two types of humans who would be participating on the 3D earth: volunteers and Light Workers. When Earth was in the 5D field, all Higher Dimensional Consciousnesses entering physical forms were participating as volunteers. Volunteers enter a form for the sole purpose of experiencing physicality and shifting into higher dimensional fields within physicality. Earth was holding a high enough frequency that she did not need assistance from human forms to shift into the 6D or 7D field.

The Light Worker

The Earth was now vibrating in a 3rd dimensional frequency. We knew she would need assistance in shifting back into the 5D field. We knew we could use the human body to assist the Earth based on what we had witnessed for millions of years.

The human form was able to shift Earth and humanity down into lower dimensional fields. We recognized the powerful relationship between the human's energetic frequency and the Earth's energetic frequency. If the human body could shift the Earth and humanity from the 5D field to a 3D field, then we knew the human body could assist in shifting Earth and humanity back into the 5D field. The human physical form would be crucial in the evolution of Earth and humanity.

This was the beginning of the Light Worker. Higher Dimensional Consciousnesses could now choose to incarnate into the human form to assist Earth and humanity in evolving back into the 5D field.

The Volunteer

All Higher Dimensional Consciousnesses within the 12D grid that simply wished to experience Earth, physicality, and the 3D field would incarnate onto the Earth Plane in human forms as volunteers. The volunteer would not hold the role of assisting in increasing the human collective's frequency. They would simply experience the human journey. Choosing to be a Light Worker required a very different experience on the new 3D Earth with an underlying task at hand; because of this, most Higher Dimensional Consciousnesses at this time chose to incarnate as the volunteer.

8.3 The First Call for Light Workers

It was at this point in Earth's history, approximately 15,000 linear years ago, we sent out the first call for Light Workers. A call is an energetic pulse that moves out into the quantum field holding an intention. We sent a vibrational pulse out to all Higher Dimensional Consciousnesses within and outside the 12D grid offering an opportunity to assist Earth and humanity in evolving back into the 5D field.

We opened the 12D grid to allow any Higher Dimensional Consciousnesses outside the grid to participate. This was the first and only time we opened the Earth's 12D grid since she began as a 5D form millions of years ago.

The call was sent out, Higher Dimensional Consciousnesses entered the grid, and we closed the grid. This happened in a single moment within the quantum field.

The Higher Dimensional Consciousnesses that entered the 12D grid during this call had never experienced Earth before. They entered the grid and moved into consciousnesses or collective light systems similar to what occurred when we initially opened the 12D grid. If they came from a consciousness or collective system that was already within the grid, they would enter that system. If they were a new Consciousness to the 12D grid, they would hold themselves within a new light system.

For instance, there were Sirians that had been existing outside the 12D grid who chose to come in and participate when we sent out the call. They entered the grid and moved their Consciousness into the collective system called the Sirian light system. However, there were many new Higher Dimensional Consciousnesses that came into the 12D grid at this time to assist Earth, including the Antares system and the Avians.

We had thousands of Higher Dimensional Consciousnesses ready to participate as Light Workers. Many had never incarnated into the human form, and many had experienced the human form in the 5D. What was unique about all these Higher Dimensional Consciousnesseses is that they were all incarnating for the sole purpose of assisting the Earth.

8.4 Two Groups of Light Workers

There were two groups of Light Workers that assisted during this first call we sent out. Each type played a unique role. The Higher Dimensional Consciousnesses chose one of the two groups to participate in when they incarnated into the human form.

Group 1

The first group of Light Workers would simply be anchoring high frequency light into the human form. Their human body would be an extremely potent conduit of light. Their blueprints were less about *work* and more about *anchoring* and *holding light* in the human form. Most Higher Dimensional Consciousnesses that intended to play this role had just entered the 12D grid when we sent out the call. They had never experienced Earth in the 5D field and had never been in a human form.

The Higher Dimensional Consciousnesses that chose this type of light work played a significant role in shifting the 3D Earth into higher frequencies.

Currently, on the Earth, only a small percentage of these Light Workers are incarnated into the human form. The majority are assisting from off-planet.

Group 2

The second group of Light Workers had a more hands-on role. They would be working with the human and the Earth through physical abilities, skills, or tools. They may choose to teach, heal, communicate, or educate, either through their own voice or through art, music or the natural elements. There are many different ways this second group could choose to assist during their human journey.

All Higher Dimensional Consciousnesses choosing this type of light work had existed within the 12D grid since Earth began in the 5D millions of years ago. Most of these Light Workers had experienced themselves as 5D humans and were on the Earth Plane when we cleared her.

Currently, on the Earth, most of these Light Workers are incarnated into human forms. They have experienced more human lives than any other Light Worker, in both the 5D and 3D fields. They would be what many humans consider *old souls*.

The role the Higher Dimensional Consciousness chooses for their light work is encoded into their Blueprint as part of the Akashic Record and held within the humans' DNA. The blueprint can be accessed at any now moment by the human. How and when they access this blueprint depends on what they created within their Akashic Record to experience in their lifetime. Therefore, many humans feel as if they have a purpose for being on the Earth Plane, but it hasn't been shown to them yet. It is within their DNA.

The Higher Dimensional Consciousness may complete their blueprint in one lifetime, or it may take multiple lifetimes. If they complete their blueprint, they can either chose to incarnate with a new blueprint or no longer incarnate.

If they do not complete their blueprint in a lifetime, they can choose to incarnate again with the same blueprint, choose a new blueprint, or no longer incarnate. It is always a choice to incarnate whether the Higher Dimensional Consciousness completes their blueprint or not.

8.5 The Impact of the Light Worker

Earth and the human form were holding a frequency of 3.0 when hundreds of thousands of Light Workers began incarnating onto the Earth Plane. Earth's intention was for humanity and herself to shift into a 5.0 frequency.

A 3.0 frequency is very dense. The Higher Dimensional Consciousnesses knew they would most likely remain in amnesia while in the human body until the Earth and human form were holding higher frequencies.

131

Therefore, in the beginning, most of the Higher Dimensional Consciousnesses incarnating as Light Workers chose group one to just hold and anchor as much light as possible into their bodies. The more light the humans anchored onto the Earth, the easier it would be for Earth to shift into higher frequencies.

This blueprint did not require the human to wake up out of amnesia. The human could perform their work in an unconscious state because the Higher Self was connected to the blueprint and the physical body was connected to the Higher Self.

It was the human body that was essentially doing the work. The body knew how to anchor the light through the assistance of the Higher Self. It did not need a conscious human to perform this task. An unconscious human could live a very normal life as an unconscious Light Worker and still shift Earth's frequency. It was the easiest way to make the fastest impact while Earth was still in a very dense frequency.

It took thousands of years and hundreds of thousands of Light Workers simply anchoring light through their bodies to slowly shift the Earth and the human collective from a 3.0 to 3.1. For the sake of this book, we will use linear numbers to describe Earth's energetic shift. However, please know that energy cannot be measured; it can only be felt. The human form was so dense it could only anchor a very small amount of light into a body. It was a slow process. However, as Earth and the human form began to increase their frequency, it became easier and faster to shift into the next highest frequency. It took around 3000 years to shift from a 3.0 to a 3.1 and only around 1000 years to shift from a 3.1 to a 3.2.

Although there were two types of Light Workers at this time, due to the density of the Earth and the human collective, it was the Light Workers anchoring the light that made the most impact for the first 6000 years. As the frequencies began to increase on Earth and the human collective, both types of Light Workers began to play equal and significant roles.

Summary

The first call that we sent out around 15,000 linear years ago brought in some of the most impactful Light Workers we have ever seen. For 10,000 years, they were able to pull the Earth and Humanity from a 3.0–3.6 in frequency and move Earth's light quotient from 1–48%. They did a tremendous amount of work in a very short period of linear time. If you are one of these Light Workers, and many of you reading this are, we applaud you and commend you for your diligence, commitment, and love for the mission, Earth, and Humanity.

Chapter 9

THE OPENING OF THE EARTH'S FIFTH DIMENSIONAL GRID

Approximately 10,000 linear years into Earth's evolutionary process, Earth and humanity went through one of the most devastating and intense times in its 3D history. Many difficult events and experiences unfolded that lasted until around the 1920s in linear time.

If you remember, one of the universal laws states that when Earth holds 50 percent of her light quotient, it is impossible for her to shift down into lower frequencies or a lower light quotient. Earth would be on a trajectory into the 5D field regardless of what is occurring on her physical form.

This is an important universal law. Until she reaches 50 percent of her light quotient, if Earth is being pulled down into lower frequencies, we are not able to interfere. Free will allows for anything to occur on the Earth Plane. Earth and we have to allow everything to play out regardless of the consequence.

The only way we can intervene is if Earth asks for our assistance—and that assistance does not interfere with the free will on the Earth Plane. She can co-create any reality with our Federation so long as it allows for free will.

Around 5000 linear years ago, Earth sent out her first and only request. It was an energetic pulse that held the intention of shifting her light quotient to 50 percent. In that moment, her light quotient was at 47–48 percent. She knew the impact holding 50 percent of her light would have on the evolution. She knew she was close, and she wanted to be energetically pushed into 50 percent.

She was requesting that we open the 5D grid to allow Higher Dimensional Beings and collective consciousnesses to physically enter the Earth Plane to assist her in shifting her light quotient.

This meant allowing them to physically be on the Earth Plane with humans and non-humans. She knew their physical impact could potentially increase her light to 50 percent as well as increase the frequency of the human collective.

We knew we had to honor her request. Unfortunately, what occurred through this one simple intention created some of the most destructive times in your history.

9.1 The 12D Grid

Before we begin, let's briefly review the 12D grid around the entire Earth experiment. This grid protects Earth's entire experiment and Earth herself. All Higher Dimensional Consciousnesses that agreed millions of years ago to participate in Earth's experiment are held within the 12D grid.

Once a Consciousness enters the 12D grid, they have free will with regard to how they want to experience themselves in the grid. They can volunteer on the Earth Plane as a volunteer or a Light Worker. They can assist off-planet within their collective consciousness. They can move through the many different dimensional fields and explore other Consciousnesses within the 12D grid, or they can exit the grid at any time. Once they exit the grid, they cannot re-enter unless we reopen the 12D grid.

Within that 12D grid is the 5D grid around Earth. To participate on the Earth Plane, all Beings must move through the 5D grid.

There are thousands of collectives that exist within the 12D grid that have been energetically assisting Earth and humanity off-planet. Earth was requesting physical assistance from these Higher Dimensional Consciousnesses, both individual Beings and collectives within the 12D grid. Some familiar collectives and Beings are the Pleiadians, Sirians, Arcturians, Lyrans, Orions, Cassiopians, and Andromedans. There are many more.

9.2 Energetic Assistance

Prior to us opening the 5D grid, all assistance from the Higher Dimensional Beings and collective consciousnesses were energetic. They would assist by energetically connecting to the human form and Earth Plane from higher dimensional realms within the 12D grid. All interaction and communication between these Consciousnesses and Earth and humanity was through free will and intent. The human or Earth had to agree and intend for any connection to occur. All Higher Dimensional Beings and collective consciousnesses followed free will. They could not assist unless the human or the Earth requested it.

Connection with the Earth was through her energetic field. The Earth was always conscious of the connection and assistance and was able to integrate the energetic assistance quickly into her human form.

9.3 Connecting with the Human

Connection with the human was through the human's energetic field, inter-dimensional travel, or the dream state. The human was either conscious or unconscious of the connection and communication with the Higher Dimensional Beings and collectives. In a conscious human, the information would be received and integrated to upgrade their life. A human who was unconscious of the energetic connection and assistance had a much more difficult time receiving, integrating, and upgrading their life.

Conscious Connection

Conscious connection requires the human to intend and participate with the Higher Dimensional Beings and collectives. The human invites the Being or collective into their awareness. The Higher Dimensional Being or collective energetically receives the intention. They then move their energy into the human's field, such as a specific room, office, or home. Once the Being or collective enters the human's space, the interaction begins.

The human can consciously interact and communicate with Higher Dimensional Beings and collectives through the human's channel or through their energetic field.

The human channel is an energetic field inside the human form that is designed to move energy in and out of the human body. The human connects and communicates with Higher Dimensional Beings or collectives through the channel by pulling the energetic message from the Beings or Consciousness through and into their channel. Once the energy is in the channel, the human translates the energy into information, such as words, feelings, visions, or sounds.

The human's energetic field is another way they consciously connect and communicate with Higher Dimensional Beings or collectives. The energetic field extends about eighteen inches out from the human and creates a 360-degree circle around the body. It allows the human to connect and feel all energies around them.

If the human uses their energetic field to connect and communicate, they will feel into the energy of the Being or Consciousness around them and pull the energy through the energetic field and into the human body. The energy will be translated by the human into words, images, sounds, or emotions. Using the energetic field as the communication tool is much more physical and palpable than using the human channel as the tool to communicate. The channel is a funnel whereas the energetic field is the entire physical body feeling the energy.

Unconscious Connection

It becomes very challenging for the human to receive information and guidance if they are unconscious. The human is unaware of the Higher Dimensional Beings or collectives. Any guidance received will come through their Higher Self or in the dream state through their etheric body. Most unconscious humans are also unaware of the Higher Self, so the guidance must be loud enough that the human can't ignore it.

The Higher Self brings the guidance in from the Higher Dimensional Beings or collectives through the human channel. The human unconsciously receives the information as a voice in their head or as intuition. Many times, the human will hear that voice and either ignore it or mistake it for the ego. If the human is not aware there are Higher Dimensional Beings, collectives, or a Higher Self, they will assume the guidance or information is from their ego and mind.

The dream state is another way the unconscious human connects to Higher Dimensional Beings and collectives. The human's dream state is when the etheric body exits the physical form and travels into higher dimensional realms. This is also known as astral travel. During the dream state, the etheric body experiences many higher dimensional fields, allowing the human to unconsciously connect, engage, receive, and learn from Higher Dimensional Beings or collectives.

9.4 Connecting with the Earth

Earth had a very different relationship and connection with the Higher Dimensional Beings or collectives that were assisting her. She remained conscious of their assistance and knew how to receive their guidance. She understood there were specific collectives and Beings that were assisting, supporting, and guiding her into the 5D field, including ourselves.

Earth was always energetically receiving guidance from these collectives and Beings through her energetic grids. They would work with her by energetically tapping into and adjusting the grids in and around her form.

Many of the collectives that worked with Earth had created councils of Higher Dimensional Beings holding specific intentions. There are security councils that protect Earth's energetic grids. There are peace councils that ensure there aren't any energetic wars that break out on Earth. There are environmental councils that, while still upholding free will, ensure that the least amount of damage is done to the Earth Plane.

9.5 Physical Assistance

When we opened the 5D grid, allowing Higher Dimensional Beings and collectives to enter onto the Earth Plane, their assistance shifted from energetic to physical.

Imagine the 5D grid like a gate around a house. The house is Earth, and the gate is the grid. When the gate opens, the Beings and Consciousnesses can enter the yard. However, the house is still closed. The only way to enter the house, or be on the Earth Plane, would be to walk through the door, which would require the Being to move down into the same vibrational field.

The Beings and Consciousnesses entered through the grid with their entire consciousnesses in their energetic or physical form. Once through the grid, they had to shift their entire energetic field down into the 3D field to be seen on the Earth Plane. They had to energetically match the frequency of the Earth Plane and human collective.

Opening the 5D grid allowed the Beings and Consciousnesses to physically move on and off the Earth Plane by shifting their frequency down into either a 3rd, 4th, or 5th dimensional frequency. All three of these dimensional fields allow for physicality. Any Being or Consciousness that wanted to physically assist at this time had to shift down to at least a 5D field. However, the human can only see the dimensional field their human body is standing in.

Most humans at this time were standing in a 3D field, holding 3D frequencies within their body. Therefore, if a Being or Consciousness wanted to be physically seen by the human, they would have to shift their frequency down into the 3D field or shift the human's frequency up into a 4th or 5th dimensional field. The human body and the Being's or Consciousness's body must match frequencies.

It is challenging for a Higher Dimensional Being or consciousness to shift their body down into a 3D frequency. It is a slow, dense, and heavy frequency. The Beings and collectives choosing to physically assist Earth and humanity would have to continuously hold that lower 3D frequency to be seen. This takes a lot of energy especially if the Being or Consciousness is coming from a much higher dimensional field and frequency, The higher the frequency of a Being or Consciousness, the more difficult it is to remain in a 3D physical form on the Earth Plane.

For instance, if a Being enters the Earth Plane from the Lyran system, they are vibrating around a 13th–15th dimensional field. When they shift onto the Earth Plane and physically engage with the human, they must slow their frequency down tremendously and hold that 3D frequency while engaging with the human. They would only be able to stay in physicality for a few minutes due to the amount of energy it took to hold that lower frequency. The Lyran would have to move back into its 13th dimensional frequency.

Due to the density of the 3D field, most of the Higher Dimensional Beings and collectives that chose to physically assist Earth and humanity at this time did so in a 4D or 5D form. When they wanted to appear physically for the human, they would bring themselves down into a 3D frequency for a short period of time and then shift back into the 4D or 5D form.

9.6 Zones

The Beings and collectives had to build areas all over the Earth Plane where they would physically connect, teach, activate, and guide the human. We call these areas *zones*.

Zones are areas of land that have physical structures on them, and these structures open portals. A portal vibrates in a very high frequency, allowing energetic access into higher dimensional fields and frequencies. It is a gateway or a shortcut into the quantum field. Every zone created had multiple portals on it. The portals maintained a very high frequency on the land.

There are two reasons why zones were essential for the Beings and collectives to connect with and assist the human:

1. Zones allow the human to anchor more light into their bodies.
2. Zones allowed the human to gently shift into the 4th and 5th dimensional fields.

When the human is standing in a zone, their bodies naturally begin to hold more light. The longer a human is in the zone, the more light their bodies will integrate and anchor. If a human is holding more light, it is easier for the Higher Dimensional Beings and collectives to connect with and assist the human.

Zones also allowed the human to gently shift into the 4D and 5D fields to physically connect with the Higher Dimensional Beings and collectives. It was challenging for Beings and collectives to move down into a 3D field. They could not stay in that low of a frequency for very long. They chose to remain in a 4D or 5D field. To connect and work physically with the human, they needed the human to also shift into a 4D or 5D field. The Higher Dimensional Beings and collectives could then engage with the human form for longer periods of time.

When the human steps onto the land and into the zone, their body will immediately shift into the 4th and 5th dimensional fields. The portals on the land are anchoring so much light that the human form can access that light and gently move into higher dimensional fields. As soon as the human walks away from the zone, their bodies will naturally and slowly move back down into the 3D field.

Higher Dimensional Beings and collectives began creating zones all over the Earth Plane. The zones emerged as structures, such as rock formations, pyramids, domes, amphitheaters, small cities, sacred geometrical vortexes, and many other such structures. All zones were created in the 3D field yet were holding much higher frequencies.

Any human can visibly see the zones, but as soon as they enter the zone, their bodies shift into the 4th and 5th dimensional fields, and they can see the Higher Dimensional Beings and collectives. A human standing outside the zone is not able to see the Beings and collectives.

The zones were created through intent and energy. The structures built in these zones defy human logic and gravity. They were created using energy and intention. A human didn't move rocks into the creation of a structure. The Beings and collectives intended a structure into being and used the manipulation of energy to shift it into a physical 3D form.

The structures were created almost instantaneously in the 3D field. The Beings and collectives shifted themselves down into a 3D frequency to stand physically in the zone. They intended the specific structure they wanted to create. Holding that intention, they pulled in high-frequency energy from the quantum field and merged the energy into physical forms, such as stones, rock, and crystals. Rock, stone, and crystal were used because they are perfect conduits for high frequency light. Their density can hold and anchor high-frequency energy while allowing that energy to move through its form. These physical forms anchored the energy and intention and created the structure.

The structures were designed from these high-frequency rocks, stones, or crystals. This not only allowed the structures to be held in a high frequency, but the land the structure was on could also hold that high frequency. This is what created the portals within the zones. The structures opened the portals.

For instance, if they wanted to create a pyramid, they would hold the intention of a pyramid, pull in high frequency light from the quantum field, and merge that light into rocks. Through their intention, along with the high-frequency energy anchored into the rocks, the physical structure would emerge. The intention connects into the energy of the rocks, and together, the rocks energetically move and build a pyramid. The pyramid is literally high frequency light, and these high frequencies create a portal within and around the pyramid. Every structure in every zone was created in this manner, and they were placed all over the Earth Plane.

Each zone was intentionally placed on specific energetic grid lines on Earth. The placement of each zone allowed the physical structures to connect directly into Earth's twelve energetic centers within her form.

The grids are all connected and energetically run along the outside of the Earth Plane. They cannot be seen by the human eye. Every grid line holds frequencies within it and connects into one of the twelve energy centers within the Earth. The grids deliver energy along the outside and inside of the Earth Plane. The Higher Dimensional Beings and collectives accessed the grids by energetically connecting to the frequency of the grids.

9.7 Physical Connection with the Human

Once the structures were in place and connected into the specific grid lines and energy centers on the Earth Plane, the Higher Dimensional Beings and collectives were ready to engage with the human.

The law of free will played a pivotal role in this phase of humanity's history. This law states that all Higher Dimensional Consciousnesses create their reality. Nothing and no one can interfere with another's free will and choice without a conscious or unconscious agreement. The human must agree to engage and receive assistance from the Higher Dimensional Beings and collectives entering onto the Earth Plane.

The Beings and collectives sent out an energetic call to the human. Imagine it as a vibrational pulse or signal. The human's energetic field feels the pulse, and the human then feels a pull to one of these zones. The human experiences the pulse as intuition, internal guidance from their Higher Self, or a *knowingness*. They then find themselves being guided to a zone.

The humans answering this call were the Light Workers holding the blueprint within their bodies to be of service to humanity and the Earth in the evolution of Consciousness. Not all of these humans were consciously aware they were Light Workers, but most of them felt the pull or call to connect with these structures, Beings, and collectives.

As the humans discovered these structures, the Beings and collectives carefully began to engage. They knew that if they appeared in physicality, it could shock the human, so they remained in a higher 5th dimensional frequency until the human was ready. Most humans were unconscious to the remembrance of these Beings and collectives. Seeing a Higher Dimensional Being could cause psychosis, a mental breakdown, or physical ailments in the body from the intensity of light the Beings and collectives held.

They had to introduce themselves gently with energetic interaction, then telepathic interaction, and then physical interaction. This introduction could take hours, days, or weeks depending upon the human. Most human bodies needed time to acclimate to the high-frequency energy in the zones.

The first step was to engage with the human energetically. The human would walk into the zone, and their bodies would immediately begin to integrate the high frequencies from the land. They could feel these energies moving into their body. The Higher Dimensional Beings and collectives would energetically move near the human body. This would gradually allow the human to begin to feel their energy.

For instance, a human would walk into the zone and find a rock structure. The human would stand there and instantly begin to feel high-frequency energy coming from and surrounding the rocks. Their bodies would begin to increase in frequency. The Beings or collectives would begin to energetically appear. The human could not physically see them, but they had the ability to feel their energy. If the human began to feel them, then telepathic communication would begin. If the humans did not feel the Beings' or collectives' energy, they would wait until the human was more comfortable with what they were feeling. A Being or collective knew a human was connecting to their energy field by the energetic response of the human. They could read and feel the human's energy field.

The longer the human is on the land, the easier it is for their body to acclimate to the high frequencies and energetically connect to the Beings and collectives around them. Once the human feels their energies, they can begin to have a telepathic conversation with them.

The Beings and collectives send energetic pulses out from their energetic field to the human. The human receives the pulses either through their channel within their body or through their energetic field. They then translate the energetic pulses into words, information, sounds, and visions. The human naturally knows how to do this because their bodies are anchored into higher frequencies. They are out of the ego and trusting their body to communicate with them. The human begins to trust and communicate with Higher Dimensional Beings and collectives they cannot see.

Once the human became comfortable connecting with the Beings and collectives telepathically and their body was comfortable in higher frequencies, the Beings and collectives slowly began shifting down into a lower 5th and 4th dimensional field. They would move themselves into a more physical form, allowing the human to see them. Then, the Beings and collectives would gently shift the human into the 4D and 5D fields. The human body became comfortable in the high frequency light and could shift more easily into the higher dimensional fields.

Both the human and the Beings and collectives were able to connect at the same frequency, and this allowed for physical contact. This was the first time the human and the Higher Dimensional Beings and collectives were standing in a 3rd dimensional field together, vibrating in a 4th or 5th dimensional frequency. All communication remained telepathic, but the interaction became physical. It was a powerful moment for us, for the Beings and collectives, and for the human.

146

9.8 Working with the Human

Once their physical connection and strong telepathic communication was established, the Higher Dimensional Beings and collectives could begin to assist and work with the human. The Beings and collectives began teaching the human how to evolve and live in higher states of consciousness within the 3D field. They taught the human how to access advanced technologies not available in the 3D field. This included manipulating energy to create physicality as well as healing the physical body of any disease or ailments. They taught the human how to build advanced civilizations in these zones and how to manifest and intend all they would need within these sacred civilizations.

They also showed the human how to create stargates. Stargates are powerful energetic portals created by physical structures on the land. Most stargates were created from rocks and were circular in formation.

Stargates allowed the human to connect to higher dimensional fields, as well as Beings and collectives off the Earth Plane. They were like quantum airports. The humans were able to move in and out of the 3rd dimensional field through a stargate. Their physical bodies could be teleported off the Earth Plane and into higher dimensional realms, including craft within the 5D grid.

During this time, civilizations within these zones were being built all over the Earth Plane. Hundreds of thousands of humans were creating and living in these advanced civilizations, learning and connecting with the Beings and collectives while evolving into higher states of consciousness. Their bodies were naturally beginning to hold 4D and 5D frequencies. As the human body began holding higher frequencies, the Earth began holding higher frequencies. She was slowly beginning to move closer to holding 50 percent of her light quotient.

9.9 Closing the 5D Grid

As Earth and humanity began shifting into higher frequencies and these civilizations were expanding, we noticed other activities on the Earth Plane that were occurring at the same time.

When we opened the grid, not only did Higher Dimensional Beings and collectives enter, but 4th dimensional races came in as well. These 4D Beings were unable to access the Earth Plane for 10,000 years because of the 5D grid. As soon as we opened the grid, free will allowed them to enter the Earth Plane.

The 4D races had very different intentions for entering the Earth Plane. While the Higher Dimensional Beings and collectives were assisting humanity in creating advanced civilizations and raising the frequency on the planet, the 4D Beings were choosing to experiment with the human form and the manipulation of energy in physicality.

We realized at this moment that humanity was about to experience an energetic shift down into lower frequencies. We knew we had to honor free will, but we were unsure what would take place for humanity.

As soon as we recognized what was occurring, we closed the grid to reduce the influx of 4D Beings entering the Earth Plane. All of this occurred for us in a now moment; the civilizations were built, 4D Beings began experimenting with human bodies, and we closed the grid. However, in human linear time, the grid closed about 500 years after we opened it.

When we closed the grid, 4D Beings could not continue to enter through the 5D grid and onto the Earth Plane. It also meant that all 4D Beings that were currently within the grid and experiencing the Earth Plane were unable to exit out of the 5D grid. They were vibrating in a frequency lower than the 5D grid, and thus could not penetrate it.

They had free will once inside the grid. We could not force them to leave. If we energetically moved them out, we would be interfering with their free will. From our perspective, it was consciousness experiencing itself in different frequencies. This is hard for the 3D human to accept because they are existing in a dualistic, polarized consciousness. There is right and wrong, good and bad. From our higher perspective, it is merely consciousness playing out its energetic signature. Allowing free will to play out in a dense dualistic field of consciousness can create chaos, and yet that is what we had to allow. The only thing we could do was close the grid.

Once the grid was closed, the Higher Dimensional Beings and collectives continued to assist the humans and the Earth in increasing their frequencies. At the same time, the 4D Beings were beginning to pull the frequency of the Earth and humanity down.

They had created programs and tactics for infiltrating the human form and experimenting with lower states of consciousnesses, such as fear, greed, and control. These programs and tactics were able to pull the Earth's frequency down much faster than the Higher Dimensional Beings and collectives could pull it up.

Regardless of the assistance the Higher Dimensional Consciousnesses were offering humanity and Earth in raising their frequency, the 4D Beings were impacting the collective frequency at a much faster rate.

The 4D races, and the humans these races had control over, were destroying many of the advanced civilizations. Thousands of advanced humans were dying. The Higher Dimensional Beings and collectives recognized that they were not going to be able to continue assisting the human and Earth in these civilizations. They knew the 4D Beings were taking over humanity. They honored free will and knew they could not stop the impact the 4D Beings were having on the human. They also could not destroy them, as that would go against the law of free will. Their only option was to either continue to build the structures and civilizations as they were simultaneously being destroyed or leave the 5D grid and assist off-planet in higher dimensional fields.

The Higher Dimensional Beings and collectives chose to exit the 5D grid as soon as we closed it. They would be assisting humanity, once again, from outside the grid.

For the next 4500 years, the grid was closed. It would take a cata-clysmic event that could potentially destroy the Earth to allow us to intervene once more. Until then, we watched as free will allowed the 4D races to pull Earth and humanity into lower frequencies while the Higher Dimensional Beings and collectives assisted from off the Earth Plane.

Chapter 10

4D RACES

Thousands of 4D Beings and races remained within the grid and carried out programs and tactics that pulled the Earth and humanity down in frequency for nearly 4500 years. These programs and tactics included abducting humans for experimentation, creating hybrid races, and infiltrating the human body to manipulate and control humanity. This was one of the most chaotic times we had ever seen on the planet. We would like to provide detail on what unraveled during these 4500 linear years, but before we do, let us explain the 4D Beings.

If you remember, 4th dimensional Beings were designed and created millions of years ago when Earth was in a 5D field. They were created to exist as 4D Consciousnesses, not Higher Dimensional Consciousnesses experiencing themselves in a 4D body.

There was a variety of different 4D races created at that time. They all held a frequency within the 4D spectrum. As we have explained, a dimensional field holds a spectrum of consciousnesses creating experiences. Lower dimensional fields, such as the 3rd and 4th, allow for many more experiences than higher dimensional fields, such as the 8th and 9th. This is because as consciousness slows its frequency down or moves into lower frequencies, it stretches, and there is more to be experienced within that one consciousness. Duality and polarity are created through this stretching of consciousness. The spectrum of available experiences increases as the frequency of a dimensional field decreases.

The 4D field is similar to the 3D field; however, the 4D is in a slightly higher frequency, allowing Beings within that field to remember how to access the quantum field. They understand how energy works. When a Being understands how energy works, they can manipulate energetic fields. They can create instantaneously. They can move themselves between lower dimensional fields. They can alter physical realities through energetic intent.

Where a 4D Being's frequency exists within the 4D spectrum dictates the way they experience their reality. The higher a Being's frequency within a dimensional spectrum, the more they will experience and feel higher dimensional aspects of that spectrum. They will start to experience higher states of consciousness. The higher a 4D Being's frequency, the closer they will be to a 5D field and the farther they will be from the 3D field.

For example, if a Being were holding a high 4D frequency (4.7–4.9), it would experience unity consciousness, benevolence, neutrality, oneness, and peace. It would be very close to the 5D field and 5D consciousness. If a Being were holding a low 4D frequency (4.0–4.2), it would be experiencing individuality, duality, separateness, greed, or fear. One side of the 4D spectrum is unity consciousness, and the other side of the spectrum is individual consciousness. A 4D Being's frequency, just like a human's frequency, dictates where they are along the spectrum of 4D Consciousness, which dictates their reality.

The reason we share this with you is because the 4D Beings that came into the 5D grid were in the lower frequencies of the 4D field. They did not hold the same intent as the Higher Dimensional Beings and collectives that entered the grid.

Their intention was drastically different. They wanted to understand and explore the physical reality within the 3rd dimension. They wanted to learn as much as they could about the 3D human body. They were fascinated by it. How did the human form work within a dense field of consciousness? How did it hold energy? How did the Higher Dimensional Consciousness within the human form stay connected to its light? How did the human form shift into higher states of consciousness?

These particular 4D Beings had been watching Earth and humanity evolve in the 3D field for the last 10,000 years. Once we opened the 5D grid, they entered the Earth's field and began to experiment with the human body and manipulate physical reality.

10.1 Entering onto the Earth

The 4D Beings entered onto the 3D Earth by shifting their frequency down slightly to a 3D frequency. This was not difficult as they were vibrating in the lower spectrum of the 4D field and could access the 3D field and the physical Earth Plane with ease.

They had the ability to physically appear on the Earth; however, if they showed themselves to the human, they would have a difficult time exploring and dissecting the physical reality and the human form. They remained unseen as much as possible.

The 4D beings knew how energy and consciousness worked and could manipulate their own energetic fields, allowing them to shift in and out of the 3D and 4D fields with ease.

When they shifted down into the 3D field, they always appeared in their 4D physical forms. They did not look human, and they could be seen physically by the human. When they shifted back into a 4D frequency, the human—who could not hold the same 4D frequency—was unable to see the 4D Being. That being was still standing in front of them, but from the human's perspective, the Being disappeared. The Being shifted their frequency higher and moved out of the 3D field and into the 4D field. They could simply appear and disappear in a blink of an eye. These Beings used this ability to their advantage.

10.2 The Galactic and Reptilian Beings

There were two specific types of 4D Beings that were on the Earth Plane at this time, the Galactic Beings and the Reptilians. These two groups experienced the 3D Earth Plane and humanity differently.

There was a variety of races within each group. A race is a large group of Beings or Consciousnesses that hold similar characteristics and frequencies dictating the way they experience a dimensional field.

All the 4D races were created from Higher Dimensional collectives that held the same names. For instance, the 4D galactic Anunnaki descended and were designed from a 9th–11th dimensional Anunnaki collective. The 4D galactic Gray races descended and were designed from 8th–11th dimensional Gray collectives. Most of the 4D Reptilian races originated from the Orion, Lyran and Sirian Collectives.

These higher dimensional collectives designed unique races that would exist in their own collective field of consciousness and experience themselves as that consciousness—not linked to any other collective system. They are NOT holding an aspect of light from a Higher Dimensional Consciousness. They are the consciousness they are existing and vibrating as, in that dimensional field.

There has been much confusion around 4D races that hold the same names as Higher Dimensional collectives. It is important to understand that the 4D races are experienced very differently than the much Higher Dimensional collectives that designed them.

Remember, from our perspective, Beings, collectives, and races do not have names. They are energetic signatures and are recognized through that signature. Humans create names to understand their reality. The 4D races may have the same names as the Higher Dimensional Consciousnesses that created them, but they are distinctly different in their frequencies, how they experience themselves, and their reality.

The Galactic Races

The Galactic races were highly intelligent, advanced in their technology, and scientific in nature. A few common Galactic races were the Anunnaki, the Grays, and the Zetas. They interacted with the human form through experimentation, technology, and education. They wanted to understand how high-frequency Consciousness could exist within a human form. They wanted to dissect it and understand its design so they could replicate the same type of form.

They were also intrigued by the human mind and egoic structure. They wanted to learn as much as they could about how these structures worked within the human form and if it was possible to control the human mind.

The Reptilian Races

In contrast, the Reptilian races were all about manipulating and feeding off the human energy field and high frequency light within the form. They understood how the quantum field works and knew how to energetically pull the light out of the human form. They would deplete the human body of its energetic force. The human would either become weak and sick or die.

These races would also infiltrate the human form. They would energetically move themselves into the human body and take over the energetic field and human. A few familiar Reptilians races were the Dracos, Lizards, and Manatees.

Summary

What unraveled between these two distinct 4D groups was the creation of many programs and tactics that impacted the human being in ways we never saw coming. These programs were experienced by the human as abductions, hybrid beings, mind control, implants, infiltration of the human form, and feeding off the human's light.

It is important that, as we begin to describe what unfolded over the next 4500 years on Earth and with humanity, you try to hold this experience in a neutral field. This can be challenging, as this was one of the most terrifying and dark times in humanity's history. However, from our perspective, it was just consciousnesses expressing their energetic signatures in a 3rd dimensional field.

There is no right or wrong in the way Consciousnesses, races, or Beings express themselves. There is no evil or dark. It is Consciousness choosing to express itself and, in this case, express itself in a dense, dualistic 3D field.

We understand how challenging this may be from your perspective; however, we hope that you can remember that all was and is divine and perfect. Let us share with you what can only be described as some of the most intense moments in Earth's 3D history.

Chapter 11

ABDUCTION, HYBRIDIZATION, AND IMPLANTS

The Galactic races created and ran the abduction, hybridization and implant programs. They were interested in learning as much as they could about the human form and the Consciousness held within that form. This curiosity led to creating similar physical forms in higher dimensional frequencies as well as controlling the human through their mind.

11.1 The Abduction of the Human: A Three-Step Process

The two largest programs that were experienced during this time were the abduction and the hybridization programs. The Galactic races had a three-step process when they began these programs. First, they needed access to human forms that were vibrating in a low 3D frequency. Second, they had to shift the human body into a 4D field. Third, they had to teleport the body through a portal and into a 4D field that held the rooms where the experiments would take place.

Step 1: Accessing the Human Forms

The Galactic races needed access to the human body without the human's conscious awareness. If the humans were aware of what was occurring, it would create emotional, mental, and perhaps physical distress.

It would be challenging for the programs to take place. They needed to override free will through the manipulation of energy.

The human was residing within a 3rd dimensional physical field. They had free will and the ability to create and choose their reality. The density of the 3D field, however, created amnesia, and the human forgot they had a choice. They forgot they could choose and stop any experience that might be occurring within their reality.

The 4D Beings were at an advantage over the human. They understood how to create realities from energy. They knew how to access the quantum field and manipulate energy in different dimensional fields. The 4D Beings could increase or decrease their own frequencies to move between the 3rd and 4th dimensional fields. They also knew how to shift the human form between the 3D and 4D fields by increasing or decreasing the frequency of the human body.

Most humans were not aware of how the quantum field worked; therefore, they were unable to stop or shift out of any experience created by the 4D Beings.

The Beings knew that in order to access the human form, they would need to shift its frequency out of the 3D field; otherwise, the human would be aware of the experience. It was crucial the humans were not aware of what was occurring to their bodies. They wanted as little conscious contact with the humans as possible. The less humans remembered, the easier it would be for the 4D Beings to continue to experiment on and manipulate the human.

To ensure the human would remain unconscious during the experiments, they chose human bodies that were holding low 3D frequencies. The lower a 3D human form's frequency, the further away the human will be from the 4D field and the more difficult it would be to feel the 4D Beings and remember the experience. The higher a human form's frequency, the closer it will be to the 4D field and the easier it will be to sense the 4D Beings.

For example, imagine the human is in an energetic bubble—the 3D field—and this bubble holds a frequency that creates a reality for the human. The energetic bubble exists within the 3rd dimensional field and has access to the entire spectrum of consciousness within that field. However, its reality—what it experiences—is based on the body's frequency.

If the bubble is holding a 3.2 frequency, it will be difficult to experience and feel a 4.1 frequency. If the bubble is holding a 3.6 frequency, it will be easier to access a 4.1 frequency. The human in the energetic bubble of a 3.6 will have a better chance of feeling and seeing the 4D Beings if and when these Beings access the human body.

If the human felt or saw the 4D Beings, it would be very difficult to shift the human form out of the 3D field. The 4D beings knew it was imperative to access bodies that were in a low 3D frequency to be successful with their experiments.

The 4D Beings knew which human bodies were in the lower frequencies by tapping into the human's energetic field. They would energetically hover over thousands of humans and scan the collective field. Each human form would pulsate out a specific frequency. The 4D Beings would energetically identify the human bodies with the lowest frequencies and access them for the experiments.

The 4D Beings were able to scan the collective field without being seen by the humans because they were in a 4D field holding 4D frequencies. It was impossible for the human holding 3D frequencies to see them.

Once they knew which bodies they were going to be accessing and experimenting on, they had to shift the human body into the 4D field.

Step 2: Shifting the Human Form from 3D to 4D

There are three reasons the 4D Beings shifted the human body into the 4D field:
1. They did not want to hold themselves in the 3D field to perform the experiments. As we have discussed, it takes energy to lower

their frequency down into the 3D field for extended periods of time.

2. They did not want to be seen by the humans or allow the humans to have conscious awareness of the experiments. Shifting the human body out of the 3D field meant the human would not be able to see the Beings and would be unconscious to the experiments. It would be almost impossible to experiment on a human body if the human was conscious of the experience.

3. They would have access to their advanced technology to perform the experiments. They needed the higher frequency tools that were in a 4D frequency to perform the experiments. For the advanced technologies to be successful, they needed the human body to be holding a 4D frequency to match the frequency of the tools.

The 4D Beings shifted the human forms into the 4D field during the human dream state. They chose this state because this is when the human's ego and mind are quiet. The human is in a state of being where all decision-making and choices are at rest. It is a perfect time to access the human form.

The 4D Beings would enter the human's room either energetically or physically in their 4D form. Most of the time, they entered the rooms energetically. They remained in a 4D field and accessed the body energetically. If they chose to enter into the room physically, they would move their frequency down into a 3D field and appear in their unique form. The reason for entering a room physically would be to allow the 4D Beings more direct and physical contact if they were having difficulty shifting the human form.

Once they were in the room, they energetically accessed the light (frequency) within the human form. They would begin to spin the light, increasing the frequency of the human body into the 4D field. They did this through intention without physically touching the human form.

Once the body was in a 4th dimensional frequency, they would pull the 4D human form out of the 3D human form. There would be two distinct human forms in the room—a 3D form and a 4D form. The 3D human form remained in the room while the 4D human form teleported into a 4D field to be experimented on.

This is challenging to understand. In the quantum field, all possible aspects and frequencies of the human Being exist. There can be a 3D, 4D, or 5D human form existing at the same time, depending upon what frequency the body is holding. Time and reality are experienced very differently depending upon the frequency and dimensional field of the human body.

When a human body is shifted out of a 3D field, it moves out of the slow linear time that is experienced in the 3D field. The 4D body exits the 3D body and field, enters the 4D field, and is experienced separately. The 3D body remains in the 3D field, experiencing the time-space continuum within that field. The 4D human body could be with the 4D Beings in the 4D field for linear hours or days, but the 3D human body might only experience it as a few hours or minutes.

In this case, the 3D human form would remain in the 3D field experiencing linear time while the 4D human form would be shifted into the 4D field, experiencing a different reality and a different version of time. The 4D human form and 3D human form are almost identical in nature except for the frequency each is holding and the way they experience time.

It can be challenging for the 3D human mind to conceptualize and understand how both bodies exist in the same now yet are separate. The human mind works with tangibility and physicality, what it can see and hold. You can't see the quantum; you can only feel it. It is only when the human is holding higher frequencies that it will understand this concept. Until then, we offer the remembrance that all realities exist in the now within the quantum field and a physical form can be in multiple dimensional fields at the same time.

Step 3: Opening the Portal

Once the 4D Beings had the human form shifted into the 4D field, they then had to open a *portal* to teleport the human form into the 4D field where the room or space was located and the experiments were performed. A portal is a pocket of energy that opens into higher dimensional fields. Portals are a way to move through dimensional fields within the quantum field. To enter a portal, the Being or physical form has to hold the frequency of the higher dimensional field it is entering.

In the human's room, the 4D Beings created portals that would open into the 4th dimension. Once the body was in the 4D field, the 4D Being would shift itself and the human body through the portal. It is a now moment when one moves through a portal.

One minute, the human form was in a 3D physical bedroom, and the next, it was in a 4D room. The portal was the bridge between the human's 3D physical reality and the 4D Being's physical reality. The 4D rooms existed within the Earth Plane, not off-planet. This is a somewhat confusing concept, but we will explain.

The portal that was created within the human's room opened into an energetic field, similar to a black hole. When the Being and human moved into and through the portal, they would step out into a space—a room—that was held within a 4D field within the Earth's form.

For example, imagine a Russian doll. There looks to be only one doll; however, when you pull the first doll out, there is a smaller doll within it. You pull that doll out, and there is a smaller doll within it. You originally only saw one doll, yet there were multiple dolls within that one doll. This is how the multi-dimensional field works within Earth. The most physical field is the first layer, the 3D. When you go a bit deeper or to a higher frequency, you can access another dimensional layer or field, such as the 4D. The portals that the 4D Beings created provided access into the next dimensional layer or field within Earth.

These rooms within the 4D field were where the experiments would take place. There were hundreds of these rooms, and they made up multiple small structures similar to buildings. The rooms were physical in nature just as the 4D Beings were physical in nature. The 4D field is physical; however, the only way to see the physicality of a 4D Being or room would be to hold 4D frequencies. Any human or Being that was in a lower dimensional field, like the 3D field, would neither be able to access nor see these rooms or these Beings.

Again, this is how the quantum field works. All dimensional fields exist to the Consciousness or Being existing within that field. It may be difficult for the human to conceptualize rooms within a 4D field that were being used to experiment on human forms, but there are many realities occurring right now that the human is unable to see or access because their frequency is not in that dimensional field.

The 4D Beings increased the frequency of the 3D human into a 4D frequency. They moved the human form through the 4D portal and into these 4D rooms. They experimented on the human and then shifted the human form back through the portal and merged the 4D body back into its 3D form without the human's awareness.

These 4D rooms were necessary in order for the programs to be successful. They allowed the experiments to be carried out for thousands of years without conscious awareness on the part of humanity. Most humans experimented on did not remember or know what was happening. They were asleep as they were shifted into a slightly higher vibrational field. If they did wake up, their ego took them back to the dream state out of sheer shock, fear, and the inability to comprehend what was occurring.

Rarely were the 4D Beings seen on the Earth Plane. It made very little sense to allow the human to see them, as it would only create chaos and confusion. Their intention was to learn as much as possible about the human form. Engaging with the human in the 3rd dimensional field would not provide such answers. It would frighten the human and cause possible harm to both human and 4D Being.

Contrary to what many believe, the 4D Beings never wanted to harm humans. They were strictly interested in experimenting on and learning how to manipulate the human form. If they wanted to harm or torture a human, they would have allowed the human to be conscious during the experiments. They would not have taken measures to ensure the human form was in a 4D field. They would have just teleported the 3D body regardless of the impact on the human.

We understand from the human's perspective that these experiments and abductions were invasive and created much pain, fear, and chaos. We also know that it could have been much worse had the 4D Beings chosen to create a more harmful experience. The 4D Being's state of consciousness was curiosity not harm.

The 4D Beings kept themselves in the 4D field for thousands of years. During this time, they mastered the art of teleporting the 4D human form out of the 3D form without human awareness. This allowed the abduction and hybridization programs to expand during these 4500 years. We watched as hundreds of thousands of experiments took place involving dissecting the form, impregnating the form, and implanting the human form.

11.2 The Abduction Program

The abduction program was the largest program conducted at this time. It was created to dissect and study the human body. Hundreds of thousands of humans were abducted out of their beds for the purpose of experimentation.

The 4D Beings were very intentional and cautious during the experiments. They did not use physically invasive 3D techniques or instruments during the experiments. Again, their intention was not to harm the human form but to study the human form.

These Beings were highly intelligent and had access to advanced technology and instruments that would work energetically on the human form. They used high frequency light technologies to enter the human form. This resulted in very little physical damage to the human body. They did not need to cut into the human form. When the body is in a slightly higher frequency, it's easier to access the inside of the form.

Most of the time, they would enter the human body through the eyes. This ensured there were no marks on the human form. They would move energetic probes or light Lasers into the human eyes and investigate the human form. Once within the form, they would dissect and study tiny portions of organs, tissue, muscle, blood, and DNA through an energetic laser.

During these 4500 linear years, the 4D Beings learned everything they could about a dense physical body holding a Higher Dimensional Consciousnesses. Through these experiments, they became curious about how the human form was designed and wondered if they could create their own hybrid human. This is how the hybridization programs began on the 3D Earth.

11.3 Hybridization Programs

The hybridization programs were designed to create new races of Beings from the human prototype. The 4D Beings wanted to create physical forms that were half human and half galactic. These programs were much more complex than the abduction program and had both a negative and positive impact on the human. Thousands of humans were traumatized while thousands of humans benefitted from the program.

The hybridization programs took place on the Earth Plane in the same 4D rooms used for the abductions as well as off the Earth Plane on planets within the 5D grid.

When we closed the 5D grid, the 4D Beings accessed planets to reside in while in the 5D grid. The planets were in 3D, 4D, and 5D fields. This meant they could be experienced in three distinct dimensions. The 3D human would experience the planet as a round, dense physical form in the sky. The 4D and 5D Being would experience the planets as a physical form that could be used to create their physical reality. Most 4D races chose to use the planets near the Earth Plane as the location where they would reside while in the 5D grid.

The planets held 4D life for thousands of years. They just couldn't be seen in a 3D field by the 3D human. The 4D Beings used these planets to build the hybridization programs. They teleported the human body to these planets using the same 4D Portals that were created for the abduction programs. It was just as easy to move the human body onto a 4D planet as it was to move the human body into a 4D room within the Earth Plane. The portals had access to multi-dimensional fields and locations within the quantum field.

Once the body was shifted into 4D frequencies, it could be moved into any 4th dimensional field, whether off-planet or within the Earth Plane. The 4D Beings often chose the 4D planet option because it was easier to control and create the hybrid within their own familiar environment.

11.4 Creating the Hybrid Being

The hybridization program began through the abduction program. It was during experiments on the human body that the 4D Beings discovered eggs and sperm. When they studied the eggs and sperm, they found human DNA within these structures. As we have discussed, all human DNA holds light codes that hold information. The 4D Beings found that the specific light codes within the egg and sperm DNA created the 3D human body.

They knew they could dissect these light codes to create new physical forms. They also recognized that merging an egg and sperm created the 3D human body. They were learning how to create new physical forms. They understood they could merge the DNA of a 4D Being with the DNA of a human Being to create a hybrid Being. The physical form would hold 50 percent Galactic DNA and 50 percent human DNA.

They explored two options in creating the hybrid physical forms. Option 1 was implanting the human egg or sperm into a 4D Being. Option 2 was implanting the DNA of a 4D Being into the egg or sperm of the human.

Option 1: Impregnating a 4D Being

The first option required the light codes in DNA from the human egg or sperm to be implanted into a 4D Being.

166

The process of implanting the human light codes was not difficult. They used high frequency light technologies similar to the ones used by the Beings performing experiments on the humans. These high frequency light tools could remove the eggs and sperm without physical harm to the human body.

First, they would remove the egg or sperm from the body. They would then energetically remove the light codes from the egg or sperm DNA and implant the codes into specific DNA within the 4D Being.

The 4D Beings held DNA similar to the 3D human. Remember, these races were designed millions of years ago by Higher Dimensional collectives. These collectives knew how we designed and created the 5D human. They knew how light codes could condense down into structures that could create physical forms.

The Higher Dimensional collectives created all 4D races using the same DNA prototype as the human form. The prototype contains light codes holding an intention that shifts down into the frequency of the form being created and moves into DNA that will create that physical form. All 4D races and Beings within the 5D and 12D grid were designed and created using the DNA prototype.

Depending upon the race, the structure of the DNA would be slightly different. Some DNAs are held in strands similar to the human form. Some are held in energetic geometric shapes. The 4D races that were creating the hybrid Beings held unique geometric strands of DNA. Within this DNA were specific DNA strands holding light codes that created the 4D physical form.

The humans also hold specific DNA that creates the human form. The difference is that the egg and the sperm hold these specific DNA codes. A human form is created when the egg and sperm merge.

A 4D physical form is created when two 4D Beings come together and energetically merge their specific DNA (light codes) designed to create the form. Instead of an egg and sperm merging, the DNA merges. One of the Beings holds the merged set of DNA just like one of the humans would hold the merged egg and sperm.

167

To create the hybrid Being, they had to merge the light codes from the egg or sperm with the specific DNA that is designed to create the 4D form. They took the light codes from the egg or sperm and inserted them directly into the specific DNA within the 4D Being's physical form.

An energetic merging takes place when the light codes from the human's egg or sperm connect with a 4D Being's DNA. Each set of DNA light codes holds different frequencies. The 3D light codes merge with the 4D light codes. When they energetically merge, they create a unique combined new set of light codes that becomes new DNA. This new set of DNA creates a new physical form that is half human and half 4D Being. It is what the human calls a hybrid.

The hybrid Being is created in a 4D frequency, not a 3D frequency. This is because the 4D Being is holding the merged set of DNA light codes within their form, and they birth the hybrid in a 4D field.

Option 2: Impregnating the 3D Human

The second way they created a Hybrid Being was by implanting the 4D Being's DNA into the human egg to impregnate the human. This method created a hybrid that would look more human than galactic. The hybrid fetus would naturally begin to hold more 3D human characteristics because the 3D human initially held the two sets of DNA light codes within its body.

The merged DNA began to grow within 3D frequencies and a 3D field (the human body). The 4D Being's DNA codes would naturally adapt to the 3D frequencies within the human body. This is similar to what happens when the light codes from the egg or sperm adapt to the 4D frequencies within the 4D Being's form. The first three months the hybrid fetus was within a 3D human form, the merged DNA formed a more 3D physical body. The same could be said about the galactic fetus. When the DNA is implanted into the 4D Being, the 4D hybrid will look more galactic. The frequency of the physical form the fetus is growing in will predict the stronger characteristics of the hybrid. The 4D Beings didn't realize that implanting the human with the 4D Being's DNA would create a more human physical form. They discovered this as they were experimenting on humans.

The 4D Beings knew they could never allow the 3D human to birth a hybrid. It would be catastrophic for the hybridization program. If a human birthed a Hybrid Being, it would remain in 3D field. The human would have no reference point to how it came into being. It would create chaos, psychotic breaks, and hysteria. It would also become more difficult for the 4D Beings to access the 3D human forms. The humans would be aware of something unusual occurring. The hybrid races were created to exist in the 4D field with other 4D beings, not with the humans.

To maintain anonymity, they only let the hybrid fetus gestate within the human body for three months. They would then remove the hybrid fetus from the human and implant it into the 4D Being. The 4D Beings always intended for these physical forms to exist in the 4D field, and thus, they had to grow within the 4D Being and be birthed into that 4D frequency.

They used advanced high frequency light tools for these procedures. There were very few, if any, marks or incisions on the human body. They held every intention to prevent harm to the humans. This is the reason humans never saw the hybrid races in the 3D field. They were birthed and experienced within the 4D field.

The human body that was holding this hybrid fetus would either think they were pregnant or have no idea they were pregnant. If they thought they were pregnant, they would have no idea it was a hybrid. When the 4D Beings extracted the fetus from the human body, the human would experience what is called a miscarriage. However, it wasn't the passing of a fetus that occurred; it was the passing of tissue that remained from the empty sack the fetus had been held in.

It was much more complicated, however, to implant the human than it was the 4D Being. The 3D human had a very difficult time holding the 4D DNA in their body. It wouldn't always connect and merge with the egg. The human was vibrating in a lower 3D frequency, and it was challenging for the body to hold higher dimensional light codes.

They had to experiment on many humans to have one successful implantation. What the 4D Beings began to do was find human forms that were vibrating in a higher frequency. They knew if they had human bodies that were holding frequencies closer to the 4D field it would be easier for the human to hold the 4D DNA. Their frequency and field were closer to the DNA that was implanted into their form.

Over the next 4500 linear years, the 4D Beings were able to use thousands of humans, without their conscious awareness, to create new hybrid Beings.

11.5 The Human and Hybrid Connection

Most humans who were part of the hybridization program, whether being impregnated or having sperm or egg dissected from the body, were unconscious to any participation their bodies had with the program. There is, however, a unique energetic connection between the human and the hybrid Being that they were part of creating. There is an energetic cord that is created from the human's light codes to the Hybrid's light codes. This cord moves through dimensions connecting the 3D human to the 4D hybrid.

For example, if a male's sperm was used to create the hybrid Being, they both shared the same DNA. The light codes within the shared DNA created the energetic cord connecting the hybrid to the male.

The bond becomes even stronger if a woman carried the hybrid fetus within her body for a few months. Not only does the woman share the same DNA, and thus is connected through the shared light codes, but she held the fetus within her form. The woman may not have any awareness of being pregnant or losing the fetus, but there will always be an energetic connection as well as an unconscious feeling that she has a child who is not physically with her.

This energetic cord is usually unconscious; however, it is possible for the human to be awakened into a memory. They may feel as if they had a child who is not with them or there is a child they are connecting with but are not sure how, why, or where.

It's a strange feeling for a human to connect to a hybrid child. The human is awakening into a memory, but it's so unconscious and surreal they rarely recall any experience of being in the hybridization program. It is uncommon for any human to reconnect with a hybrid child, but it is possible.

If a human consciously recalls being a part of the hybridization program, it will feel like a dream. They won't have physical proof, but they can feel it. This is because the hybrid child and the human are connected through the energetic cord.

If there is any contact at all, it is in the dream state through the etheric body. This is because most 3D humans are not holding high enough frequencies to physically see a 4D hybrid on Earth. All contact must be in the 4D field until the human body is anchored into the 4D field while on the 3D Earth. Until then, the dream state is the access point for contact. During the dream state, the Higher Self assists the human's etheric body into the dimensional field and the planet the hybrid child is on, and they connect. The human will wake up and and either remember what occurred or will have no memory of the experience. The 3D human will only be able to physically engage and see a hybrid in the 3D field when the 3D human collective is anchored into higher frequencies.

We would like to preface here that currently there are 4D, 5D, and 6D hybrid Beings on the 12D grid. We are not discussing the history of how all of these hybrids were created. We are merely sharing what occurred in the last 4500 years on the Earth Plane as it had a significant impact on where humanity finds themselves now.

11.6 Implants

While the abduction and hybridization programs were occurring, another powerful experiment was taking place. The 4D races began implanting the human form with devices allowing them to gain control over humanity. The implantation program began about 1000 linear years ago, and it had the most devastating impact on the Earth and humanity. Implanting humans with devices to control them pulled the Earth and humanity's frequency down quicker than any other program. It also played a pivotal role in physically destroying parts of the Earth Plane.

This program was designed by the 4D Beings with the intention of controlling and participating in the 3D field without being in the 3D field. They knew they couldn't physically appear; it would create too much chaos. They had to find a way to be a part of the 3rd dimension without physically being in it. They discovered that high-frequency devices implanted into the human could allow the Beings to control the human and thus participate and impact the 3rd dimensional field.

You can imagine the implants as remote controls. The 4D Beings could control and manipulate human behaviors, thoughts, and even emotional states while they remained in the 4D field. Each race created their own devices that held unique energetic pulses. The device, once implanted into the human, would send out an energetic pulse connecting the 4D Beings to the human. Only the race that connected energetically to the pulse could control and activate the implant. This allowed for exclusivity between races and their specific impacts on humans.

The 4D Beings implanted the device into the human body using the same techniques as the abduction and hybridization programs. They accessed the human body during the dream state, shifted the body into a 4D field, moved it through the portal, and performed the experiment in the same 4D rooms created for the abduction and hybridization programs.

The devices were physical for the 4D Beings but translucent, almost transparent when inserted into the 3D human body. The 3D human would not be able to detect or see these devices within them. The 4D Beings would surgically insert the device under the skin of the human. The surgery was energetic, not physical. They use advanced high frequency light instruments to open the skin and move the device into the body. There wasn't any tearing or physical intrusion of the skin. The device was

172

in a higher frequency than the human body, so it was almost impossible for the human to detect it.

Once the device was within the human form, these Beings could access the brain and the energy fields within the human body. They could alter the brain chemistry and manipulate the way the human evaluated an experience and the response the human would have with that experience. This allowed them the ability to alter the humans' behaviors, thoughts, emotions, and beliefs.

They could also shift the human's energetic field down into lower frequencies, impacting how the human experiences the world. When a human's body is in a lower frequency, they are not in as much control over their free will and choice. They are in a heightened sense of amnesia and powerlessness. The human is unconscious to the amnesia. They believe they are in control of their choices; however, the lower a body's frequency, the less conscious a human is to the choices they are making. The 4D Beings knew that to lower a human's energetic field is to lower their ability to control their choices. This allowed the Beings to control the choices of the human.

The human with the implant would not be consciously aware of what was occurring. They would be in an unconscious state, believing that how they were feeling and experiencing their world was a choice they were making. They would feel as if they were in control. Humans around them, however, would notice a difference in their behavior. They would feel as if that human had been taken over by something or someone else. The 4D Beings were able to control the human's thoughts, behaviors, and emotions through their mind and energetic field.

Hundreds of thousands of humans were implanted with these devices over the last 4500 years. The power and control these Beings had over humanity led to war, physical destruction of the Earth, and the destruction of civilizations. It was the most powerful mind control we had ever seen.

It was the humans who created war and destroyed the Earth and civilizations. The 4D Beings simply controlled these humans from the 4D field. We had never seen anything like it before and had not anticipated that the 4D Beings would introduce this type of advanced mind control into the 3D field.

The abduction, hybridization, and implant programs all played a significant role in slowly pulling humanity and the Earth Plane into lower frequencies. However, another group of 4D Beings on the Earth also played a significant role during this time. Humanity refers to these Beings as the Reptilians.

Chapter 12

THE REPTILIANS AND THE HUMANOID

The Reptilian's intentions for entering the 5D grid were to understand the energy within the human form. They were curious about the way energy was held within the human body and how to access and use it for their own purposes. They knew that energy was light, and light was a life force for other Consciousnesses, including Reptilians. Light created more power or more abilities for a Consciousness.

If Reptilians could pull energy from the humans, they could then increase their own life force and create more power. When we talk about power, we don't mean control. Instead, we are referring to a Being feeling more energetic frequencies within their own form, becoming more alive and electric. It would feel similar to the human receiving a burst of endorphins, so their body feels *high* or in an altered state. This is what occurs for the Reptilians when they access the energy within the human form.

12.1 Pulling Energy out of the Human

The Reptilian races began to experiment with the human by energetically pulling energy out of the human form through the 7th energy center, the Crown Chakra. The humans were unaware this was occurring.

The human body is in frequencies that provide amnesia. Remember, the lower a human body's frequency, the higher the human's amnesia. The human's ability to feel and understand what is occurring within and around their energetic field is limited. They are unconscious to their sovereignty and ability to control what moves in and around their field.

The Reptilians were able to infiltrate the human body without conscious consent because of the human's amnesia. This was very different from the abduction, hybridization, and implantation programs. The Galactic races performed experiments on the human body. They never took the human's energetic life force. The Reptilians energetically moved into the human's energetic field and pulled the human's light out through their channel. This type of engagement with the human was much more invasive and destructive than any of the Galactic programs.

The Reptilians entered the human's energetic field in such a way that has caused many humans in their current lifetime to have a hard time opening their 7th energy center, and trusting they are safe and sovereign in their body. They have cellular memories of lifetimes where these Reptilians had infiltrated their field and body to pull their life force out of them.

The Reptilians technique was simple. They did not have to shift the human's or their own energy field. They merely energetically entered the human's energetic field, accessed the human channel through the 7th energy center, and then gently pulled the light from the human body out through the channel. Once the Reptilians understood this technique, they began pulling the light from thousands of human bodies. They watched as their own power and energy within their forms increased.

The human was unaware of the energy being drawn out of them, but they did experience many physical symptoms. The act of pulling light out of the human body caused the brain to slow down, which caused disorientation, nausea, headaches, dizziness, flu-like symptoms, vertigo, or zombie-like behaviors. They would have difficulty finishing sentences or doing daily tasks. There were many physical, mental, and emotional symptoms of Reptilians infiltrating their bodies and pulling out their life force.

It was rare but, in some cases, the human body died. The human body runs on light. Although it was never the intention of the Reptilians to shut down the human body, if they were not careful, they could pull too much of the human's light out of their body, which would shut it down completely.

12.2 Entering the Human Form

The Reptilian races would also move directly into the human form and remain within the body. This allowed them continual access to the human's light. It was a much more potent and powerful way to obtain the energy. It also provided the Reptilian with the ability to control the human's mind, which inadvertently controlled their emotions, behaviors, and thoughts.

This technique of moving into the human body was much more challenging than just pulling energy from the human body. Entering the human form required that the Reptilians hold themselves in the body energetically. They experienced themselves in the human form. This was all done energetically, not physically. Once in the body, they would take over the body. The Higher Dimensional Consciousness that incarnated into the human body would be overlaid by the reptilian consciousness. It was as if the Higher Dimensional Consciousness was in a timeout while the reptilian energy was in the body.

Remember, the human is unconscious to their free will and innate ability to remain sovereign and command these Beings out of their bodies. The Higher Self may try to get the human's attention through guidance, but if the human is unaware of this guidance, they won't make the decision to command the Reptilian out of their bodies.

Although the human was generally unaware of what was occurring, many had an unconscious response to the reptilian energies within their body, experiencing a purging process like a flu. The Reptilians combated these physical reactions by energetically manipulating the human brain to quiet the mind and the energetic connection the human was having to the reptilian energy within their body. It was not easy for the reptilian energy to be in the human body. Many Reptilians chose to pull the energy out of the human instead of residing in the human body.

The Reptilians that did move into the human form did so not just for the constant flow of life force, but to control the human's emotions, thoughts, behaviors, and choices. This simple action of Reptilian energies moving into the human body was by far the most devastating experience for humanity. It had the largest and longest impact for the human collective.

12.3 The Creation of Humanoids

After a few thousand years of interacting with the human form, the Reptilians eventually began to create their own Hybrid race called Humanoids. They saw how the Galactic races were creating new races and wanted to follow suit.

They abducted human forms and created the hybrid being in a way similar to the Galactic races' methods. They entered the human's room and shifted the body into the 4D field. However, the Reptilians had their own portals they created and accessed to shift themselves and the body into the 4D field. The portals led to 4D rooms within the Earth Plane and the 4D planets the Reptilians existed on while in the 5D grid. Both the rooms and the planets were used to perform the experiments.

Once they had the human body in the room or on the planet, they extracted the light codes from the egg or sperm and implanted it into a Reptilian. The Reptilian light codes merged with the human light codes, and a humanoid began to form within the Reptilian. Once the humanoid was completely formed, the Reptilian birthed the hybrid into the 4th dimension.

The original Humanoids looked more Reptilian than human. They were vibrating in a lower 4th dimensional field and existed in that dimension.

Most original Humanoids were birthed and lived on the 4D planets even if they were created in the 4D rooms. There were many planets at this time that held the thousands of humanoid races being created by the Reptilians.

Over time, the Reptilians began implanting the Humanoids with human DNA to create a new race of Humanoids. This new race was in a lower frequency than the original Humanoids. After a few thousand years, as the Reptilians continued to implant new Humanoid races with human DNA, they created a race that was in a high 3rd dimensional frequency. This Humanoid was no longer being birthed in the 4D field; it was birthed in the 3D field.

A new 3D Humanoid race was created that could exist and be seen by the human eye. They looked human and were able to walk among the humans; however, they still had reptilian DNA and could tap into the lower 4D field. The reptilian DNA kept them connected to the 4D field while the human DNA kept them anchored in the 3D field. We were astonished by what they were able to create.

The Humanoids innately held within them the same desires to experiment and control the 3D field as the Reptilians. Once the new 3D Humanoids were in the 3D field, they began participating in greed, control, manipulation, war, and more. Many of these Humanoids were able to control large groups of people. They were able to persuade them to do, think, and believe as they wished. They excelled in mind control.

Humanoids were human but held slightly different characteristics. They could be charismatic, but many were robotic in nature. Many did not socialize with the human population. They could feel very dark or what the human called evil. They didn't quite fit in and had odd reactions and responses to the way the world operated. When humans encountered a Humanoid, most would not feel comfortable around them. After thousands of years, the Reptilians were able to create Humanoid races that were in the 4D field on 4D planets and a few unique 3D Humanoid races that were able to walk among the humans. Of all the programs that occurred during this time, it was the Reptilians entering into the human and the creation of the 3D Humanoids that had the most devastating impact. In fact, to this day, humanity is still being controlled by not only Reptilians that entered into the human form but 3D Humanoid races.

Summary

Over the last 4500 years, the 4D Galactic and Reptilian Beings were slowly pulling humanity and the Earth into lower frequencies. We watched as hundreds of thousands of human abductions and experiments took place. Over sixty hybrid races were created. Implants were used on thousands of humans to control and manipulate their behavior. The human life force was being pulled out of them by the Reptilians. There were race wars in the 4D field, and new 3D Humanoid races were physically on the Earth Plane.

This was, by all accounts, the most tumultuous and traumatic time in Earth's 3D history. We refer to this as *Earth's second fall from grace*.

It was the first time since Earth began in the 3D field that her light quotient and humanity's collective frequency shifted down. We watched as humanity went through the most destructive period of its 3rd dimensional existence.

Chapter 13

SECOND FALL FROM GRACE; SECOND CALL FOR LIGHT WORKERS

As we've discussed, a fall from grace occurs when Earth's light quotient is pulled down into a lower percentage and the human collective's frequency is pulled down into lower frequencies.

During this second fall from grace, Earth's light quotient shifted down from 48 percent to 41 percent. Humanity's collective frequency shifted from 3.4–3.5 down to 3.2–3.3. This doesn't seem like a large shift; however, we use linear numbers to describe frequencies. A shift in the human body from 3.4 to 3.3 can feel very drastic, and it can take tens, and sometimes hundreds, of linear years to shift back up.

The second fall began around 4500 years ago when we opened the 5D grid and 4D races entered. It lasted until around 1920.

As we have stated in previous chapters, as soon as we opened the grid and recognized the 4D races entering onto the Earth Plane, we closed it. Once it was closed, the 4D Beings were stuck within the 5D grid. They were unable to vibrate out of the 5D field due to experiencing themselves in 4D frequencies.

Shortly after closing the grid, the Higher Dimensional Beings were aware of the potential energetic destruction that was beginning on the Earth Plane and made the choice to pull out and assist from off the Earth Plane. It was at this point, a few hundred linear years into opening the 5D grid,

181

when we realized we would need assistance from more Light Workers to combat what became the inevitable shift down in humanity and Earth's frequency. The Light Workers from the first call were not able to make the impact needed to shift the frequency on the Planet. We had to send out a second call for Light Workers.

We sent out the second call approximately 4500 years ago. All Light Workers answering this call incarnated with the sole intention of combating the impact 4D beings were having on Earth and humanity's frequency as quietly as possible.

During this second call, the Earth was holding 47 percent of her light quotient. This was significantly higher than the first call 10,000 years ago when she was holding 1 to 5 percent of her potential light. Humanity was also holding much more light in their bodies during the second call. This allowed the Higher Dimensional Consciousnesses incarnating into human form to bring in a higher percentage of their light. The higher the light quotient a Consciousness can bring into their incarnation, the higher the probability of remembering who they are and accessing their blueprint.

13.1 The Unique Role of the Second Call Light Worker

We knew that all Light Workers during this second call could and would hold blueprints that would activate early in their life, allowing their mission to have the highest impact.

The Light Workers in the second call were unique. They had the potential to be in higher states of consciousness from the moment they incarnated into the human form. Many were able to hold 5D consciousness throughout their entire human journey. They would align and connect to their Higher Self, *I Am* Presence, and Guides early on in their human journey. Many of these Light Workers would actively and consciously work with higher dimensional Beings to fulfill their blueprint.

Their work made a powerful impact on Earth and humanity in a very short period of time. They incarnated knowing they were in a human physical form, connected to their blueprint, and held in higher states of consciousness. They were very powerful Light Workers and to this day are well known by many of you as *ascended masters.*

Most of the ascended masters that the human collective is aware of incarnated into human forms during the second call. These masters include Jesus, Saint Germain, Mother Mary, Mary Magdalene, Quan Yin, Kathumi, Babji, Buddah, Merlin, and so many more. Although in your history you are only aware of perhaps a handful of these humans, there were thousands of masters walking the Earth Plane at this time.

They incarnated with the intention of either holding the 5D consciousness in their form or evolving into 5D Consciousness while in the 3D body. They played significant roles in teaching the human how to hold higher states of consciousness and how to awaken into their multi-dimension potential. Many of these Masters incarnated multiple times, while some chose to incarnate only once.

The Light Workers were incarnating into a chaotic moment on Earth. They were holding higher frequencies than the collective of humanity, but it was still challenging to be a Light Worker.

They were walking through some of the most destructive times we had ever seen on the planet. From as far back as 4500 years ago, to as recently as 80 years ago, the Light Workers from the first call and the second call were working diligently to combat the powerful impact the 4D Beings were having on Earth's light quotient.

During this time, the Earth's light quotient moved from 48 percent down to 41 percent. It was holding steady around 41 percent, but the tactics and programs the 4D Beings were performing were growing more complex. Although the Light Workers were able to slow down the decrease in frequency of Earth and humanity, they were not able to stop the 4D Beings from slowly destroying the Earth Plane.

The more 4D Beings learned how the 3D field worked, the more their technology advanced; the more intense their human experiments became, the more they were able to manipulate and take over the human form. This is what pulled the Earth's light quotient down so quickly.

These last 4500 linear years have been the most intense on the Earth. We watched as another energetic war played out between the light workers and the 4D Beings. It wasn't until around the 1920s that we knew we would be intervening and assisting Earth.

At this time, humans, under the mind control of 4D Beings, began creating nuclear devices that were designed to destroy humanity and inadvertently destroy the Earth Plane. These designs eventually culminated into what was called the atomic bomb.

We knew what was going to occur next. We had seen this unravel millions of years ago during the first fall from grace. If you remember, one of the universal laws the Earth holds is that if she is ever going to be physically destroyed, we, the GFOL, can intervene and assist. We knew we were about to intervene once again.

Chapter 14

CLEARING THE EARTH

It was around the linear year of 1920 that we began to prepare for three things:

1. We intended to energetically clear the 4D Beings from the Earth Plane.
2. 4D Beings were beginning to shift themselves down into the physical 3D form creating very traumatic experiences for the human.
3. We sent out a third call for Light Workers.

All three occurred at the same time. We will begin with the clearing of the 4D Beings.

What we are about to share with you may be viewed as unbelievable. We lovingly understand the trauma, pain, and fear that occurred for so many humans during the past 4500 years, and most recently, in the last 80 years. Many humans are still tied to the experiences that existed during this time, and we understand and acknowledge the beliefs created from these experiences.

We preface this next section with the reminder that you are deeply loved regardless of your truths, beliefs, and experiences. We honor and respect each of you for the courage it takes to be in your human form. We ask that you feel the energy of our words and always follow your own resonance.

When the human and—more importantly—the 4D Beings began to experiment with nuclear bombs with the intention of using them in a destructive manner, there was a high probability that Earth could physically be destroyed. We knew at this moment in Earth's history that we had to intervene. We would need to clear out the cause of this destruction, which stemmed from the 4D Beings. Although it was humans who created the bombs, it was the 4D races that were controlling and navigating the potential destruction of humanity and Earth.

It was not necessary to clear the entire Earth Plane as we had 15,000 years ago. What was unraveling was not as complicated. The humans and Earth were not shifting down into lower dimensional fields. They were remaining in a 3D field; however, there was a timeline humanity was moving down that would eventually physically destroy the Earth. We simply needed to clear the 4D races and Beings off the planet to shift that timeline for Earth.

14.1 The Process

We cleared the 4D Beings energetically. You can imagine it like an energetic vacuum pulling the Beings out of the 4D portal, off the Earth Plane, and out of the 5D grid. We would do this in four steps:

1. Connect to the 4D Beings' energetic field.
2. Create a bubble of light around their form.
3. Increase the light within that bubble, which would increase their frequency.
4. Pull the bubble of light and their form out of the 5D grid and back into their 4D field within the 12D grid.

We had to shift them into the 5D field to move them through the 5D grid. Therefore, we began by connecting to the 4D Beings' energetic field. Then we encased them in a bubble of light. Once encased, we increased their frequency into a 5D field in order to move them out of the grid.

Once pulled out of the 5D grid, they would find themselves back in the 4D field outside the Earth Plane within the 12D grid. This is the same 4D field they were in for thousands of years after the first fall from grace. Once we pulled the 4D races out of the 5D Earth grid, they could no longer impact the human in the same palpable and physical way.

Remember, as 4D Beings, they are unable to access any dimensional field higher than the 4th. They would have to vibrate at that field or higher to access it. Therefore, they could not access the 5D grid around Earth. The 5D field protected humanity and the Earth from these Beings. Once we cleared these Beings out of the 5D grid, they were no longer participating with the human in the same physical way.

We cleared most of the 4D Beings off the Earth Plane in approximately seventy human years, from the 1920s through the 1990s. During this time, the interaction and engagement these Beings had with the humans became much more physical.

14.2 4D Beings Shifting into 3D Forms

As we began to clear the 4D Beings off the Earth, we noticed that many of these Beings started to shift their energetic field down into a lower vibration to vibrate in the 3D field. This meant it was much more difficult for us to pull them out of the Earth's 5D grid. In addition, they would be seen by the 3D human because their forms were now vibrating in that 3D field.

The way in which these Beings shifted themselves into a 3D field was by intentionally slowing down the spin of their energy within their form. As we have explained, the slower energy spins, the denser the form becomes. These Beings would slow their frequency down into the 3D field and find themselves in a 3D physical form.

It is much more challenging for us to pull a dense 3D form out of a 5D grid. It is not impossible, but it takes a bit longer as we have to shift the dense physical form out of two-dimensional fields. There is more energetic resistance from the Being when they are in a 3D form.

Imagine throwing a sixty-pound rock compared to a ten-pound rock. The heavier rock is denser and it's harder to throw. The lighter rock is less dense and easier to throw. This is like pulling a 4D Being or a 3D Being out of the 5D grid. There is less resistance with a higher frequency Being.

The 4D Beings knew slowing their frequency down and shifting into a denser 3D form would not only create a challenge for us, but they would be able to remain within the 5D grid for a much longer period of time. As we began pulling these Beings out of the grid, many started shifting themselves back and forth between the 3rd and 4th dimensional fields. When they shifted into the 3D field, they held the same physical features as their 4D body. They did not look or become human. They merely shifted their bodies down into a more physical form.

They used *craft*, or what humans call spaceships, to move in and out of the 3D field. Craft made it easier to move between dimensional fields and remain in the 3rd dimensional field for longer periods of time. As we stated in an earlier chapter, a craft is a device created for inter-dimensional travel. It moves through dimensional fields with intention and energy. The Being controlling the craft intends the craft into a dimensional field and with energetic precision, shifting the energy of the craft higher or lower in the dimensional field; the craft will then shift itself into the intended field.

Craft also hold advanced technologies to manipulate frequency and energy. Craft are highly intelligent devices that are beyond current human understanding.

The reason 4D Beings used craft is because a craft allows for the Beings to move into the physical 3D field without having to engage, interact, or be seen very often by the human. Another reason for using craft is they are the easiest form of transportation into lower physical dimensional fields.

The 4D Beings would shift themselves and their craft into the 3D field by moving their craft's energetic field down into the 3D field. They could then be seen by the human. However, these Beings were very careful and creative when manipulating and traversing the 3D field. They knew how to vibrate along a frequency that was low enough to be in the 3D field but high enough to still be out of sight by most humans. Imagine, if you will, seeing a light that disappears and then appears again as if it's playing tricks on you. That is how these Beings traversed the 3D field. They would appear and yet not appear. They could be seen and yet not be seen.

We want to make it clear that these Beings weren't physically walking among the humans during this time. They weren't flying their physical craft among the airplanes. It was much more subtle. Although they were in the 3D field and more physical in nature, they were able to disguise themselves by constantly moving in and out of the 3rd dimensional field.

They were essentially playing chase with us like a game of inter-dimensional hide and seek. They would appear in one dimension (3D), disappear, and then appear in another dimensional field (4D).

14.3 Physical Contact with Humans

Around the 1950s, the experience between the human and the 4D Beings shifted drastically. We began pulling the 4D Beings off the Earth while they were inter-dimensionally traveling. They could no longer hide from us. The response from the 4D Beings was to remain within the 3D field for longer periods of time. The longer they were in the 3D, the more physical in nature they became and the harder it was for us to pull them out.

Once they started moving into the 3D field for longer periods of time, several things began to occur. The most prevalent consequence is that humans were beginning to encounter these Beings in ways they never had before. They began seeing the Beings more often both in their bedrooms and during the abductions.

The 4D Beings started performing all experiments and programs in lower frequencies within the 4D Portal. They were holding themselves in a lower frequency, and they shifted the rooms where the experiments and programs were being held down into a low 4D–high 3D frequency. This made it more challenging for us to remove them, but even more detrimental was the impact it had on the human.

Humans began to remember these abductions and experiments in ways they never had in the past. The Beings were now in a low 4D or high 3D frequency, making them more physical. The human body was also in a low 4D or high 3D frequency. This allowed the human to wake up during the experiments more easily. The closer the human body is to their original frequency, the easier it is to wake up.

For instance, if a human body is vibrating at a 3.5 frequency and the Beings shift their body to a 4.5, the body is now holding a significantly higher frequency. The human will have a harder time waking when it's put into that frequency. If a human body is vibrating at a 3.5 frequency and the Beings shift their body to a 3.9 frequency, the human is much closer to their original state of frequency. The probability of waking up in that frequency increases.

Humans were becoming aware of the 4D Beings. They were seeing them in their bedrooms and in the operating rooms; they were even hearing them speak. Most humans kept this to themselves, but as the linear years progressed, these Beings and their programs began to come out.

Another consequence of the 4D Beings holding themselves in the 3D field for longer periods of time is that some humans began to see craft in the sky. It was inevitable that their craft would be seen by the humans. They had no choice. If they wanted to avoid us and continue with their experiments and programs, the craft were eventually going to be seen.

What we didn't expect were the craft that accidentally crashed onto the Earth. The more the Beings held themselves and their craft in the 3D field, the higher the probability of a crash. This was rare, but it did occur. It is not easy to move in and out of dimensional fields physically, and to be in the 3D field, you have to hold a dense form. The 4D Beings weren't just shifting a craft energetically and physically, but they were also shifting themselves at the same time. They were moving themselves and their craft physically in and out of the two dimensions. It takes a lot of energy to shift a physical form from the 3D into the 4D field.

Additionally, the more time spent in the 3D field, the more difficult it becomes to shift out of it. It is much easier to move in and out of a 3D field quickly. The longer the Beings held themselves in the 3D field, the heavier they and their craft became.

Holding lower frequencies for longer periods of time is like putting on weight. They became heavier, and the heavier they became, the more difficult it was to return to the higher frequencies. It was rare but occasionally, the Beings would have difficulty lifting the craft back into the 4D field. The craft would lose its frequency, spin, and crash to the ground.

Once humans began discovering these craft, governmental systems all over the world got involved. They created secret programs in order to explore, learn, and engage with the 4D Beings. These programs were kept out of the public eye.

These secret programs existed from the 1950s until the 1990s. All of the programs were held on secret bases. These bases were built near mountains, underground within the mountains, or in the deserts. All the bases were kept hidden from the human.

Governments examined the craft and 4D Beings to learn as much as possible. They also created agreements among the 4D Beings to learn about their advanced technology. The 4D Beings knew they were going to be seen more by the 3D human. They were forced to be more physical and in the 3D field because we were pulling them out of the grid at this time. They knew it would be much easier if they worked with the human.

The 4D Beings agreed to share their technologies. In exchange, the governments would keep these Beings and craft hidden from the public and allow the Beings to continue to travel in and out of the 3D field.

Not all governments chose to work with the 4D Beings. Some governments wanted solely to experiment on the craft and Beings that were deceased from the crash. Once a craft crashed, a government would collect the craft and any Beings within the craft and experiment on both. The location of the crash on the Earth Plane would dictate which government had access to the craft and Beings. These governmental programs covered up any findings. They made the human believe any craft seen in the sky was designed by the government. Humans were misled, controlled, and programmed into believing that these Beings never existed. The less the humans knew, the easier it was for the government programs to work with the 4D Beings.

The governments that were choosing to work with the 4D Beings would physically engage with them; however, physical interaction was rare. It could only occur when the 4D Being chose to shift down into the 3D field to be seen. The Beings would do so to connect with humans in the bases and share the information requested. They would speak through symbols and signs. Each visit only lasted a few minutes to an hour. The 4D Beings did not like holding themselves in the same field as the 3D humans. There was very little trust between the two groups.

It was during these exchanges that disagreements broke out between the Beings and the humans. They occurred strictly within the underground bases. These disagreements turned into small battles that began around the 1960s and ended around the 1990s, once the Beings were completely cleared off the Earth Plane.

We were not surprised that the humans began to engage in war-like behavior with these Beings. The humans wanted to learn more from these Beings and believed the technology they were receiving was not enough. They also wanted to experiment on these Beings. The 4D Beings were not giving them what they wanted. They were not going to allow the human to experiment on them even though they had been experimenting on the human for thousands of years. The only way a government could experiment on a 4D Being was if that Being crashed with the craft. Otherwise, the 4D Beings were not allowing any conscious experimentation.

Conflicts broke out all over the Earth Plane within the underground bases. There were battles that took place with 4D Beings and humans killing each other. It was tragic and traumatic for both humans and 4D Beings.

Eventually, around the 1990s, we were able to clear almost all the 4D Beings off the Earth Plane. When this occurred, these battles abruptly ended. Most of the secret governmental programs halted or slowed down. Any programs currently active are working with past historical data.

It was as if the Beings just vanished. Overnight, everything stopped. The 4D portals were gone. The Beings were gone. Craft were rarely seen in the sky. Nothing was left but the physical remnants of what had taken place.

Currently, in your now, these specific 4D Beings that had been on the Earth Plane for 4500 years are not interacting with governments or the human. All abduction and hybridization programs have stopped. 4D Beings cannot penetrate the 5D grid and, therefore, can no longer access the Earth Plane.

14.4 The Clearing of the Reptilians

By the 1990s, almost all 4D Beings had been pulled from the Earth Plane. It was more difficult, however, to remove the Reptilians off the Earth. Many had infiltrated and energetically moved into the human form. We had to be careful how we pulled their energies out of the human body. If we extracted the reptilian energy out of the human too quickly, it could pull the energetic life force out of the human and end their life. We had to be careful, and thus it took more time.

There were two steps we had to take to remove the Reptilian from the Earth Plane. First, we had to identify the humans infiltrated by the reptilian energies. Second, we had to pull the reptilian energy slowly out of the human bodies without harming the humans. It was a delicate process.

Most of the human forms that had been infiltrated by Reptilians had around 30 to 40 percent of the reptilian energy in their bodies. Although we had to be careful pulling the energy out, we knew we could do it. However, we noticed cases in which the Reptilians had taken over much of the human form. Instead of the humans holding 30 percent of the reptilian energy, they were holding around 70 percent. This created a larger hazard for us. The humans with 70 percent of their body holding reptilian energy had a higher probability of being harmed when we pulled the reptilian energies out.

Of all humans infiltrated by the Reptilians, only around 10 percent were holding a high percentage of reptilian energy. We chose to leave those humans alone and focus on the humans holding 30–40 percent of reptilian energy. This meant the reptilian energies within that human body would remain in the body, on the Earth, and impacting the human collective.

We knew that the Light Workers would continue to shift Earth and humanity into higher frequencies. The light quotient on the Earth would increase, and the frequency within the human body would increase. As the human form continued to hold higher frequencies, the reptilian energies would not be able to remain within those forms. The high frequency light anchoring into the body would do the work for us. The light would naturally begin to pull and clear the denser reptilian energies out of the human form. We had to allow this process to unravel through the work of the Light Workers.

14.5 The Clearing of the Humanoids

Another obstacle we ran into when clearing out the Reptilians was the humanoids. Humanoids, as we have discussed, were a hybrid of human and Reptilian. These Beings held the intentions and DNA of the Reptilians but were in a 3D human form. We understood and followed free will; however, we also knew that these 3D human forms were created and embedded with 4D Reptilian DNA. This DNA is what enabled the humanoid to create and design the chaos and destruction on the physical 3D Earth Plane.

The Humanoid Beings were the most dangerous creations on the Earth Plane. They were humans walking the Earth Plane, yet they held the intentions of the reptilians through their DNA. They were different from the humans who had been infiltrated by reptilian energy. The Humanoids were more intentional and powerful. The Reptilians that infiltrated the human body had to navigate the human's energy and frequency. They were trying to control a body that was holding other frequencies. The humanoid was a Reptilian through DNA but standing as a human body in the 3D field.

We knew we had to pull as many Humanoid Beings off the Earth Plane as possible, and we did so in a unique way. Humanoids were holding a much denser form than the 4D Beings. They were essentially human bodies with 4D DNA. They had the potential to exist in the 4D field based on their DNA. Therefore, we had to pull the entire physical form out of the 5D grid and allow these Beings to exist in the 4D field within the 12D grid.

The only way to do this was to shift their entire physical form into the 4D field. Once they were holding a 4D frequency, we could move them energetically through the 5D grid and into the 12D grid. It took a long time to pull the Humanoids off the Earth Plane. There were thousands of Humanoids. We had to energetically connect to each one and then begin to shift them through intent into a 4D field. We typically did this at night when other humans could not view the shift. Their form would literally disappear from the 3D field. The Humanoids began shifting off the Earth Plane and back into the 4D field within the 12D grid outside the 5D grid.

When a Humanoid was taken off the Earth Plane, humans would experience it as a disappearance. The person would just disappear. For instance, if a human had a friend who was a humanoid, and we pulled the humanoid off the Earth, the human on the Earth Plane would experience it as their friend disappearing or vanishing. There were only a small percentage of Humanoids on the Earth compared to the entire population, so their disappearance did not cause a reaction among humanity. It was rarely noticed.

We were able to clear about 90 percent of the 3D Humanoids off the Earth Plane by the early 2000s. Currently on the Earth, there are about 10 percent of Reptilians left in the human body (a few thousand humans) and about 10 percent or a few thousand of the 3D Humanoids left. That number is decreasing as the human form continues to shift into higher frequencies and the human collective continues to evolve into higher frequencies. The Reptilian energies will not be able to remain within the human body and the 3D Humanoids will no longer be able to control the human. It will not be long before all reptilian energies will be completely banished from the Earth.

As of your now moment, the 4D Beings are not entering the 5D grid, and they are not continuing to perform the hybridization, abduction, or implantation programs. All of these programs have halted. The only 4D Beings left on the Planet are the 10 percent Reptilians in the human form and the 10 percent 3D Humanoids.

If a human currently on the Earth Plane had an implant in them, it has either been removed when the 4D Being was taken off the Planet, or the implant will naturally dissolve as the human form continues to hold higher frequencies. Either way, with the 4D Being outside of the 5D grid, the implant is not capable of being accessed. We understand that the human has many vivid and cellular memories of these Beings and experiences; however, they are no longer interacting and engaging with the human in the same physical manner. It has been quiet on your Earth Plane for over fifteen years in your linear time.

14.6 Engagement with 4D Races Off-Earth

The 4D Beings are unable to access the 5D grid energetically. The Earth is held in the 5D grid. Therefore, any interaction a human has with these 4D Beings must be outside of the 5D grid thus off the Earth Plane.

The human is going to believe it's happening on the Earth Plane only because they are unconscious of how interaction works with these Beings.

Let us explain.

Any current interaction a human has with a 4D Being is done through free will and the etheric body. Most humans are unaware of how these two concepts work. Let's begin with the etheric body.

Most humans' bodies are currently unable to physically shift dimensional fields. The frequency within the form is not high enough to move through the 5D grid. All interaction with 4D Beings must be done outside the Earth's 5D grid within the 4D field. Therefore, the human must move through the 5D grid to access these Beings. Since the human form can't do this, the human must use their etheric body to travel into the 4D field.

The etheric body holds an aspect of the consciousnesses that incarnated into the human form. It was designed for multi-dimensional travel. It allows the consciousnesses within the human form to experience and travel inter-dimensionally.

The etheric body can shift out of the 5D grid and into the 4D field easily. This is most often done unconsciously. It can move into any dimensional field and have a multitude of experiences including engaging with 4D Beings. The etheric body shifts out of the physical form, moves out of the 5D grid, enters the 4D field, and engages with 4D Beings. Again, this is all a choice, albeit most of the time, an unconscious one.

The etheric body typically shifts out of the human body during the dream state when the ego is resting but not always. However, humans can also be conscious and awake when the etheric body travels into other dimensions. The human calls this *bilocation*.

Whether conscious or unconscious, most interactions with 4D Beings through the etheric body feel like a dream. If the human is conscious, they have a higher probability of remembering the dream. If they are unconscious, they will most likely not remember the interaction or may have unclear memories of that dream. It will feel as if something happened to them, something that they did not choose.

Most of these interactions are perceived as if they are occurring on the Earth Plane, yet all are occurring off the Earth Plane, outside the 5D field, within the 12D grid. The human may filter the experience through their consciousness as having taken place in a 3D room or wherever else it may have occurred, but that is the 3D mind trying to understand this concept. Most humans will process the experiences as happening on Earth.

Along with the etheric body, it requires choice (free will) to engage with any 4D Beings. This can be difficult to understand, but nothing is occurring in a human's life that is not dictated by choice. The human chooses to engage with the Beings. They are either conscious or unconscious of that choice. If they are conscious, they are aware that they are desiring an interaction with these Beings and thus are choosing it. If they are unconscious, the Higher Self is choosing the interaction to fulfill an unconscious desire of the ego. The ego may hold a desire—that the human is unaware of—to have a certain experience. The Higher Self hears that desire and creates the experience for the human. The human is unaware that they chose the experience. They feel like it happened *to* them instead of *for* them.

Most humans engaging with these Beings right now are doing so unconsciously. The Higher Self is playing out an unconscious desire of the human's ego that the human is not aware of yet. The human might consider themselves a victim of the experience and will feel as if they had no choice, yet they always create the experience through choice.

We understand there may be some hesitation or difficulty in holding this reality. Humans have had a traumatic history with these Beings, and to believe that they are now choosing to engage with them can be impossible to believe.

During the past 4500 years, when the 4D Beings were within the 5D grid and on the Earth Plane, they had the ability to override humanity's free will through energetic manipulation. We have detailed this in the previous chapter. The Beings could shift the human body's frequency to infiltrate it and perform experiments. In your current now, humans who are unconsciously engaging with these Beings outside the 5D grid may feel as though they are being infiltrated. However, these Beings are no longer in the 5D grid. They cannot infiltrate, attack, or take over the human's energetic field or body. All interaction is a choice by the human.

It is hard to understand why a human would choose to engage with Beings that may not have their best interest at heart. We do not have the answer. It's possible that the human has had many past experiences with them, and so there is still a desire to connect. It's possible that the human is hoping to gain some advanced information or knowledge. It's also possible the human enjoys the interaction even though the experience may not be filtered through the ego as enjoyable.

There are many reasons why the human chooses to engage consciously or unconsciously with the 4D Beings. Regardless of the choice, as humans begin to hold higher frequencies within their bodies, the choice to engage stops. This is because the intention the 4D Beings held was never for the higher good of the human. The interaction never served the human's highest potential. When the humans evolve into higher states of consciousness, each choice they make is for their highest good and highest potential.

In your now, we have been witnessing significantly less engagement between the human and the 4D Beings. It is not only because they no longer exist within the 5D grid but also because the evolving humans are choosing to no longer engage.

We share this with you so you can begin to remember that you are always choosing your now moments. All 4D Beings are off the Earth Plane and outside the 5D grid. Only approximately 10 percent of the reptilian energy remains in human bodies, and 10 percent of the 3D Humanoids remain on the Earth. All programs and experiments have halted. The experience many humans have had with these Beings for the last 4500 years has come to an end. We encourage humanity to begin to embrace these remembrances.

Chapter 15

THE CLARION CALL:
THIRD CALL FOR LIGHT WORKERS

As we began clearing the 4D Beings off the Earth Plane, we made the decision to send out a third call for Light Workers. Humanity has referred to this moment as the Clarion Call. It was the most impactful call we ever made.

The Earth's light quotient and humanity's collective frequency had been pulled down by the 4D Beings for the previous 4500 years. Although we had sent out a second call during those 4500 years, we needed many more Light Workers to enter onto the Earth Plane to assist in increasing her light quotient and humanity's frequency as we began to pull the 4D Beings off.

We knew that intervening by clearing the 4D Beings off the Earth Plane could potentially create more chaos and hostility on the planet. We were unsure what would unravel or how many linear years it would take to pull these Beings off the Earth. We wanted to ensure that, regardless of what unraveled, Earth would continue to increase her light quotient.

We sent out the Clarion Call with the intention of increasing Earth's light quotient to 50 percent as quickly as possible. As we have stated before, once Earth is holding 50 percent of her light, she begins to physically anchor the 4D and 5D fields. She also cannot be pulled back down into lower frequencies. The 4D Beings would no longer have the ability to pull her or humanity into lower frequencies regardless of how long it took for us to remove them off the Earth.

When the third call went out, millions of Higher Dimensional Consciousnesses answered. They were either Light Workers incarnating back into the human form after a break between their human lives or first-time Light Workers who had never incarnated into a human form.

Light Workers that had been continuously assisting Earth and humanity since the first call 15,000 years ago or the second call 4500 years ago were not part of the Clarion Call. They have been incarnating after each lifetime and are currently assisting the Earth. However, there are many who answered the first or second call and then chose to take a break from incarnation.

A break is viewed as time through the eyes of the human, but the Higher Dimensional Consciousnesses don't experience time. They merely choose to have an experience. They chose not to go directly back into a human form after their last lifetime. A break can be a year or 5000 years. It's all a choice by the Higher Dimensional Consciousnesses.

All Higher Dimensional Consciousnesses have free will. They do not have to continue to incarnate unless they choose, and that choice occurs after each life. There is no karmic cycle tying a Higher Dimensional Consciousness to reincarnation. We will discuss this in more detail in Chapter Eighteen.

We also had a significant number of Light Workers that had never incarnated into human form now answering the Clarion Call. These Higher Dimensional Consciousnesses were in the 12D grid assisting from off-planet but had never chosen to incarnate.

At the time of the third call, the light quotient on the Earth Plane was around 47 percent. This was the same quotient she was at around 5000 years ago when we sent out the second call for Light Workers.

The frequency on Earth was high enough that all Light Workers answering the Clarion Call could hold between 9 and 11 percent of their light quotient in the human body. This also meant that any other Light

Workers incarnating at this time from the first and second call were entering into human forms holding that same amount of light.

When a Light Worker brings in more of their light quotient, it is easier for the human to align and connect into their channel. This allows the human to wake out of amnesia much faster. They will also be able to connect to their light, Higher Self, and divine blueprint more easily.

The Clarion Call was the most impactful call to date due to the unique assortment of Light Workers that answered and the body's ability to hold more light. Three specific types of Light Workers chose to incarnate.

15.1 Three Groups of Light Workers

All Light Workers answered the Clarion Call at the same now moment. However, this call was different from the first two calls. When we sent out this call, we wanted three unique groups of Light Workers to incarnate to ensure the quickest shift in Earth and humanity's frequencies.

Each group would hold a unique blueprint and incarnate at a specific time. Each group had a specific time frame in which they would incarnate into the human form. The Higher Dimensional Consciousnesses answering the call would choose which group they would participate in, and the blueprint or service they would provide to humanity and Earth would be dictated based on that group.

As we discuss the three groups below, please remember these are approximate linear dates. They are not to be held firmly. We are dealing with a time-space continuum in the 3rd dimension, and both ourselves and all Higher Dimensional Consciousnesses do not reside within this linear frame.

15.2 The Beacons of Light

The first group of Light Workers incarnated into the human form around the linear years of 1920–1960. They held approximately 9 percent of their light quotient within their human form. Their blueprint was to hold as much light as possible in their physical body to increase Earth's light quotient. We call them the *Beacons of Light* for Earth and humanity.

The human considers a Light Worker someone who is offering a service, creating a difference that can be seen or felt by the human collective or Earth Plane. This first group did not fit that narrative. They were on the Earth Plane courageously holding the light and impacting humanity through that light every day. Their blueprint wasn't contingent on a specific career they held, on how they lived their life, or whether they were conscious of their purpose. Their bodies were doing the work for them by holding and anchoring the light.

These Light Workers often created conventional lives. They held careers that many, including themselves, would not consider spiritual. For instance, they worked at grocery stores, banks, restaurants, schools, governmental agencies, healthcare industries, financial institutions, and more.

This created much frustration and doubt if or when these Light Workers woke up. They looked around at their life and questioned why they weren't making an impact, why they weren't fulfilling their purpose. What they forgot was that they chose to serve within this first group, the Beacons of Light. They chose to allow their bodies to anchor higher frequencies of light for the sole purpose of increasing Earth's light quotient and humanity's frequency. That act alone was extremely significant, yet it was hard to see the impact their role had on humanity and the Earth.

The first group's blueprint was so significant that not only did it increase Earth's light quotient and the humans' collective's frequency quickly, but it allowed the other two groups within the Clarion Call to successfully activate and fulfil their blueprints with more ease.

The first group was, and still is, imperative to Earth and humanity's current evolution in Consciousness. They were and are the Beacons of Light.

15.3 The Soldiers

The second group incarnated between the years of 1960 and 1990. Just like the first group, they are holding around 9 percent of their light quotient in their physical form. They hold blueprints that were designed to assist humanity and Earth in the physical evolution that would begin around 1987. We will discuss the physical evolution in Chapter Seventeen.

We call the second group *The Soldiers*. We use this term to reflect the power and focus these Light Workers had on the Earth Plane. It is not meant to reflect war or any variation of war.

Many Light Workers in this group knew early on they had a purpose on the Earth. They just weren't sure what it was yet. If the Light Worker does not awaken on their own, they will experience an external awakening that will jolt them into the remembrance of who they are within the human form.

The first group of Light Workers could remain unconscious and still do their work. Most Light Workers within the second group are designed to wake up. They need to be conscious of their blueprint to fulfill it.

The blueprints held by the second group are based on the physical evolution. They are incarnating to assist humanity and the Earth in clearing density from their physical forms and shifting into higher dimensional fields. These Light Workers could choose from an infinite number of roles that would allow them to fulfill this blueprint. Some of the roles included healer, writer, channeler, teacher, activist, artist, musician, grid keeper, and so much more.

The second group is also responsible for waking up many of the Light Workers who are still in amnesia. They are essential in catapulting the human collective into their first massive shift into higher states of consciousness. Unlike the first group, their work is seen and felt by humanity, Earth, and themselves. They can see the impact they are making through their blueprint.

The second group is very committed to their blueprint. Their purpose and mission are at the forefront of their lives. This often creates a sense of overwhelm and exhaustion, yet they never stop. They put a lot of pressure on themselves to show up for humanity and the Earth. Their fortitude is honorable.

Many Light Workers find themselves searching for the next opportunity to serve. They will expand and grow in their service, moving from one role to another. They may begin as an energetic healer and a few years later, or many years later, find themselves teaching and writing books. Many continue to evolve in their work and how they show up for the world.

The second group is forging the path for humanity and the Earth. They are currently standing on the front lines, physically shifting humanity into higher states of consciousness. They are the Soldiers.

15.4 The Pioneers

The third group of Light Workers incarnated between the 1990s, and your current day. They are continuing to incarnate, and play an extremely important role in assisting humanity into the higher dimensional realms. We call this group the *Pioneers*.

The Pioneers are unique in that they can incarnate with around 11 to 14 percent of their light quotient. They bring in more light than the workers in the first two groups because they are incarnating at a time when the Earth is holding more than 50 percent of her light quotient. We will describe when Earth hit the 50 percent mark in the next chapter.

The human form is at a much higher frequency and thus capable of holding a higher percentage of the Higher Dimensional Consciousness's light. Although it's only a small percentage higher than the other two groups, the Pioneers experience the human journey and being in the human form very differently.

Many Light Workers in this group have a difficult time adjusting to being human. They feel as if they do not fit in with the world around them and are often desiring to go home. They have a hard time understanding how and why the world is the way it is. Many Pioneers feel claustrophobic in the body and just want to escape.

Humanity may see the Pioneer Light Workers as disconnected, confused, dissociative, or unable to adapt to the world around them. There are many labels that have been used to define and understand these powerful and courageous Light Workers, including ADD, ADHD, bipolar, schizophrenic, autistic, Asperger's, and others.

There are also millions of humans holding these labels that do not belong to the third group of Light Workers. However, these labels are common among the Pioneers. They are holding so much more light than the rest of humanity that they experience reality very differently. The key is to remember there is nothing wrong with them. They merely incarnated with a higher percentage of light quotient than most of humanity.

The Pioneer is designed to do their work in the higher dimensional fields. They are on the Earth Plane to walk humanity into the 4th and 5th dimensional fields with ease and grace. They hold within them the abilities, knowledge, and technology that will show the way into the next two dimensional fields.

Pioneers have everything within them without ever needing to learn anything. All the knowledge, gifts, and abilities they hold are available within their DNA, and they can access these abilities the moment they incarnate. They are born with a knowingness, and they hold memories that most humans are not capable of remembering. They can recall past lives, experiences with higher dimensional beings, being on a craft, and so much more. They are designed to remember so that they can begin to show the way into the higher realms.

Many of these Light Workers are born awake, and it's their free will that pulls them through the process of navigating who they are and how they will unravel their blueprint. To activate their blueprint, they have to hold the same frequencies as that blueprint. Their work begins once their physical forms match the blueprint.

This is different from the other two groups of Light Workers. The Beacons of Light and the Soldiers can activate their blueprints regardless of the frequency their body is holding.

Most of the Light Workers in the third group will need their bodies to match their blueprint, and then they will begin their work. This can happen the moment they incarnate, or it can take linear years to activate. The process of waiting for their bodies to match the frequency of their blueprint can create frustration for many Light Workers in this group.

The challenge for the Pioneers is to remember that they have chosen a very potent blueprint. They must find patience in the remembrance that their body's frequency must match their blueprint's frequency. As soon as this occurs, they will naturally know what they are here to do and all the gifts and abilities they hold within them.

Often, these Light Workers will experience a spontaneous awakening. Their bodies are pushed or jolted into the higher frequencies to match the blueprint, and the body may not be completely ready. The Higher Self is ready, the human ego is ready, but the physical body has not yet been able to hold the higher frequencies.

The Higher Self creates an event that catalyzes the awakening. It will shift the human body into the higher frequencies, activating the blueprint and awakening the human into their purpose. This can happen through a tragic event, a trauma, a kundalini awakening, a walk-in, a drug-induced experience, or another significant occurrence. Once the event happens, the Light Worker almost instantaneously recognizes their innate gifts and abilities. They remember or slowly unravel their blueprint.

Regardless of whether these Light Workers are awake as soon as they incarnate, experience a spontaneous awakening, or slowly awaken into their blueprint, the Pioneers are the group that will be playing a crucial role in assisting humanity into the higher dimensional fields.

Summary

All Light Workers that have been assisting humanity for the last 15,000 linear years play a significant role in the current evolution in consciousness. Whether a Light Worker came in 15,000 linear years ago during the first call, 4500 years ago during the second call, or 90 years ago during the third call, all of these courageous Higher Dimensional Consciousnesses are working to ensure that Earth and humanity shift into the 5th dimensional field.

Chapter 16

THE HARMONIC CONVERGENCE

The Harmonic Convergence was a turning point for Earth and humanity. It occurred in the linear year of 1987, and it was the moment when Earth held 50 percent of the light needed to anchor the 5D field. Another way of saying this is she hit 50 percent of her light quotient. One of the universal laws we had put into effect was that when Earth was holding 50 percent of her light, she could not ever get pulled back down in frequency. Earth and humanity would inevitably shift into the 5D and eventually, into the 7D. Nothing can occur on the Earth Plane from this moment forward that would pull her trajectory down and stop her and humanity from evolving.

There were three significant events that occurred during the Harmonic Convergence: the individual and collective Higher Dimensional Consciousnesses entered back into the 5D grid, millions of Light Workers awakened, and the Earth Plane anchored into the 5D field.

16.1 Higher Dimensional Consciousnesses Entering the 5D Grid

Earth was now holding 50 percent of her light. This would catapult Earth and humanity into their physical evolution. Physical evolution occurs when the physical body begins to anchor into the next highest dimensional field. This was a transformational moment because both Earth and Humanity would begin to physically experience the 4th and then 5th dimensional fields. We knew it would be imperative for Earth and humanity to receive more assistance from individual and collective Higher Dimensional Consciousnesses during this shift.

We also knew most of the 4D Beings were cleared off the Earth Plane, and it was safe for the Higher Dimensional Consciousnesses to enter back into the 5D grid. These Higher Dimensional Consciousnesses are the same Consciousnesses that assisted Earth and humanity around 5000 years ago when we first opened the 5D grid. There are thousands of these individual and collectives that wanted to participate in the Harmonic Convergence. Some of them include the Pleiadians, Sirians, Arcturians, Lyrans, and Orions.

When it was time to allow these Higher Dimensional Consciousnesses to enter back into the 5D grid, we chose to do it differently than we did the first time. We were not going to open the grid. Instead, we sent out an energetic call or invitation allowing individual and collective consciousness vibrating above the 5D field to enter through the 5D grid without having to energetically open the grid. This would ensure the 4D Beings and races could not enter back in.

The reason these Higher Dimensional Consciousnesses never entered the 5D grid until this time is because all Consciousnesses understand and abide by free will. Earth chose through free will to not allow Higher Dimensional Consciousnesses to physically enter through her 5D grid. So, although these individual and collective consciousnesses could shift themselves through the grid, they followed the law of free will and honored Earth's choice.

Prior to sending out this call to invite the Higher Dimensional Consciousnesses back into the 5D grid, communication between the human and the Higher Dimensional Consciousness was much more challenging. There were many dimensional fields that had to be accessed or moved through to connect. Most contact between humans and these Consciousnesses was etheric. The human used their etheric body to experience and connect with the Higher Dimensional Consciousnesses outside the 5D grid. The higher in dimensional field a Consciousness resides in or is holding themselves in, the farther they are from the 3D field and the more difficult it is to connect and communicate with the human.

For example, if a collective consciousness were held in a 9th dimensional field, they would be separated from the human form by six dimensions. The more dimensions separating the human and collective consciousness, the more difficult it is to connect and communicate.

By allowing the Higher Dimensional Consciousnesses to move into the 5D grid once again, they could access the human with much more ease. They only needed to penetrate two dimensional fields. The human would be able to connect and engage more easily. However, unlike 5000 linear years ago when the human could physically see and engage with the Consciousnesses, this time contact would begin energetically.

It is like visiting a human's home without physically entering the home. Imagine a gate has opened, allowing access to a person's property. You step into their front yard or back yard (5D grid), yet you do not enter their physical home. You stay outside the home. The Higher Dimensional Consciousnesses would be staying outside the home (Earth) but in the yard. They will be closer to the home (Earth) but not physically on it. This allows them to remain in their energetic frequency and yet have an easier time communicating with the human. The communication will be energetic, not physical.

Once the Higher Dimensional Consciousnesses entered into the 5D grid, only two dimensional fields separated them from the human.

The intention for each individual and collective Consciousness entering the 5D grid was to assist humanity and Earth in physically anchoring the 4th and 5th dimensional fields into their bodies. They knew they would need the support of the millions of Light Workers currently incarnated on the Earth Plane, and so they began to awaken them.

16.2 Awakening the Light Worker

As soon as the Higher Dimensional Consciousnesses entered the 5D grid, they were able to awaken hundreds of thousands of Light Workers. They had access to the human in a way they hadn't for thousands of years.

All communication between human and Higher Dimensional Consciousness is telepathic (energetic) and occurs within the human channel. The Higher Dimensional Consciousnesses now had access to the human in a way they did not outside the grid. The Higher Dimensional Consciousnesses could now send much clearer energetic messages to the human's channel because of the proximity in dimensional fields. Telepathic communication became easier.

The Higher Dimensional Consciousnesses cannot access the human channel without permission from the human. They receive permission through the Higher Self. The human is either aware (conscious) or unaware (unconscious) of this permission. The state of awareness a human holds is dependent upon the frequency the human body is holding at that moment.

Regardless of the human's state of awareness, the Higher Dimensional Consciousnesses work with the Higher Self to awaken the human. The Higher Self becomes the bridge between the human and these Consciousnesses. It takes all communication, guidance, knowledge, and messages from the Higher Dimensional Consciousnesses and filters it through the channel. The human will experience this assistance as either their own voice, knowingness, or "gut" guiding them, or they will feel it as guidance from outside of themselves. Either way, the human has free will and can choose how they want to navigate the information they are receiving.

If the human chooses to follow the guidance, they will begin to awaken. They will start to remember their blueprint and become the Light Worker in human form. The Higher Dimensional Consciousnesses will also begin to clear density out of the human body through activations and energetic upgrades. The guidance and the upgrades will assist thousands of humans to awaken during this time and begin to assist humanity and the Earth in anchoring into the 5D field.

16.3 Earth Anchored into the 5D

The Harmonic Convergence not only allowed Higher Dimensional Consciousnesses to enter into the 5D grid, allowing them to awaken thousands of Light Workers, but it was the moment Earth hit 50 percent light quotient within her form and began to physically anchor into the 5D field. Up until that point, she was continuing to acclimate and assimilate high frequency light. Once she hit 50 percent light quotient within her form, she was able to begin to physically anchor into the 5D. This is the *physical evolution.*

Physical evolution occurs when a form—the Earth Plane, in this case—begins to physically anchor into the next highest dimensional field. The form is holding the frequencies of that field, and that field becomes their new reality. This can only occur when Earth is holding more light in her form, increasing her frequency, while simultaneously clearing out the density or lower frequency light from within her form.

Earth holds *densities* within her form. Densities are lower frequency energies or consciousnesses that are created by the human collective. We call these densities within the Earth's form *collective consciousnesses.* The human collective has an external experience that is naturally digested into the Earth's form. Anything that occurs on Earth will be digested by her physical form.

Examples of density or collective consciousness digested and held within the Earth Plane would be fear, hate, greed, rage, murder, control, and so much more. These consciousnesses were caused by human behaviors in external experiences, such as wars, genocide, chemical warfare, destruction of her land, poisoning of her air, and so much more. The Earth digested these experiences simply because they were on her form and she held them within her body. Many collective consciousnesses have been digested by the Earth and created density in her form.

The density is cleared in two ways: either the Earth clears it through her conscious awareness of the density and then purges it out through her form, or the human Light Worker clears it.

The Earth clears large collective consciousnesses from her form through external physical movement. This is called a *purge* and occurs in what the human calls a natural disaster. Volcanic eruptions, floods, tsunamis, and earthquakes are all ways in which Earth purges density within her form.

For instance, if she was intending to purge *fear* out of her form, she would take that collective energetic consciousness and move it through and out of her form through conscious intent. It may appear on the surface of her form as a tsunami or a volcanic eruption or a large tornado. The human would see this as a physical experience, as a natural disaster caused by something external and physical. The Earth would experience it as a purging.

Earth will also use islands to purge the density. Islands provide more space for the energy to move out of her form. Depending on their location and size, an island might have the least amount of impact on humans and all other Beings on the Earth. There is also water surrounding the island, which assists in lubricating density, allowing it to be released with more ease. Water is a beautiful and powerful conduit for moving energy.

Once the dense collective energies are out of her body, the energies alchemize as light back into the quantum field.

Many Light Workers incarnated at this time with the blueprint of assisting Earth purging her density. The second way density is cleared through the Earth's form is with Light Workers. They are known as the *grid keepers*. They use Earth's energetic grids, their own physical bodies, crystal activations on the land, and many more unique techniques to assist Earth in purging the density.

The Light Worker must energetically see and feel the dense collective consciousnesses within the Earth's form, energetically pull it up into the external collective field, and clear it for the Earth. This role of clearing Earth's density can be challenging and tiresome; it requires the human to feel heavy collective consciousnesses, which the human typically does not feel within their own body.

Over the next eighteen linear years (1987–2005), Earth and the Light Workers cleared the density out of Earth's form to assist her in anchoring into the 4D and then the 5D field.

When the Earth Plane anchors into the 4D field, her entire physical form is holding 4D frequencies. She cannot separate from that field. She is now experiencing the 4D field while simultaneously is able to access the 3D field. Both dimensional fields are accessible and available for her to experience. This is the quantum field.

When the Earth Plane anchors into the 5D field, her entire physical form is holding 5D frequencies. She cannot separate from that field. She can now experience herself in the 3rd, 4th, and 5th dimensions. Her form is anchored in the 5D field, so her reality is that field, but she also exists within the 3rd and 4th dimensional fields. Once a form anchors into another dimensional field, they will always have access to any lower dimensional field.

Currently, in your now, Earth is anchored in the 5D field while remaining within a 3D and 4D field. Imagine it as three clouds that are around the Earth form. Each cloud is a dimensional field, and it holds Earth in that dimensional frequency. They are not three separate physical Earths. There is one Earth experiencing three distinct dimensional fields. They all overlap. Earth's reality will be seen through the lens of the dimension she is anchored in—the 5D—but she still has access to and is in the 3D and 4D fields. This is how the quantum field works.

The human has access to all three dimensional fields on Earth as long as their physical body is anchoring that dimensional frequency in their form.

Through the eyes of a human, it can seem impossible that Earth has shifted into the 5th dimensional field. This is because the human is still anchored in a 3rd dimensional field.

If the human form were anchored into the 5th dimensional field, they would see the 5D Earth. Reality is dictated by the human form's frequency. The frequency will dictate the dimensional field the human is standing in, and that dimensional field will create the lens the human uses to perceive their reality.

Currently, in your now, the human is viewing what looks like more corruption, abuse, war, raping of the Earth's land, dismantling of human rights, and so much more. It can look very dark for the human during these times. They are feeling and seeing a large amount of the dense consciousnesses that Earth is clearing out of her form.

Humans may be experiencing despair. In these moments, we want to remind you that Earth is okay. Earth has already cleared the density that the human is currently still experiencing. Humanity is essentially living out a past moment that Earth has already moved through. This is quantum understanding.

Earth is anchored in the 5D field while most of humanity is still in the 3D and 4D fields. Humans are unable to experience another field of reality until they are anchored into that field.

This is a challenging concept for the human to understand, but one that is imperative to begin to hold. As humanity continues their physical evolution, anchoring higher frequencies into their form and clearing density out of their form, they will eventually catch up to Earth and find themselves anchored into the 5th dimensional field.

Summary

The Harmonic Convergence was the turning point for Earth's and humanity's evolution. There would never be a shift back into lower frequencies. Light Workers on the Earth Plane would continue to awaken at quickening speeds. Earth shifted into the 5D field. Humanity is currently experiencing their physical evolution, and Higher Dimensional Consciousnesses are reconnecting with humanity to assist in this shift.

Chapter 17

THE PHYSICAL EVOLUTION

The Harmonic Convergence was the catalyst for humanity to finally begin their physical evolution. The human body would begin to anchor into higher dimensional fields.

When a human body is anchored into a dimensional field, the consciousness within that field dictates their reality. The process of anchoring into the next dimensional field requires the body to acclimate, assimilate, and then anchor the light tethering the body. It takes linear time to anchor a human form into a higher dimensional field.

The human body initially acclimates or holds the high frequency light moving into the body. The body then begins to assimilate or absorb that high frequency light into all physical aspects of the body. Eventually, the body holds most of the light that is required to anchor into the next dimensional field.

To anchor into another dimensional field, 80 percent of the light held in the human body must be at the frequency of that dimensional field. For instance, if a human body is holding 60 percent 3D frequencies and 30 percent 4D frequencies and 10 percent 5D frequencies, the body is anchored in a 3D field. However, because the body is also holding 4D and 5D frequencies, it can access states of consciousness within those two other dimensional fields.

217

The human body must clear out all lower frequencies or density in the body in order to anchor into the next dimensional field. Trauma is one of the largest densities stored in the body. Trauma is created through an external experience or event, and all external experiences create energies allowing the human to understand the event. The energies are filtered through the human as emotions, thoughts, beliefs, and behaviors. If a human encounters an experience that creates energies filtered into the body that do not feel good, the human will suppress the energies. The emotions, thoughts, beliefs, and behaviors created from the event will not be felt through the body in their entirety. The energies will store in the body as lower frequencies or density. The trauma is the density held in the body.

The more trauma a human experiences and stores in their body, the more density held within the body. Through the process of acclimation, assimilation, and anchoring of light in the body, the density or trauma begins to clear out, allowing the human form to hold more light and to anchor into the next highest dimensional field.

Trauma is released when high frequency light passes through the human body and pulls the consciousnesses held within the trauma into the human's awareness. A human must be conscious of the trauma for it to clear the body.

You can imagine the trauma as a heavy block of mud and the light as water. As the light (water) moves into the body, it hits the block of mud (the trauma) and begins to break it up. The mud begins to move through the human body, allowing the human to feel the trauma that had been locked or stored within the mud. When the light hits the density, it breaks up the trauma and the human has the opportunity to feel the emotions and become aware of the thoughts, beliefs, and behaviors associated with the trauma.

The only way a human can anchor into higher dimensional fields is by consciously and courageously choosing to release the trauma that is holding the density. A human can release the trauma by simply choosing to feel, without attachment or judgment, the emotions connected to the trauma. They also must choose to acknowledge the thoughts, beliefs, and behaviors connected to the trauma without attachment or judgment and then choose new thoughts, beliefs, and behaviors.

When trauma begins to clear from the body, the human may experience intense and uncomfortable emotions—such as grief, anger, rage, depression, fear, and sadness—that have been suppressed for many years.

They may recognize thoughts or beliefs they never knew they held, such as: *I am not worthy. I am not loveable. I am not safe. I am not capable of success. I do not deserve to be seen or heard. I am stupid. I am ugly,* and many more.

They may start to recognize behaviors they have been doing that are not for their highest good, such as abuses to their body, abuses to other people, obsessive-compulsive behaviors, passive aggressiveness, addictions, people-pleasing, lack of boundaries, and more.

Along with the emotional, mental, and behavioral symptoms, the physical symptoms can sometimes be the most confusing and challenging for the human to experience. Like we said above, trauma is lower frequency energy stored within the body as density. As it builds up over time, the energetic density can create physical illness, disease, and pain in the human form. When the density begins to break up and move through the body, the illness, disease, and pain can become amplified. Attention is brought to the parts of the body that were impacted and affected by the density built up through trauma.

The human may feel more of the illness, disease, or pain. The human may believe they are getting sicker, or their health is getting worse, when in actuality, they are healing. As the density holding the physical pain, disease, or illness is dissolving, this can create the illusion of worsening health.

Physical symptoms can also appear for humans who do not have an illness, disease, or pain in the body. As trauma and density releases, the energy of that consciousness moving through the body can cause physical pain. It is energy moving through physicality. It can and does create physical discomfort.

There is an infinite number of possible physical symptoms a human can experience as they move density through their body and anchor more light. For instance, they can feel headaches, nausea, dizziness, memory loss, blurry vision, aches and pains, exhaustion, blotchy skin and rashes, weight gain or weight loss, ringing in the ears, and so much more.

The process of physically evolving requires the human to be courageous and compassionate with oneself as they feel the trauma within the body. The human must become the observer; they must be aware of all that is being released, feeling it and loving it through their form. They must detach from any judgment around the density clearing, as they are learning to move it through with eyes of neutrality. All that is occurring is energy, spinning in a lower frequency, being pushed out of the form from the influx of much faster spinning energy coming into the form.

The key is for the human to hold the remembrance and knowingness that they are consciously and courageously clearing emotions, thoughts, beliefs, behaviors, disease, illness, and pain that were created from trauma and are naturally designed to move through their body. If the human can simply remember to feel, acknowledge, and allow, without attachment or judgment, all to move through the body, it will release. The body will gracefully shift and anchor into higher states of consciousness. It is impossible for the consciously evolving human to bypass, deny, or skip this powerful and necessary step.

17.1 The Multi-Dimensional Human

As the body physically evolves and anchors into higher dimensional fields, the human begins to become multi-dimensional. They begin to experience themselves within multiple dimensions in any one moment.

As the body releases trauma and increases its frequency, light codes that were dormant within human DNA become activated. The activation allows the human to remember how to be in the next highest dimensional field. The codes provide the human with new abilities, information, and knowledge they did not have prior to the DNA activating.

As we have stated in previous chapters, the human form is only able to access light codes that reflect the body's current frequency. As the human body holds more light, its frequency increases. The DNA assimilates the higher light frequencies, which in turn activate the light codes with that same frequency. This is the natural process of physical evolution. Dormant DNA naturally activates, allowing the human to access higher dimensional fields.

As the 3D human body begins to increase its frequency and the light codes within the DNA activate, they will start to become multi-dimensional. The human will experience anchoring into the 4th and eventually 5th dimensional fields while still experiencing the 3rd dimensional field. The human does not leave the 3rd dimension. They are in the 3D field while simultaneously anchoring into the 4th and then the 5th dimensions.

When the human anchors into the 4D field, 80 percent of their body is holding 4D frequencies. The lens of perception will be 4D, meaning most of their states of consciousness will be in the 4D. They are also simultaneously standing in the 3D field. They can see other humans in 3D states of consciousness.

When the human anchors into the 5D field, 80 percent of their body is holding 5D frequencies. Their lens of perception will be in 5D. Most of their states of consciousness, which create their reality, will be in the 5D. They will, however, be standing in a 4D and a 3D field simultaneously. They can see and access these fields in each now. They can see other humans in both the 3D and 4D states of consciousness.

The process of the human body anchoring into the 4D and then the 5D fields takes many linear years and is a very subtle shift. The human experiences these shifts as an energetic movement back and forth between very different states of consciousness. The human is energetically shifting from a 3D to a 4D field, a 4D to a 5D field, and a 3D to a 5D field throughout their day. Humans will experience themselves moving through a variety of different states of being in any given day. This shift creates a back-and-forth pull between dimensional fields.

Eventually the human body anchors into the next dimensional field, and the human's reality and states of consciousnesses are derived from that dimensional field.

The shifts and the anchoring itself are energetic. Most humans will not be aware of what field they are in at any given moment. It is their state of being and state of consciousness that will dictate what dimensional field they are accessing throughout their day.

If 80 percent of their thoughts, beliefs, behaviors, and emotions are in a 3rd dimensional frequency, they are anchored in that field. If 80 percent of their thoughts, beliefs, behaviors, and emotions are in 4th dimensional field, they are anchored into that field.

The human must be able to feel and observe not only their states of being and states of consciousness but also the frequencies of the different dimensional fields within their body. The human must play a participatory role in their physical evolution. They must be connected to their bodies and observing their states of being and consciousness. This will allow the human to continue to choose how they wish to be in the world, what their body is requiring, and what is for their highest good. If the human is aware and conscious of both their choices and the energies that are being expressed and experienced within their bodies, they will be actively participating in their own evolution. If the human is unconscious and unaware of their choices, their states of being and consciousness, and the energies expressed and experienced in their body, they will be slowing down their evolution. Stepping into multi-dimensionality within the human form requires both the human and the body to work side by side.

17.2 The Multidimensional Experience

The human has never experienced the current physical shifts within their body. They do not have a reference point. It requires patience, surrender, trust, and most importantly, being the observer.

When the human becomes the observer, they begin to see themselves *in* the human journey instead of *being* the human journey. They begin to choose. They begin to feel without attachment. They begin to experience frequencies within their body, and they begin to notice the subtle shifts in their states of consciousness.

Once the human becomes the observer, they begin to experience themselves embodying their multi-dimensionality. They feel and see their shifts between dimensional fields, and they will start to notice when they have anchored into another dimensional field. There are many ways the human will experience their multi-dimensionality. We will list a few below.

One of the first experiences had by the human as they step into their multi-dimensionality is reconnecting and embodying all fragmented aspects of the human's light Consciousness—the spirit—that left the body due to trauma. The human releases all trauma, pulls in all fragmented aspects of themselves, and begins to become whole once more.

Another experience the human will have as they step into their multi-dimensionality is feeling their resonance. Resonance is the frequency the human body is holding in any now moment. It is designed to navigate the human through the energetic world. It is the human's compass. Everything is energy and as the human becomes multi-dimensional, they begin to trust resonance over thoughts, beliefs, and the external world.

The human will also become more present and in the now. The human will find themselves experiencing presence more often. They will release the attachment to the past or the future. They begin to trust the now moment as the only moment that needs attention. The human will find themselves in a more surrendered state, not trying to control or create a desired outcome. They will detach from all experiences. Detachment does not mean they do not feel or desire experiences or outcomes. Detachment means the human no longer associates themselves as the experience or outcome, but instead, simply experiences each now.

As the human practices presence, they will begin to experience neutrality. Neutrality is another aspect of becoming multi-dimensional. The human begins to step out of duality, which creates the illusion of separateness and right or wrong, and into neutrality.

Neutrality allows for the natural expression of all consciousness—thoughts, beliefs, programs, paradigms, and behaviors—without judgment. The multi-dimensional human stands in the one unified quantum field where all experiences and consciousnesses exist without separation. The human understands everything in the external world is its own unique expression of source consciousness; therefore, there is no judgment.

Another experience of multidimensionality is sovereignty. When a human is in their sovereignty, they are aligned with their energetic signature and their resonance. They are completely embodied and feel safe within their physical form. The sovereign human understands that the external world cannot impact them unless they allow it. Sovereignty releases any aspect of victimhood. They express themselves freely and with both a power and a knowingness. The sovereign human is creating their reality from an empowered state, free within their form. They allow all other humans to express and be without an attachment to changing them. A sovereign human knows they are worthy and free to be all of who they are without being impacted by the external world.

The multi-dimensional human also begins to connect and align back into their channel. The human embodies their Higher Self and *I Am* Presence. They trust and follow the guidance of the Higher Self over the ego.

The human also gains access to all their multi-dimensional senses. They hear, see, feel, and receive higher frequency energies. There are many experiences the human has as they discover their multi-senses, but a few common ones are:

1. Connecting and communicating with their guides
2. Bi-locating into other dimensional fields
3. Seeing energies in colors, shapes, and waves

4. Receiving energy from higher dimensional realms and unpacking it as information
5. Feeling energies around their body and in rooms
6. Seeing visions or scenes from the non-physical realm
7. Telepathic communication with other humans
8. Knowing things before they happen

Humanity is currently navigating this miraculous and courageous physical evolution in Consciousness. The above examples are just a few of many experiences the human will have as they step into their multi-dimensionality. These don't happen overnight. It takes baby steps and requires the human to have compassion and patience as they learn how to become multi-dimensional.

Summary

The human is navigating a miraculous and courageous present moment. We have been waiting thousands of years for this moment. You have been waiting thousands of years to be able to finally experience this physical shift in consciousness within your human form. There are light codes within your DNA that will activate and are activating, allowing you to step into the multi-dimensional human.

It is no mistake that you are reading these words. You are remembering why you are here in the human form. You have chosen to experience the physical shift in consciousness within a dense physical form. You are doing this courageously and exactly how you designed it to be. Many of you have worked diligently as Light Workers for thousands of years and hundreds of lifetimes to get Earth and humanity to this now moment. You are honored, loved, and held as you physically anchor into the 4th and 5th dimensional fields.

Chapter 18

THE QUANTUM FIELD

To understand humanity's current physical evolution, it is important to discuss the quantum field. As the human becomes multi-dimensional, they will be accessing and experiencing this field. We have briefly discussed many of these concepts in previous chapters. However, we wish to go into depth on how you, the human, experience and navigate the quantum field.

18.1 Review: The 12D Grid

Before we begin, let us briefly review the 12D grid. All experiences and realities by any human, Higher Dimensional Consciousness, or race that existed within, on, or above the Earth, since the moment she intended herself into a 5th dimensional form millions of years ago, has been held in the 12th dimensional grid.

All physical forms on and off the Earth Plane, including everything seen in the sky, are within the 12D grid. The entire human experience, everything the human sees, knows, and understands in any lifetime, on or off the planet, is within the 12D grid. Any Higher Dimensional Consciousness participating with the Earth is within the 12D grid.

This grid holds ten dimensions within it, 3D to 12D. Currently, the human is in the lowest dimensional field within the 12D grid, the 3rd dimension. They are experiencing a reality through a 3rd dimensional lens. Everything the human sees, feels, hears, and experiences is filtered through this dimensional field. However, there are nine other dimensional fields existing within the 12D grid. Each dimensional field is holding distinct and unique spectrums of consciousness to experience. A human, or any other Consciousness or Being, will experience one of the ten dimensional fields based on its frequency.

For example, if a human was holding 5D frequencies, they would be in a 5D field, and the lens used to experience their reality would be in the 5th dimension. If a human was holding 7D frequencies, they would be in a 7D field, and the lens used to experience their reality would be in the 7th dimension.

The 3D field works in physicality. All that is real to the human is seen with the physical eye. Truths and facts are created within this physical reality. A human believes that which they can see. That which cannot be seen is challenging to accept or prove in the 3rd dimension. However, all physicality is energy in its purest form. Energy is alchemized into matter, and matter creates physicality. The entire 12D grid and all ten dimensional fields are within the quantum field.

18.2 What is the Quantum Field?

The quantum field holds all possibilities that ever have been, will be, and are currently existing now. It is the realm of infinite possibilities.

When consciousness splits from Source, it enters the quantum field as a unique energetic expression within its own energetic field. It expresses itself and creates its experience through the spin of its energy. The spin creates a frequency. Through choice and free will, it begins to spin into a desired frequency. That frequency moves the consciousness into a dimensional field correlating to the frequency.

For instance, if the consciousness intends to experience itself in a 25th dimensional field, it will spin its energy higher or lower to move into that dimensional field. The faster an energy spins, the higher its frequency and dimensional field. The slower an energy spins, the lower its frequency and dimensional field. The frequency a consciousness holds will dictate its dimensional field.

The dimensional field has a spectrum of consciousness within it that creates experiences for the individual energetic consciousness (IEC). Every dimensional field is within the quantum field, and all IEC's that hold the same frequency will experience the same dimensional field. For instance, if an IEC is holding a 9th dimensional frequency, they will be in a 9D field within the quantum field. They will have the ability to connect with all Beings that are vibrating in a 9D field.

The spectrum of consciousness that exists within a dimensional field increases as the dimensional field decreases, meaning the lower a dimensional field, the larger the spectrum of consciousness that can be experienced and the more experiences one can have within that field. A low 5th dimensional field has a larger spectrum of consciousness to be experienced than a 15th dimensional field.

This is because consciousness stretches as its frequency or spin slows down. When consciousness is in a lower frequency, it spins slower. That slow spin creates a stretching of the consciousness. That stretching creates a larger variety of experiences to be had within that consciousness.

The lower a dimensional field, the slower all consciousnesses within that field will be spinning, creating a larger spectrum of consciousness— a stretching—to be experienced by the human. The higher a dimensional field the faster all consciousnesses within that field will be spinning, creating a smaller spectrum of consciousness to be experienced by the human.

Any consciousness, including the human, can experience both the quantum field and their own dimensional field in each now moment. The ability to experience both fields is based on the frequency the consciousness is holding. For the human, it is based on the frequency of their physical body. The higher a human or a consciousness's frequency, the easier it is to experience both the dimensional field and the quantum field. The lower in frequency, the more difficult it becomes. This is because the quantum field is experienced energetically, not physically. It cannot be seen, only felt. When a consciousness chooses to shift into lower frequencies, it becomes denser and can experience itself as physical. Once physical, it can be challenging to experience and remember the quantum field.

The 7th dimensional field and lower fields create physicality. Any consciousness that chooses to be in a 7D field or lower will be experiencing themselves in some sort of physical form. A consciousness in the 7th, 6th, 5th, or 4th dimensions can still tap into the quantum field as they are in the quantum field, but the lower in frequency and dimensional field a consciousness moves the denser, more physical, and more challenging it is to feel the quantum field.

A human in the 3D field has the most challenging time experiencing and remembering the quantum field because their bodies are in a very low frequency. As the human's body begins to hold higher frequencies, the human will start to feel and understand the quantum field.

Micro- and Macro-Quantum Fields

There is only one unified quantum field. However, we are breaking it down into two to allow the human's linear mind to conceptualize and understand their experience on the Earth Plane within the 12D grid.

There is a micro field experienced within Earth's 5D grid and a macro field experienced outside the Earth's 5D grid. Both fields, which can be experienced by the human at any now moment, exist within the one unified quantum field.

The micro field holds the current experience on Earth within the 5D grid. It consists of the 3rd, 4th, and 5th dimensional fields. All three dimensional fields exist in the now. The human can tap into the 3D, 4D, and 5D fields in any now moment while in their physical form. This is the quantum realm existing on Earth that the human can access within their physicality. These are the dimensional fields Earth has already anchored into, and they are the fields that the human is anchoring into now.

The macro field is everything that exists within the 12D grid and outside the 12D grid and all infinite possibilities and dimensions beyond the 12D grid. It is everything within the 5D grid, within the 12D grid, and outside the 12D grid. It is all that ever is, was, and will be.

18.3 Humans and the Micro-Quantum Field

Typically, in the quantum field, Higher Dimensional Consciousnesses choose through intent what dimensional field they want to experience. Once they choose, they shift their frequency to match that dimensional field to experience the realities found within that dimension. However, due to the physical density of the human form coupled with the design and intention of Earth's experience, the human accesses the quantum field in a different way. Remember, the entire purpose of the Earth's experiment is to remain within the physical form yet shift into the next highest dimensional fields by holding higher frequencies within the form. The human form must hold and anchor the frequency of the dimension they are intending to shift into. This process takes many linear years to accomplish and is the *evolution in consciousness.*

The human experiences the micro-quantum field by holding higher frequencies within their form. As their body's frequency increases, their energetic field begins to tap into the 4D and 5D fields in the micro field.

When a human's energetic field taps into another dimensional field, the human can access the spectrum of consciousness within that field. The consciousnesses within that spectrum are what allow the human to experience that dimensional field. They are the emotions, thoughts, behaviors, beliefs, programs, and paradigms: all the potential ways of being in that dimension. All consciousnesses within that spectrum are holding the frequency of that dimension. For instance, in the 4th dimension, there is a spectrum of consciousness that holds frequencies vibrating from 4.0 to 4.9. Any frequency not in that vibration will not be experienced in the 4D field. When the human taps into the 4D field, they will access the specific consciousness or states of being, feeling, doing, and thinking found within that field.

A human can only tap into consciousnesses within a dimensional field if they are holding the same frequencies as that dimensional field. Tapping into the field allows the human to experience the field. However, if a human wants to physically stand in that dimensional field, their body must anchor into the field. The body anchors the next dimensional field by holding most of its frequency in that dimensional field.

For instance, for a human body anchored in a 3D field, to anchor into a 4D field, 80 percent of its frequency must be at a 4D frequency. This is called the *vibrational set point*. The majority of frequency held in the physical form will dictate the dimensional field the human is anchored into.

The 3D human anchored into the 3D field experiences their reality through the lens of the 3rd dimension. As their body begins to hold frequencies in the 4th and 5th dimensions, they begin to tap into the spectrums of consciousness found within the 4D and 5D fields. The human starts accessing states of consciousness within these two fields. They begin to change the way they live and experience their lives. As soon as the vibrational set point within the body is at the 4D field, the human will anchor into that field. The lens creating their reality will be in the 4D. All experiences will be viewed from the 4D field.

The 3D human is now a 4D human in the micro quantum field. They can physically see the 3D field around them, but they are standing in the 4D field. A human can see and experience any dimensional field they have anchored into. The 4D human already anchored the 3D; therefore, in the micro quantum field, the 3D field doesn't disappear. It is visible and available for the human to experience in any now if they choose to do so. The human is anchored into the 4D field. Every moment is experienced, seen, and filtered through the lens of the 4th dimension. The human is also tapping into states of consciousness within the 5D field as their body continues to increase in frequency.

232

Eventually the 4D human anchors into the 5D field, and they become a 5D human. Their reality is filtered through the lens of the 5D. The 5D human, like the 4D human, will still see and have access to the 3rd and 4th dimensional fields through choice and free will but will be experiencing their now moments in 5D states of consciousness.

All three dimensional fields are accessible and can be physically seen by the human at any moment, based on the human's frequency and the dimensional field they are anchored in. For example, the human anchored into the 4D is seeing the 3D field, experiencing their reality through the 4D field, and accessing the spectrum of consciousness within the 5D field. When they walk outside, they are anchored into a 4D field. Every experience they have is filtered through the 4D lens, yet they are also seeing a 3D field and being in 5D states of consciousness. They are experiencing three dimensional fields in a now moment.

Regardless of what field the human body is anchored in, the conscious human is energetically oscillating between three dimensional fields. The human form is anchored into a lower field (3D or 4D) yet holding higher frequencies in the body (4D or 5D). The human will experience lower states of consciousness and then higher states of consciousness throughout their day. It can feel confusing as the human moves through many different emotional, mental, and physical states of consciousness, but it is how the human form evolves into higher dimensional fields within the micro quantum field.

18.4 Creating in the Micro-Quantum Field

The micro quantum field allows the human to tap into an infinite amount of possibilities and aspects of themselves existing in another now moment within this lifetime. The aspect or possibility the human steps into in each now moment depends on free will, frequency, and choice. This is how a human consciously navigates the micro-quantum field. The human calls this *manifestation*. We call it being a creator.

When humans become conscious and are aware of what they are feeling, thinking, and doing, they can begin to choose. They consciously observe who they are and who they want to be.

When a human chooses or intends who they want to be or what they want in their life, they are tapping into a version of themselves that exists energetically in the micro quantum field. The aspect of themselves they are choosing to become holds a specific frequency. That frequency may be similar to or higher than the frequency the human is currently holding in their body.

They become, or step into, the intended aspect of themselves when their body holds the same frequency as the aspect they are choosing to become. Most of the time, this occurs unconsciously. The human is not aware of what is occurring energetically in the micro quantum field. The more conscious a human can be of how their choices and intentions work in the micro field, the easier it is to create in their life.

A distinct and separate timeline for every aspect of the human exists within the micro quantum field. A timeline holds a version or versions of the human in a specific frequency, offering opportunity, experiences, relationships, and healing. Each timeline offers new experiences. Each timeline is a new reality with new possibilities for the human.

In the micro quantum field, there are an infinite amount of timelines because there are an infinite number of aspects a human can be. A human jumps—chooses a new timeline—by both intending a new aspect of who they want to be and allowing the body to shift into that aspect's frequency. If the human is consciously choosing the jump, they will be waiting for linear time to bring them into the new timeline. There is a lag between the moment of the jump and the human being the new aspect or experiencing the new reality. It takes time. The micro-quantum field is held in linearity; therefore, all creations are experienced in time.

If the human is unconscious of the jump or creation (i.e., the ego creates it or the higher self creates it), they will not feel anything. They will not know they created or jumped; therefore, they won't be expecting or waiting for anything. This unconscious jump creates the illusion of victimhood. Many humans believe they are a victim to their reality when in fact they have always been creating in the micro-quantum field. They just don't remember. It is not their fault. The human is simply experiencing themselves in the 3rd dimensional field without the remembrance of how the micro-quantum field works.

As the human begins to hold higher frequencies within their body, they begin to awaken out of an unconscious state. They start to remember how the micro-quantum field works, and they begin to choose new aspects of themselves and new possibilities available in the field. They begin to trust the timelines they are on and shift or jump into new timelines. The human becomes the creator within the micro quantum field without the remembrance of how the micro-quantum field works.

18.5 Future and Past Lifetimes

Along with accessing aspects of the human existing in another now, the micro quantum field also holds all future and past lifetimes. The human can see, feel, and remember lifetimes they had in a past as well as lifetimes they may have in a future.

All lifetimes, past or future, are occurring in the same now moment within the micro quantum field. The human is only experiencing the lifetime that is their current now. There is only ever one now being experienced through a specific lifetime, and yet within that now there are an infinite amount of nows and lifetimes accessible within the micro quantum field.

As the human shifts into higher states of consciousness, they will begin to consciously feel and see other lifetimes existing in the micro quantum field on Earth. The human experiences these as *past* or *future* lifetimes because they are in a linear space-time continuum. There is a movement of now moments creating a past or a future. However, in the micro quantum field, all lifetimes are in the now.

Accessing past or future lifetimes—aspects of the human existing in another now as well as states of consciousness in higher dimensional fields—is experienced within the micro quantum field. The more conscious a human becomes, the more they will remember this quantum field and the creator they are within it.

18.6 Humans and the Macro-Quantum Field

The macro-quantum field holds the micro-quantum field, the dimensional fields within the 12D grid, and all consciousness outside the 12D grid that ever was, is, or will be. It holds all possibilities for consciousness to experience itself. It is the one unified quantum field.

It is much more difficult for the human to access the macro-quantum field than the micro-quantum field because the human must be able to hold, feel, and trust higher dimensional fields and frequencies within their body.

To feel and trust the macro-quantum field, the human must reenter the body, be willing to feel all that is in the body, and trust the human form as it shifts into higher frequencies. The human must trust what it feels and what it sees.

The human is always connected to the macro-quantum field and can feel or access it through their etheric body and energetic field.

The etheric body accesses the macro field during the dream state and the waking state. It energetically moves out of the human body and into the macro-quantum field, always staying energetically connected to the human body through an energetic cord.

When the etheric body travels or moves into the macro field during the dream state, most humans are unconscious of this travel. They wake up from sleep and have very little recollection of what they experienced.

When the etheric body travels or moves in the waking state, it does so through bilocation. Bilocation is when the human's physical body is in the 3rd dimensional field and, at the same time, their etheric body is in higher dimensional fields. They are essentially in two places at the same time. Bilocation can only occur through the conscious and active participation of the human. The human consciously intends to move into the macro-quantum field with the etheric body and actively experiences other dimensional fields.

The human can also access the macro-quantum field through the energetic field around their body. The human must be in the body to feel the energetic field. Once in the body, connected to their energetic field, they will feel the higher dimensional fields around them.

The human must trust the frequencies they are feeling; they will not have any physical proof of higher dimensional fields outside of the 7th dimension. Remember, after the 7th dimension, physicality no longer exists. When humans allow themselves to trust what they are feeling, they will begin to move their awareness in and out of higher dimensional fields within the macro-quantum field.

Summary

Regardless of whether the human is accessing the macro- or micro-quantum field, the human must be in their body and conscious. This is the only way the human becomes the creator in the physical body within the quantum field.

Chapter 19

PARADIGMS

Along with understanding the 12D grid and the quantum field, it is equally important to understand the three specific paradigms the multi-dimensional human will step out of as they evolve.

The entire human journey within the 3rd dimension is experienced through *paradigms*. A paradigm is a collective of consciousnesses existing as a collective energetic frequency. Paradigms are experienced as beliefs, emotions, thoughts, truths, theories, and ways of being. They are designed to assist the human in understanding how to be in the 3rd dimensional field. They are like road maps for the human.

There are many paradigms a human can experience in the 3D field. For example, *news* is a paradigm allowing humans to receive information. *Scientific evidence* is a paradigm allowing humans to gain knowledge. *Schools* are a paradigm allowing humans to learn. *Sports* is a paradigm allowing humans to play games. *Religion* is a paradigm allowing humans to search for meaning.

Every paradigm holds a collective frequency that can be visualized like a cloud. The collective frequency is created from the vibration of all consciousness held within the paradigm. A consciousness is a belief, thought, emotion, truth, and behavior. All paradigms hold a variety of consciousnesses, creating the collective frequency.

A paradigm that holds consciousnesses with low frequencies, such as fear, lack, control, or greed, will be vibrating at a low collective frequency. If a paradigm is holding consciousnesses with high frequency, such as love, joy, peace, abundance, or freedom, that paradigm will be vibrating in a high collective frequency.

A human interacts and engages with a paradigm through their energetic field. The human body's frequency, held within their energetic field, will bump up against the frequency of the paradigm. This is not physically seen. It is energetically felt. The human experiences the collective frequency of the paradigm by listening, watching, reading, or physically experiencing the paradigm. The human will then choose to either participate or not participate with the paradigm. If they choose to participate with the paradigm, it becomes their reality and creates their truths, beliefs, behaviors, and emotions.

The human's frequency dictates the paradigms they are experiencing. If a human is holding the same frequency as that paradigm, they will resonate with the paradigm and have the opportunity to step into it, allowing it to be their reality. If a human is holding a lower or higher frequency than a paradigm, they will not resonate or have a desire to experience that paradigm. The human's frequency must match the paradigm's collective frequency to have a desire to experience it.

Many paradigms are chosen for the human based on the culture or society the human is experiencing and not the human's frequency. The human is born into these paradigms. Their frequency may not align with the paradigms, but they will have to experience it because the culture they live in follows the paradigm. For instance, school and paying taxes are paradigms that many humans experience but don't necessarily resonate with and wish to participate in. Their culture requires it of them.

However, many paradigms are chosen by the human. They believe they are choosing it based on what they want to experience in their life; however, it is unconsciously driven by their body's frequency. Their frequency will always guide them to paradigms with the same frequency.

As the human increases their frequency, they will no longer resonate or feel a desire to stay in paradigms holding lower frequencies. They will naturally shift from the older paradigms into new paradigms.

This also occurs for the entire human collective. As the human collective shifts from lower to higher frequencies, older paradigms will no longer be a part of certain cultures and societies.

For example, there are paradigms from the 1950s that are no longer being experienced in 2022. The frequency of certain paradigms in the '50s are lower than the human collective's current frequency. Naturally, the human collective will move out of these paradigms.

Humans will call these paradigm shifts *advancing* in science or education or *learning from the past*. We call it energy and the evolution of consciousness. The collective as a whole is always shifting into higher frequencies. As they do, the paradigms in the lower frequencies will dissolve from the collective.

The three specific paradigms in the 3rd dimension that humanity will be shifting out of as they evolve into higher states of consciousness are karma, past lives, and the Akashic Record. These paradigms are deeply ingrained in the human conscious, however, these three paradigms, along with many others, are not part of the higher dimensional fields. They do not exist in the 5th dimension. We hope that bringing awareness and clarity to these paradigms will lead the human to have a better understanding; they will choose to step out of these paradigms if the resonance is no longer there.

Please remember that all paradigms are real and true for the human experiencing them. Our intention is not to devalue a paradigm but instead provide the human the ability to choose to step out of paradigms that were never designed to be in a 5D field.

As you read this chapter, we ask that you honor your resonance; it is of utmost importance. Whether or not you resonate with the information, there is no right or wrong. We are merely offering another perspective on three specific paradigms.

19.1 Karma and Karmic Cycles

Karma is the first paradigm we would like to discuss. It is existing within the 3D field that the human will not experience as they shift into higher states of consciousness. There are two paradigms within karma. The first states there is an energetic balance and karmic cycle in all behavior. The second states that there is an energetic balance and karmic cycle in reincarnation. Both paradigms are designed to keep the human in a cycle of action and consequence, and neither paradigm will be found in 5D or higher fields.

Karmic Cycle in Human Behaviors

The first karmic paradigm we wish to discuss states that a person's behavior will create a cause-and-effect cycle in their life. There is an energetic force that creates a balance in all human behavior. That which the human puts out will come back to them in the now or in another future now.

If the human behaves in a good or positive way, they will experience something good or positive. If the human behaves in a bad or negative way, they will experience something bad or negative. Their behavior will dictate what will be experienced either in the now or in a future now. This paradigm creates a cyclical and perpetuating behavioral response.

This karmic paradigm was brought into the human collective thousands of years ago when humans were anchoring higher frequencies within their form. They began to understand and dissect energy, human patterns, and human behavior. These humans were noticing the relationship between behavior and energy. They recognized that the frequency in their body would dictate their behavior. The body's frequency would also reflect back to them experiences in the external world. Their frequency would create their reality based on their behaviors and the reflection of the external world.

If they were interacting with another human and holding a frequency that presented as laughter, love, or joy, they noticed that their external reality would reflect that same experience back to them. Their internal frequency created their external reality. If they were in joy, they received joy. If they were in sadness, they received sadness. It was a present moment experience.

They also knew their frequency was always shifting. A now moment can't create a ripple effect in another now moment unless humans are holding the vibration of that moment. If they behaved in a specific way in a now moment based on their frequency in that now, it would create a response only from that now frequency. No cyclical response would vibrate out to create a future now moment based on the current now frequency and behavior. They knew there was no expectation for a future experience that would balance out a previous behavior. They understood that everything occurred in the now and only the now.

For example, if they were sad or angry and responded to a human in a sad or angry way, the entire experience would stay in that now moment. There would be no ripple or cyclic effect that would later call for the human to balance out that anger or sadness. They didn't expect the anger or sadness to come back to them in another now to be experienced and balanced out.

The small percentage of humans who were having these awarenesses and experiences thousands of years ago began to share them with other humans. However, because the vast majority of humans at that time were holding much lower frequencies within their body, they were unable to understand this information.

As these teachings about human frequency, behavior, and outcomes were being shared, humanity was filtering it through a dualistic, linear lens, and the paradigm you now know as karma was created. Most humans receiving the teachings did not have a clear understanding of the quantum field, the present moment, sovereignty, their own energetic field, and free will.

They believed there was a consequence to a behavior instead of it being merely a reflection of one's frequency in the now moment. They created the belief that whatever a human did in the external would be returned to them during their lifetime. There would be another moment when the human would receive *karma* for what they did in a previous moment.

Energy doesn't work this way. It is not linear, concrete, or dualistic. It does not follow or stay connected to a human. Energy is neutral and fluid and is always moving within the quantum field. It flows in and out of awareness in all directions. It is not permanent, and it does not stay or respond to a past vibrational experience. An energetic response based on a human's past behavior does not reappear in a linear now. Energy only responds to the now moment and the human's current frequency in their body.

For instance, energy doesn't say, "This human did something bad or good five months ago, so a bad or good behavior will be provided to them now." That statement reflects duality and linearity, and energy doesn't hold either of those traits. Those traits occur through the human 3rd dimensional lens.

The human that performed the good behavior in that now moment did so because they were vibrating at the consciousness that held that behavior. It's that simple. If a human has a good experience in another now, it is because they are holding the frequency that creates that good experience. It is not tied to any previous now.

If a human stole something, they did so because they were vibrating at the consciousness of that behavior (lack or unworthiness as an example). If someone steals from them in a later now, it's because they are holding a similar frequency to the behavior of theft (again, lack or unworthiness as an example). They are consciously or unconsciously, and most of the time it's unconsciously, holding a belief, such as lack, that creates the frequency in the body, which creates the experience of theft in that now. It is not due to a previous behavior. It is due to the current frequency in the body.

Any behavior, thought, or belief creates the human's current frequency. Even if those beliefs are based on past behaviors or experiences, it is still creating the now frequency. That is how energy works in the quantum field, and the human is always in the quantum field.

The way in which a human creates their next now moment is through their energetic field, their frequency. The 3rd dimensional human is unaware that this is how they are creating every now. They do not realize that the frequency they are holding in the now will dictate that now experience.

What is occurring is the natural pulse of the human's energetic field creating their reality, anew in each now moment, within the quantum realm. The human's energetic field is constantly sending out pulses of magnetic energy, and that pulse is what the human will pull into their field and experience in their reality. The human's frequency can shift in any now to create a different pulse and a new reality. Nothing is occurring in the human's now based on any previous now.

This karmic paradigm created beliefs that were rooted in fear, control, and victimhood. These consciousnesses created the collective frequencies within this karmic paradigm. When a human experiences this paradigm, they will experience fear, control, and victimhood. The original teachings around karma were never rooted in these consciousnesses.

When a human is holding higher frequencies in their body, they will no longer resonate with this karmic paradigm's collective frequency. They will step out of the belief that a previous behavior will dictate a cyclic response to a future experience. The human will connect to the quantum field and remember how energy and consciousness works. They will live in a more present moment state, sovereign, creating in the now, and not living from a past behavior. They will feel their energetic field and will understand the vibrational pulse from that field pulls experiences into their now.

The human will remember there are no cyclical patterns holding them to any past behavior. Karma is neither creating nor is responsible for any now experience; the human's frequency in that now is responsible for the experience: all beliefs, emotions, thoughts, and behaviors are responsible for the experience. This is sovereignty: taking full responsibility for your actions. Sovereignty and stepping out of this karmic paradigm occur as the body increases in frequency.

Karmic Cycle in Reincarnation

The second karmic paradigm that many humans will be shifting out of is *karmic reincarnation*. This paradigm states that each human lifetime is connected to and can impact another lifetime. The human must clear and balance out all contacts and action-reaction experiences in a lifetime; otherwise, it will follow them into the next lifetime as karma to be cleared and balanced. It will create a karmic cycle.

For instance, if a human lived a past lifetime where they physically tortured other humans, their current lifetime would have experiences of perhaps being tortured themselves, or they might be drawn to fight injustices, wrongdoings, or torture of other Beings on the Earth Plane, including humans, non-humans, and animals.

This paradigm was created thousands of years ago at the same time as the karmic cycle in human behavior. The karmic reincarnation paradigm holds consciousnesses, such as fear and control. These two consciousnesses create the collective frequency of the paradigm. When a human experiences the paradigm, they will experience fear and control.

This paradigm ties the human to beliefs that their actions in the now will have a lasting impact so deep that it will follow them into other lifetimes. The human fears what may come in a future life if they don't "perfect" or learn from this one.

They also fear that what they have done in a past life must be healed in the current life. They believe they are tied to the past. It can create a sense of punishment if the human journey isn't done correctly.

When a Higher Dimensional Consciousness exits the human body, they exit the Earth and the 3rd dimensional field. They are no longer bound to 3D consciousnesses where duality, polarity, and paradigms exist. They experience themselves in much higher frequencies outside of the 3rd dimensional field.

If a Higher Dimensional Consciousness is no longer in the 3rd dimensional field, no longer holding 3rd dimensional frequencies, and therefore no longer experiencing paradigms held in the 3D field, how can it still be tied to the laws of that paradigm? How can it make decisions in a paradigm that it isn't vibrating at or standing in? Higher Dimensional Consciousnesses do not take 3D paradigms with them when they exit the human form.

The human form, the human life, and all experiences within that life no longer exist when they leave the human body. They are not tied to its energy, behaviors, or experiences. They are only connected to and experiencing that which is in their now.

Once they exit the human form, they exit the 3rd dimension. They immediately connect into the quantum field. They remember they are sovereign and have free will. They do not experience duality, such as right or wrong, good or bad. They see all experiences from the human journey as neutral. Any choice they make is from this perspective. They recognize that linearity doesn't exist. There is no past or future; therefore, there are no past lives or future lives. It is all now moments being experienced in the now. Karmic cycles can't exist from this quantum perspective. They aren't tied to any karmic cycle or lifetime they have lived in a human form.

The Higher Dimensional Consciousness can choose whether to reincarnate or not. If they no longer wish to experience the human life, they can choose another experience. The Higher Dimensional Consciousness can choose from an infinite number of possibilities, and reincarnating into a human form is only one.

If they choose to incarnate back into the human form, that life will be separate and sovereign from any other past or future incarnation. Each incarnation has a separate and unique Akashic Record independent of any previous lifetime experienced. There are no past experiences the Higher

Dimensional Consciousness has to clear in the current lifetime. They do not bring any past Akashic Records into the new lifetime.

19.2 Past Lives

The second paradigm we would like to discuss is past lives. We wish to share a perspective on past lives that is outside of any current paradigm; this is a perspective that all evolving humans will experience as they shift into higher states of consciousness.

While we share these perspectives with you, please know all perspectives are valid and exist in the one unified quantum field. There is no right or wrong. We are merely sharing a perspective that becomes available when humans hold higher frequencies of light in their bodies and begin to experience the quantum field.

A past life is a lifetime the human experienced in a linear past on the Earth Plane. It is the same Higher Dimensional Consciousness incarnating at a different linear time on the Earth.

The karmic reincarnation cycle holds the belief that a human's past lives are connected to their current life. Certain traumas, emotions, beliefs, and behaviors in a human's current life can be connected to an experience in a past life. Therefore, clearing these traumas, emotions, beliefs, and behaviors is accomplished by addressing the experience in the past life.

They believe if they can feel and experience emotions or physical pain from a past life then it must need to be cleared or healed in this lifetime. They feel it in their now as if the consciousnesses from those experiences were still held within their body (i.e., their DNA). They then believe that their current behaviors and experiences are related to these past life experiences. Thus, to clear and heal themselves, they must clear and heal their past life experiences.

However, what is happening is the human is accessing a past life energetically in the quantum field. They are feeling experiences from that past life in their current body in the now lifetime. This is how the quantum field works. The 3D human has merely forgotten.

Let us give you an analogy to assist you in understanding the quantum view of past lives. Imagine the quantum field as a bookstore. You walk into the bookstore, and all the books you see on the shelf are unique and separate lifetimes you experienced and are experiencing on Earth, depending on how you want to see it.

Each book is written by the same author, the Higher Dimensional Consciousness. Each book is its own unique story. The story is written through the Akashic Records chosen by the Higher Dimensional Consciousness. The records are the words creating the story. Each book is a new story with Earth and the human form holding specific frequen-cies. All the books in the bookstore are occurring in the same now moment. No book is dependent on another book to write its story, shift its story, or finish its story. Every book in the bookstore is unique, honored, and having its own beautiful Earth experience. The human does not have to heal or clear any previous book other than the book they are currently reading.

The bookstore is the quantum field and, as the human shifts into higher states of consciousness, they see the bookstore. They understand how each life is experienced and existing in the now. There is no linearity. There is no cause and effect between lifetimes. Every lifetime is sovereign, and sovereignty holds each life distinct and separate from any other life. The human does not need to access any other lifetime to clear and heal what is in their now. Anything the human heals or clears is based solely on the now sovereign life they created.

Most humans are not vibrating in a frequency high enough to remember how the quantum field works. They are unable to remember that each lifetime is separate and sovereign. Therefore, many humans remain within the paradigm that past lives are connected to each other through DNA and the Akashic Record. However, as the human shifts into higher states of consciousness, they will shift out of these beliefs.

They will remember that all past lives within the quantum field are in unique and separate timelines, experienced as separate and sovereign lives. The human will remember that lifetimes do not carry over to another life, and there is no cause and effect between lifetimes. They will remember that everything the human body experiences in a lifetime stays in that human body, including the Akashic Records and the DNA. Each new lifetime creates new DNA and Akashic Records.

19.3 DNA

Every lifetime created and experienced by the Higher Dimensional Consciousness is created as a separate life, unique and disconnected from any other life, with its own DNA and its own Akashic Record. Every time a Higher Dimensional Consciousness incarnates into a human form, they design and create the human life through light codes held within the DNA. Ten percent of DNA creates the physical form and 90 percent are the aspects of the Higher Dimensional Consciousness and the Akashic Records.

The DNA creating the physical form, the 10 percent, is the same in each human form. It is the light codes that are in each human body that create and build the human form.

The light codes that always change in every single life—the 90 percent—are the Akashic Records and the unique aspects of the Higher Dimensional Consciousnesses. The Akashic Record, as you know, holds the core foundational experiences, the physical attributes, the family system, and the human contracts. The unique aspect the Higher Dimensional Consciousness brings in creates abilities and gifts the human will have access to as their body evolves into higher frequencies.

The human form is therefore holding brand new DNA in every human life and brings in new aspects of their consciousness. An Akashic Record is never connected or tied to a previous lifetime.

19.4 The Akashic Records

The third paradigm we would like to discuss is the Akashic Record. We have already discussed the Akashic Record in much detail in a previous chapter. What we would like to point out with regard to past lives and the karmic cycle is that you, as the Higher Dimensional Consciousness, choose new records every single life. The choices are based on what you want to experience in that now life. They are not chosen based on a previous or future lifetime. It is a present now decision. All Higher Dimensional Consciousnesses outside of the 3D field understand this and are not bound to any Akashic Record, cleared or not cleared, from a past life.

When a Higher Dimensional Consciousness is creating a new Akashic Record, they choose new physical attributes, a new family system, new contracts, and new core foundational consciousnesses based on what they want to experience in that life.

It is the core foundational consciousnesses that will create external experiences during the human's life. The external experiences are what create traumas stored within the human body. These traumas are what is cleared and healed during the human's lifetime. It is impossible for trauma from a previous life to be cleared or healed, as it's not in the current human's DNA.

All trauma stored in the body is from experiences in the current lifetime based on the core consciousnesses held and chosen in the Akashic Record. Therefore, all healing of trauma is from the now lifetime, not a past lifetime. The human body does not hold any consciousness that was not experienced in the now life. It is impossible.

19.5 Clearing the Akashic Record

Along with the Akashic Record being unique and separate in each lifetime, Akashic Records also clear or dissolve as the human body shifts into higher frequencies. The Akashic Record is made of thousands of light codes holding a variety of different frequencies. A large part of the Akashic Record was designed to assist the human in navigating the 3D field. We are specifically referring to *contracts* and *core consciousnesses*.

These two aspects of the Akashic Record are made up of light codes holding 3D frequencies. As the human body physically shifts into higher frequencies, the lower-frequency light codes begin to merge into the higher-frequency light codes. The records that are held in 3D frequencies will naturally merge into higher light codes within the human form. The human body will no longer hold 3D Akashic Records within their body.

The core consciousnesses and the contracts will eventually dissolve from the human's experience.

Clearing Core Consciousnesses

A human clears the core consciousnesses through the healing or re-leasing of trauma held within the body. Remember, core consciousnesses create many of the experiences the human has in their lifetime. They are held in 3D frequencies and are not designed to dictate a human's experience as they shift into higher frequencies.

As the human body holds higher frequencies, the core consciousnesses in the lower frequencies naturally begin to move through and out of the body. This is felt as the releasing or healing of trauma. The human begins to become aware of and feel all emotions, thoughts, beliefs, and behaviors that are held within the trauma.

Observing and feeling the trauma slowly releases the core consciousnesses. The human begins to create new thoughts, beliefs, behaviors, and experiences that are no longer tied to these consciousnesses. The human's entire reality changes. They begin to create from a present moment state and not from the core consciousnesses that held the human in the past.

Clearing Contracts

When the Higher Dimensional Consciousness created the Akashic Record, they chose contracts between specific humans. As we stated in an earlier chapter, these contracts allowed the core consciousnesses to be experienced.

The contracts are with Higher Dimensional Consciousness within the same soul group. The soul group is made up of what the human calls *soulmates*. We would like to preface: when we use the term *soulmate*, we are not necessarily referring to a romantic partner. We are referring to all souls within the soul group.

Soul groups entered the 12D grid together to experience Earth and incarnated into human forms together as soulmates. There are also soulmates within the soul group that have never incarnated onto the Earth Plane but instead have assisted from off the Earth as Guides.

The soul group creates the human contracts within The Higher Dimensional Consciousness's Akashic Record. Typically, the contracts are an agreement made between two Higher Dimensional Consciousnesses. Both Consciousnesses choose the role they will play in each other's lives and the core consciousnesses they will play out for the other human.

All contracts are held in 3D frequencies because they are assisting the human in experiencing core consciousnesses that are all held in 3D frequencies. As the human body shifts into higher frequencies, and the core consciousnesses are cleared, all contracts with humans will be cleared from the human's DNA.

The human that is shifting into higher frequencies will no longer hold the same frequency as the contract. They will thus begin experiencing the relationship very differently. It will become clear they need to release the contract. They can release the contract either with or without the other human participating. The other individual can be aware of the contract and clear it with the human or be unconscious to the contract and remain connected to it. Either way, the contract can be cleared.

Clearing a contract requires observation or awareness of the contract and the intention to clear it. The contract itself is an energetic cord connecting both humans to each other. That cord holds and creates patterns, behaviors, beliefs, and emotions, allowing the core consciousness to be experienced.

When the human becomes aware of the contract, they see and feel the patterns that occur between themselves and the other human. They will understand the core consciousness that played out in that contract and the trauma that was experienced as a result of the relationship.

They release the energetic cord through intention (choice), visualization (seeing the energetic cord between both humans), and feeling all that was experienced in the relationship (honoring the contract). The contract and all consciousnesses tied to the contract will release from the human's

DNA. When the contract is cleared from the human's DNA, all patterns, behaviors, and emotions that were held in the contract will be released. All lessons agreed upon within the contract are cleared, including core consciousnesses. If the human chooses to stay in the relationship, they will no longer experience the patterns, behaviors, and emotions tied to the contract. The human will feel free within the relationship. If the other human is unable to release the contract, which is the case many times, they will continue to play out the same patterns, behaviors, and emotions. The human who cleared the contract will observe this behavior but not respond. The relationship will be experienced differently for both humans. They can both remain in the relationship, but the dynamics will be experienced differently. One individual is free of the energetic cord creating the patterns, while the other individual is still connected to it and playing out the patterns.

There is no right or wrong way of navigating contracts as the human clears the Akashic Record. It is important to understand that just because a contract is cleared does not mean the human must end the relationship. There are many ways to clear contracts and still have the human in their life. However, it is also important to honor the need to leave a relationship if it is no longer for the human's highest good and the contract has been cleared. If the human tries to leave a contractual relationship without clearing the contract, the human will find themselves tied, either physically or energetically, to the other human until the contract is released.

Summary

Shifting out of paradigms is inevitable as the human evolves. Recognizing the programming in karmic cycles and past lives is inevitable as the human evolves. Clearing the Akashic Record is inevitable as the human evolves. Although we only named three, the human will naturally step out of all 3D paradigms as they shift into higher states of consciousness.

Chapter 20

FINAL STATEMENTS

As we begin to close this book and share our final thoughts, we want to remind you that you are moving through an evolutionary shift in human consciousness. In a linear time-space dimensional field and within the quantum field, Earth and all on her are evolving individually and collectively.

Regardless of the programs, paradigms, emotions, behaviors, thoughts, beliefs, and trauma you are currently experiencing in your 3rd dimensional field, there are other dimensional fields occurring now on the Earth Plane that you will anchor into. Your reality is shifting and will continue to shift.

Do not buy into the belief that the world is falling deeper into chaos. Remember what we told you: Earth has anchored a new reality, a new world. Earth is in a 5D field and is waiting for humanity to meet her there.

Remember, nothing that is occurring on the Earth in this moment, both within you and around you, is an accident. This is how an entire human collective evolves into higher states of consciousness.

You are all currently experiencing and watching the trauma or density from the human collective be pulled out of the darkness and into the light. Just like your own trauma, the human collective trauma must be seen, felt, and shifted into higher frequencies. The way you move through this is by seeing the trauma, feeling the trauma, and then choosing who you want to be right now.

Your choice and your sovereignty are your superpowers.

You always have a choice. It's all choice, layered with patience, compassion, surrender, trust, and a deep knowing that all is well in your now. You are surrounded by Higher Dimensional Beings. You are continuously anchoring the next highest version of you into your form. You are remembering your multi-dimensionality, and you are courageously showing up for yourself and humanity, putting one foot in front of the other.

You are cherished. You are light. You are Source. You are a unique consciousness playing in a human form standing on a courageous Being called Earth. All of this, this entire book, and so much more within and around you, is precious. This is all so fragile. This life is a gift.

There is so much more we will share with you. We had to start somewhere, and thus, we began with this book. We have shared an abbreviated version of all significant moments of Earth and humanity's experience as Consciousness in physical form experimenting with an evolutionary shift that is spectacular.

Whatever you are experiencing as you read these words, we hope you can feel the infinite, expanded version of you within your form. We hope you can remember through the energetic activation of these words that you chose this body you are in, and you wrote the book of this life.

We hope that you can feel the magnificence of your Beingness as you walk each step of your path, as you courageously envelop each now moment with new eyes and an open heart.

We hope that you feel us through these human words, and you remember just how deeply you are loved; not for one linear moment were you ever alone on this path.

We hope that as you move forward into each of your beautiful moments, you remember this story. Remember your story. Remember Earth's story, and remember that you hold the quantum world within your physical form.

If there is anything you take from these pages, may it be how deeply you are loved and how you *are* love. You have never been anything other than love. Perhaps after reading these pages, you understand how you arrived in this moment and just how courageous it was to incarnate into this field of consciousness. Never once have we taken our eyes off you. Never once have you been separated from Source. Never once have you done anything *wrong*. Never once have you disappointed. Never once have you been alone. In this now, as you read these words, we are watching you and loving you; you are connected to all.

Be your humanness. Be you. Devour each of your human moments; what a gift to be experiencing it all. Love yourself and the humans around you. You are all navigating this as Higher Dimensional Consciousness in dense form, all of you. Remember, all is perfect and divine. Nothing is right or wrong, and yet, in that statement, you can sit in the beautiful dimensional field that holds right and wrong.

This is the evolution in human consciousness. This is you shifting. This is you remembering the book you wrote in this lifetime. And whether this is the first book you have written on the Earth Plane, or you have a library filled with books you lived, you are consciously, courageously, patiently turning on the light, putting on your reading glasses, and remembering who you are and what you designed. And you are choosing in each now moment to create the next highest version of you.

So just be. Know you are light, and that this life will turn in a blink of an eye. Devour it like it's the only now you have. There will be a moment when you will be out of form, in a Higher Dimensional Consciousness, remembering your human life and what an absolute, miraculous gift and experience it was and is.

We love you. We are with you, and we honor you.

ABOUT THE AUTHOR

Lorie Ladd is an author, spiritual teacher, and thought leader specializing in the evolution of human consciousness. Her teachings and guidance have helped millions of people navigate the current planetary shifts, embody Sovereignty, and remember the divine design held within the human experience.

Inquisitive and intuitive Lorie found her life purpose at 13, when she simply knew she would assist humanity through the miraculous and divine collective awakening humanity is experiencing now. But it wasn't until 2015, after leading an almost normal life, which included a MA in Psychology, teaching hot yoga, a corporate job, and a fiancée, that she fully committed to her mission.

In 2015, Lorie launched her own platform, which includes master classes and online courses, and thousands of videos available on YouTube, Instagram, and Facebook. People on all continents resonated with her teachings and down-to-earth personality, gathering together in a community that surpasses a million people.

The Divine Design is Lorie's first book, and came to her as a download, during an initiatic journey to the sacred land of Machu Picchu. Designed to be a lifetime companion, the book reveals the untold story of earth's and humanity's evolution in consciousness and provides the much-needed tools for navigating the current planetary awakening.

Lorie Ladd resides in California, the state where she was born and grew up.

Printed in Great Britain
by Amazon